The *wandle*

and ***Companion***

WANDLE TRAIL GUIDE

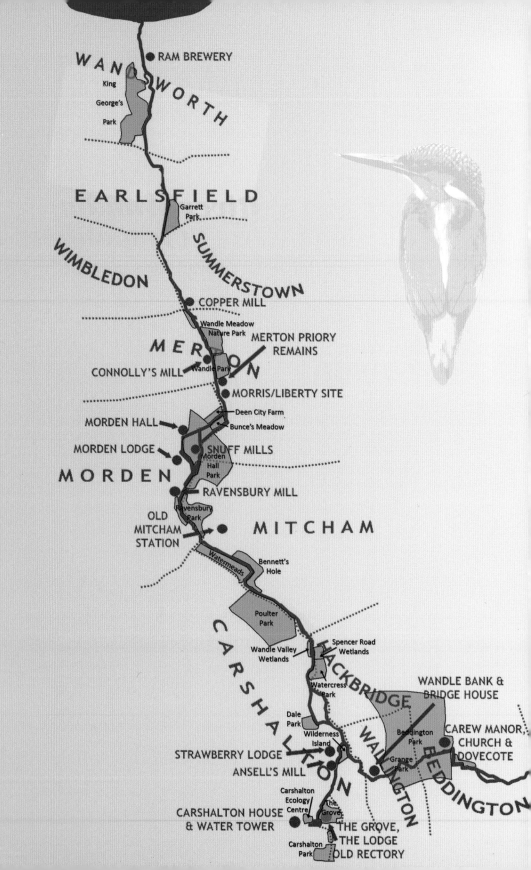

RAM BREWERY

WAN DSWORTH

King George's Park

EARLSFIELD

Garrett Park

WIMBLEDON

SUMMERSTOWN

COPPER MILL

Wandle Meadow Nature Park

MERTON

MERTON PRIORY REMAINS

CONNOLLY'S MILL

Wandle Park

MORRIS/LIBERTY SITE

Deen City Farm

MORDEN HALL

Bunce's Meadow

MORDEN LODGE

SNUFF MILLS

Morden Hall Park

MORDEN

RAVENSBURY MILL

Ravensbury Park

OLD MITCHAM STATION

MITCHAM

Watermeads

Bennett's Hole

Poulter Park

CARSHALTON

Wandle Valley Wetlands

Spencer Road Wetlands

HACKBRIDGE

Watercress Park

WANDLE BANK & BRIDGE HOUSE

Dale Park

WALLINGTON

Beddington Park

CAREW MANOR, CHURCH & DOVECOTE

Wilderness Island

STRAWBERRY LODGE

Grange Park

BEDDINGTON

ANSELL'S MILL

Carshalton Ecology Centre

The Grove

CARSHALTON HOUSE & WATER TOWER

THE GROVE, THE LODGE OLD RECTORY

Carshalton Park

River Wandle Companion

and Companion
WANDLE TRAIL GUIDE

Bob Steel

with Derek Coleman

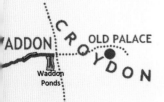

CULVERHOUSE BOOKS

Published by Culverhouse Books

© Bob Steel and Derek Coleman

First published 2012

A CIP catalogue record for this book is available from
the British Library

Printed in the United Kingdom at
Lavenham Press, Lavenham, Suffolk

Book design/typography: Dale Tomlinson
Typefaces: Kingfisher and Trilogy (typography.net)

ISBN 978-0-9572582-0-4 *hardback*
ISBN 978-0-9572582-1-1 *paperback*

Contents

Walking the river

Foreword

Down the course of the Wandle's recorded history, this very special little chalk river has enjoyed local, national and even international importance; and its identity has changed many times.

Within the last two centuries alone, as these pages demonstrate, the Wandle has been widely recognised as a famous trout stream that gave the world the idea of dry fly fishing, a power source for factories turning out every conceivable product from calico to cannon balls, a stylish water feature for wealthy industrialists' parks and gardens, a storm drain and open sewer, and more recently a green and pleasant corridor of countryside for residents of the world's first megacity. By anybody's calculations, that's a lot of identities for one little river. Sometimes they have been known to overlap, co-exist and even complement each other. Much more often, they have ended up contradictory or mutually exclusive, just like the human nature that created and modified them in the first place. And they have all been faithfully reflected in this impressive and most comprehensive piece of research and writing by Bob Steel and Derek Coleman; the first new guide to all aspects of the Wandle for 15 years.

To those who already know and love this river, many details will be familiar, but plenty of others will be new. And that's as it should be, because a great deal has changed in South London since the Wandle's previous guidebooks were published in 1974 and 1997.

Thanks to European legislation such as the Water Framework Directive, restoring the health of urban rivers like the Wandle has never been more important, or more solidly enshrined in law. John Ruskin may have been one of the first environmental volunteers to be captivated by the Wandle's battered beauty, but he certainly wasn't the last, and his famous "work never given" is now more freely and regularly donated than ever before, backed by sound science and local people taking responsibility for the stewardship of their river and its chain of nature reserves. Best of all, the Wandle has assumed its rightful place as the central artery and *raison d'etre* of the proposed Wandle Valley Regional Park – a living, flowing focus for the whole area's multi-faceted heritage.

In short, there's never been a better time for the people of the Wandle Valley to take a new look at their river, and a new pride in its history, biodiversity and different identities. For many years to come, this book will be their reliable companion and guide.

THEO PIKE
Chairman of Trustees
The Wandle Trust

Grove Ironworks, Carshalton by William Tatton Winter (1855–1928).

Preface

These are interesting times for the River Wandle: 50 years or so
after being declared an open sewer, the river is now on the verge of
becoming the focus of a linear Regional Park. It's been some 15 years
since the last book dealing with the river as a whole: in that time
both the river and the Wandle Trail have made very good progress.
Central to this success story is the steadily increasing level of awareness of and interest in the river: voluntary bodies and individuals are
at work along the length of the river improving the environment and
organising awareness-raising events like the Wandle Festival. There
are now several nature reserves as well as many parks, with bodies
like the National Trust and the London Wildlife Trust playing an
important role in maintaining and enhancing the river and riverside
environment. Water quality continues to improve, and even the
severe setback of the 2007 pollution spill which did a great deal of
harm appears to have been only a temporary reverse. Fish stocks are
recovering well, helped by a large grant from sinners-turned-saints
Thames Water. The Wandle Trust, which has handled much of the
Thames Water money, has been able to appoint a full-time development officer and carry forward several projects to enhance river
habitat as well as lead its regular clean-up days. All this activity and
interest points to a bright future for the river, and enhancement of
the river is now enshrined in the policy documents of the local
authorities through which the river flows.

    This book is a modest attempt to present the many faces of the
river over time from playground of the wealthy to industrial artery to
linear park. As a geographer I have been particularly anxious to make
good use of maps to illustrate the river's sites of interest. Old maps
have been employed at large scale to show the location of features
such as large houses and estates, mills and other factories. Many of
these have left little or no trace, but I hope the maps will help the
reader to identify their locations on the ground. In my own contribution
to the campaign against the collective identity theft of our old place

names by the modern London Boroughs I have also mapped and named the boundaries of the old riverside districts.

In writing this book I have been joined by Derek Coleman, one of the leading naturalists connected with the river. Derek has written chapter five on the wildlife of the river, including a lot more place-specific detail than has appeared in any previous volumes on the Wandle; and I am also grateful to him for proof reading, help with the index and bibliography, and numerous suggestions for improvements.

A book of this nature relies very heavily on the published work of previous researchers: they are too many to mention in their entirety, but special mention should be made of Eric Montague's detailed and thoroughgoing books on the Mitcham section of the river; the late Doug Cluett's role as chair of the Wandle Group and author of several papers relevant to the Carshalton stretch; the late Michael Wilks, erstwhile chair of the Carshalton Society and authority on the Carshalton Wandle; and the exhaustive and remarkably detailed work of Peter McGow on the mills of the Wandle.

It was a great sadness to learn of the death of John Gent, the pre-eminent Croydon local historian as this book was being prepared. Despite being unwell John reviewed my draft chapter on the Croydon Wandle, and was very helpful in directing me to other sources.

BOB STEEL, *Carshalton, 2012*

'Carshalton Village in the '80s' by William Tatton Winter (1855–1928). At this time the Wandle flowed alongside the street.

Acknowledgements

Between us we would like to acknowledge the help and assistance of a wide range of people in the compilation of this book. All the staff at the respective borough heritage services have been helpful, and we would like to thank in particular Kath Shawcross and her staff at Sutton Local Studies Centre; and her counterparts at Merton and Croydon, Sarah Gould and Chris Bennett respectively. All of these were more than helpful and generous over the reproduction of and permission to use photographs from their archives. Chris Bennett provided several other very useful introductions. John Phillips, former heritage manager for the London Borough of Sutton, has been an invaluable source of help on the Upper Wandle; and we thank Jane Howard and Val Murphy for their assistance with prints of several paintings.

We are very grateful to John Stillman, a Carshalton artist, for allowing us to use a copy of his painting 'Fishing for Tiddlers'.

Eric Montague, Peter Hopkins and other past and present members of Merton Historical Society read and corrected numerous errors on the Mitcham and Merton sections of the book. Valerie Selby, Bruce St-Julian Brown, and Shirley Passmore from the Wandsworth Society gave useful help on the Wandsworth section. Staff at the Wandle Industrial Museum kindly allowed us, with the author's consent to use references from Peter McGow's authoritative research on Wandle mills while Dave Saxby at the Museum of London enabled us to trace and use some valuable images. Peter Robinson at Wandsworth Council made the enquiries to enable us to use mapping from the Wandle Trail guide; and Maureen Patel from the National Trust at Morden Hall Park fielded several enquiries, as did Tanya Houston and other staff at the Environment Agency. In the wildlife chapter, we would like to thank the following for making helpful comments on particular sections: Martin Boyle (flora), Tom Cousins/Environment Agency (fish), Tom Langton (amphibians and reptiles), Jane McLauchlin (flora), Theo Pike (fish), Will Tall (other fauna), Peter Wakeham (flora) and to John Marchant for extracting data from surveys conducted by the British Trust for Ornithology.

Several people and institutions deserve our gratitude for allowing us to use maps and other images, for which they have been, we hope, appropriately credited. These include Wandsworth Museum, Croydon Museum and Tudor Hughes, who has also read our draft manuscript and offered suggestions.

To mention everyone who helped us in other ways during the research for this book, for example facilitating photography would lengthen this section considerably, but we sincerely thank them all. Last but not least, warm thanks to our designer Dale Tomlinson for his professionalism, patience and forbearance over the past two years. RWS, DAC

1 Introducing the Wandle

The name of the river

The earliest reference appears to be in 693, when in the Wandsworth charter (and incidentally at this time Wandsworth was known as Wendles Wurthe) it was called *hlida burnan*. This may well have been a reference to the Old English *hlyde* meaning 'loud one', perhaps implying a fast flowing stream. It was still being referred to in a similar way as late as 1470 when monks at Westminster Abbey talked of the *Lutborne*.

The earliest reference to the present name in the Latinized form *Vandalis* is in 1586, but it seems that the name of Wandle appears to be derived from Wandsworth rather than the other way round. Other variants *Wandal* and *Wandell* were also in use by the sixteenth century.

The geological background

At least two theories co-exist as to the origins of the river we now call the Wandle: it is acknowledged that in prehistoric times rivers were larger than today, particularly in the period after the last Ice Age when successive freezing and thawing created frequent flood conditions when rivers carried large amounts of material. Chert deposits in the flood plain of the river around Croydon suggest that the river could have originally developed in the Weald, like the modern River Mole, and then flowed northwards through the gap in the North Downs at Merstham. And Hobson, writing in *The Book of the Wandle* in 1924 contended that the river was a Wealden stream, which had cut the gap in the

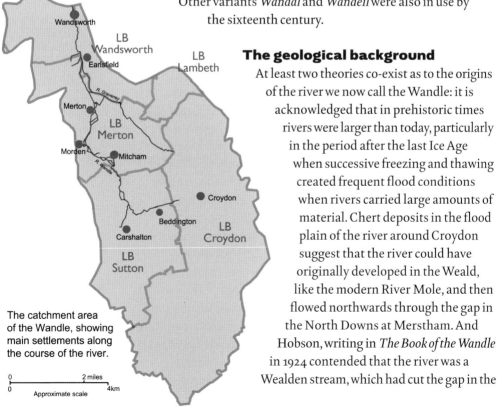

The catchment area of the Wandle, showing main settlements along the course of the river.

0   2 miles
0   4km
Approximate scale

North Downs at Merstham, and was later joined by tributary streams, which most likely originated on the chalk downs and cut the now dry valley systems, notably the Chipstead Valley and the Godstone Valley before coming together in the vicinity of modern Purley.

Most geologists today, however, contend that the river developed on the chalk of the North Downs, and was not a Wealden stream. The confusion is that the quartz-like chert deposits can occur both in chalk (where in purer form the term flint is normally used) or in other sedimentaries such as sandstone. Either way the extensive dry valley system referred to above, and shown clearly on the map on p. 3, confirms that this river system would have been a significant one carrying a far greater volume of water than the modern river. This would also suggest that the Croydon branch of the river is fluvially the more significant, since the Carshalton river is not likely to have been much longer than it is today, with a dry valley system extending only a couple of miles to the south of Carshalton Ponds. Today, the river is emphatically a chalk stream, which no longer flows on top of the chalk, but which emerges from a spring line at the foot of the North Downs and flows due north to its confluence with the River Thames.

The exceptions to this are the occasional streams, collectively known as the Bourne(s), which run through both the Caterham and Smitham Bottom (Coulsdon) valleys; really a legacy of the wider Wandle, they only surface after heavy rainfall. Legend had it that these Bournes flowed every seven years, and foretold disasters , and indeed they were sometimes referred to as 'woe waters'. Camden's *Britannia* (1586) says: "*… For the torrent that the vulgar affirm to rise here sometimes and to presage dearth and pestilence … the saying goes that 'When Croydon Bourne doth upwards ryse, disaster dyre before us lyes'*".

The Bournes cause problems intermittently, most recently in 1995 and in 2001. In normal times, a series of ditches and culverts channel the water along the valley through Purley to Croydon.

The complexity of the geology along the spring line can be seen in Beddington Park through which the Wandle flows broadly east–west along the spring line. Some areas close to the river are wet almost throughout the year: nearby archaeological excavations suggest that the reason is peat deposits along with some silts and peaty gravels. North of the river, an area of gravels deposited during the last Ice Age gives much drier soils. At the southern edge of the park close to Croydon Road, a distinct break of slope marks a gravel-covered former river terrace composed of Thanet Sands.

Right: *A detailed contour map of the Wandle headwaters. It's very plausible from this map that the Wandle was never a true Wealden stream, but that the extensive catchment of the Croydon Wandle had its origins in the chalk downs whose scarp has receded over time, creating passes like that at Merstham. The Carshalton Wandle looks insignificant in comparison. Dotted blue lines represent former watercourses.*

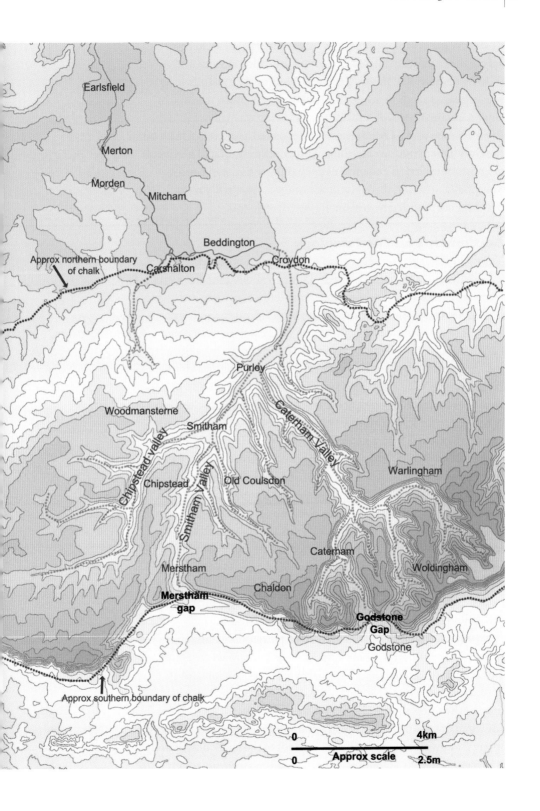

Earlsfield

Merton

Morden

Mitcham

Beddington

Approx northern boundary
of chalk

Carshalton

Croydon

Purley

Woodmansterne

Smitham

Chipstead valley

Caterham Valley

Chipstead

Smitham Valley

Old Coulsdon

Warlingham

Merstham

Caterham

Woldingham

Merstham
gap

Chaldon

Godstone
Gap

Godstone

Approx southern boundary of chalk

0

4km

Approx scale

0

2.5m

The Wandle runs onto London Clay soon after leaving the spring line, with alluvial deposits along the valley bottom and gravel formations on valley sides. The gravels were deposited following the Anglian glaciation, when the massive glacial thaw resulted in significant quantities of sand and gravel being washed out into the River Thames and its tributaries and deposited as gravel terraces on the river bank. There are also deposits of undifferentiated glacial till at South Wimbledon and on the valley sides at Earlsfield and Southfields. The soil throughout the valley is seasonally wet, deep clay surrounded by seasonally wet, deep loam.

Settlements and archaeology

The earliest human settlers in the Wandle Valley both in the Paleolithic and Mesolithic periods (i.e. up to about 4000 BC) were attracted by dry sites close to water; and plenty of evidence of settlements from these periods has been found, often in the gravel terraces of the lower Wandle and in the sandy soils of the Thanet beds between Croydon and Carshalton. Farming was introduced in the Late Stone Age (Neolithic) period from 4000 BC onwards, but in the Wandle Valley we have to wait until the Bronze and later Iron Ages for more significant evidence of settlement, in the form of weapons and fortifications. The remarkable Waddon caves are among the most significant archaeological finds in the Wandle Valley, discovered in June 1902 during the construction of sewers in the grounds of the old Waddon House. The excavations were led by George Clinch, FGS, who later presented a paper to the British Association for the Advancement of Science. He discovered three beehive-shaped chambers cut into a bed of compact sand and extending into the hillside (a fourth cave was found in October 1953, after heavy rain led to subsidence in a garden on Alton Road nearby). These caves may date from the Neolithic period but provide evidence of settlement over a long period, including Iron Age, through Roman and Saxon periods and possibly later.

Roman settlement occupied several sites in the Wandle Valley notably at Beddington, where a bath house and burials are recorded; and Roman roads crossed the Wandle Valley in Croydon and at Merton in the case of Stane Street. But it is to the Saxons we owe most of the recognisable settlement sites today, particularly from Mitcham upstream: the Croydon branch of the river flows from east to west following the spring line at the foot of the chalk downs and this was a favoured site for settlement. Anglo-Saxon villages grew up along this spring line from Croydon through Waddon and Beddington to Wallington and Carshalton. This relationship is most evident today at Carshalton, where the ponds are still fed by several sources, although the flow is less reliable and far weaker than in the past. The original settlement of Wallington was a small hamlet spread out along and around a network of springs and streams, which flowed a short distance northwards into the Wandle itself. It only moved southwards to its new location around the railway station after the line was built in the 1840s. At Beddington, land close to the river has always been susceptible to flooding, so the centre of the village was on high ground immediately to the south. This avoidance of the river's flood plain is even more pronounced in the lower course of the river where, as usual with rivers, the flood plain is wider. Thus between Merton and Wandsworth there were no significant settlements close to the river itself until comparatively recently. The hamlet of Garrett, for example, lay comfortably away to the east of the river, and Garrett

Morden Hall Park in winter.

Lane, the ancient highway connecting Wandsworth to Tooting, also kept a safe distance from the water. Wandsworth was able to take advantage of high ground, particularly east of the river. The mouth of the Wandle was, of course, an area of a marsh and mud and unsuitable for settlement, although a riverside hamlet, Waterside, later grew up along the Thames itself to the east of the Wandle's mouth.

Moving into the Medieval period, two important strands shaped the settlement history of the Wandle Valley: the transformation of much of the manorial lands of the Domesday period by a series of large pleasure estates and houses; and the contribution of the river's energy to the economic life of settlements along its banks – and nowhere more so than at Wandsworth. At the time of Domesday if we can believe the figures, the mills on the river there accounted for over half the total value of the manor of Wandsworth. In 1610 Upper Mill at Wandsworth was grinding 100 quarters of wheat weekly, 60 from Kingston market and 40 from Brentford. Of course, in the more recent past, the rapid growth of London has engulfed the area of the Wandle Valley almost entirely, and the settlements grew as a direct result of their proximity to the capital rather than because of any intrinsic locational advantages. This growth affected the Lower Wandle most profoundly in the late nineteenth century, for example, at Earlsfield where the character of Garrett Lane reflects the contemporary style of housing and development; and the Upper Wandle in the first half of the twentieth century, epitomised best perhaps by the St Helier housing estate, which transformed farmland and the semi-rural character of the area between Morden and Carshalton in the inter-war years.

To hell and back

A key part of the story of the Wandle is that of the rise and fall of industry. The river's location and steep gradient, which results in fast-flowing water, led to it becoming one of the most industrialised in the world for its size, with more than 90 mills along its 11-mile length. As Chapter 3 makes clear, the river was adapted for a very wide range of manufacturing tasks, the proximity of the London market being a major stimulus to the rise of the Wandle's industrial prowess. As long ago as 1086, the Domesday Book noted 13 mills. By the year of Trafalgar in 1805, this number had quadrupled to 12 calico works, nine flour mills, five snuff mills, five oil mills, three bleaching grounds, two dye-works, and one each of paper, skinning, logwood and copper mills.

Youngsters release trout fry into the river, 2011.

Pollution, and disputes over water usage and abusage, was commonplace in the nineteenth century. Naturally, this had a considerable impact upon the wildlife and beauty of the river, which had been an attraction for the wealthy merchants and luminaries who settled along the river and built the large houses that characterised the river banks for a while. Trout, recorded as flourishing in the Wandle as far back as the 1600s, and caught by famed anglers including Admiral Lord Nelson, began to fade out in the nineteenth century, and disappeared completely by the early twentieth century. Moreover, as water power was overtaken by steam, the factories along the river's corridor converted to producing paints, solvents and noxious chemicals, all of which eventually found their way into the water. Finally, in the 1960s, the Wandle was officially classified as a sewer. More than a decade later, local residents were still noticing how the river ran "*red, pink or blue, depending on the dye they were using*".

Since the ten-year period around 1960, probably the river's darkest decade, an accelerating momentum to clean up and rehabilitate the river has gathered pace, culminating in the creation of the Wandle Trail, and the plans for a Wandle Valley Regional Park which, funding and resolve permitting, should bear tangible fruit soon. Water quality has steadily improved, although there have been some serious setbacks. The river is being recognised as an important leisure resource, and habitats are improving along the river; the upper River Wandle in particular is still one of the finest chalk streams in the London area, according to *Natural England*, and it supports an exceptionally diverse aquatic flora for an urban stream. Interest in the river has probably never been higher.

Carshalton church from across the Upper Pond (1890), by William Tatton Winter (1855–1928).
This view was painted prior to the enlargement of the church in 1893.

The life
of the river

Detail from 'Fishing for Tiddlers' by John Stillman, b 1968.
The scene is downstream of the cascade in Grove Park, Carshalton.

2 Wandle water

The two significant aspects of the river hydrology are, of course, the discharge (the rate of flow) and the water quality. Both of these aspects have affected many other facets of the river, including economic activity, fishing and biodiversity.

The river hydrology: flow and variation

As far as the discharge is concerned, the most important generalisation that can be made is that there is less water in the river now than in the past. The river is fed (naturally at least) primarily from chalk aquifers, and these have been subject to abstraction for a considerable time. Artesian wells drilled into the chalk below the London basin have taken advantage of the shape of the water table in the chalk in the Downs, and follow the principle that water travelling through a porous rock from a higher elevation will rise to the surface through a pumpless well which appears to defy gravity. For example, the well drilled in the grounds of the Culvers estate in Carshalton around 1875 was sunk to a depth of 185' and, like tapping a vein, the water from high on the North Downs found a natural outlet here making less available to dribble out at the spring line and into the Wandle.

We are lucky that, in 1853, in one of the first surveys of its kind, Frederick Braithwaite conducted a survey of the Wandle's hydrology and water quality. This survey was published in 1861, when it was presented at a meeting of the Institute of Civil Engineers. Braithwaite's survey also provides the most reliable quantitative estimate of discharge from the more distant past. So at Garrett's Oil Mills near Earlsfield, he quotes a discharge of 9274 cubic ft per minute, or 154 cubic ft per second. This compares with an average discharge at Connolly's Mill, Merton, in the 1960s of 60 cu ft/s close to the long-term average for the past 50 years of 64.6 cu ft/s. Interestingly, the figure in 2010 at Connolly's Mill was rather higher than this at 72.9 cu ft/s. At the same time, the flow in Beddington Park was a mere 6 cu ft/s. (6.65 in 2010). When one bears in mind that today the majority, sometimes as high as 90%, of the Wandle's discharge is (admittedly clean) effluent; and given the variability in discharge (in the 1960s data the flow at Connolly's Mill varied from 8 cu ft/s to 1388 cu ft/s!), it's at least safe to say that natural discharge has declined very considerably indeed. Braithwaite also noted that the flow in the river showed great seasonal variation since evaporation, and growing plants take up water more during the summer; and, of course, there are more rapid changes caused by rainfall inputs. Moreover, the lower part of the Wandle Valley is composed of both gravels and clays, causing differential responses to water inputs. Braithwaite stated that in 1853 the supply from Waddon and Carshalton (the only reliable inputs) was found to vary between about 18.3 and 33 million gallons per day depending on inputs from intermittent springs and runoff.

Competing for water

Ironically, given the perennial concerns over flooding on the river, the interests of the millers on the river dictated that the river level should be maintained as high as possible to ensure a regular supply to the mills, especially at times when water levels were low. With the rise of industries on the river, competition for water, and in particular the construction of dams to increase the mill head at particular sites, could cause problems downstream, and one mill owner could have a significant effect upon those around him. According to the Wandsworth Historical Society, James Henckell, a city merchant who turned his hand to iron at Adkins Mill in the town, was particularly selfish. He demolished the existing mills, and built an iron mill on the site, damning up the river to provide a greater head of water, which resulted in the flooding of fields upstream from the new mill, and an irregular supply to the Upper Mills downstream. Complaints from the farmers and millers affected were heard by the Commissioners of the Surrey and Kent Sewers on 19 January 1780, and they ordered that Henckell should take measures to prevent the "*penning up of water at the said mill*". Apparently nothing was done, and complaints continued to be made for several years. This was not an isolated case in Wandsworth: one Richard Bush made representations to the Wandsworth Vestry intermittently throughout the 1790s to be allowed to improve water supply to his mill, the Lower Mill in the town; but all he was permitted to do was make his overfall weir above the mill wider. He then had to contend with the construction of the Surrey Iron Railway, planned to commence by the side of a new basin to be built immediately east

of his mill; he had more luck this time, since he managed to have
included a clause in the enabling Act, "...*that all and every sluice gate and
sluice gates, waste gate and waste gates, that may be erected by the said
company of proprietors* [i.e. of the railway] *by virtue of this Act, at or near
the said dock or bason,* [sic] *shall at all times be under the direction and
regulation of the occupier or occupiers for the time being of the said mills*".

At Merton, Braithwaite in 1853 noted that the copper mills of
Messrs. Shears and Sons had trouble with their water supply. Thirty
years previously they had brought an action against Peter Wood, the
proprietor of a silk mill upstream at Phipps Bridge, which was heard
in the Court of Common Pleas. Their complaint was that Wood had
diverted the water of the river to better serve his mill, resulting in
an irregularity of the supply to their mill, which was "*particularly
injurious to a copper mill*". Judgment was given in favour of the
plaintiffs, and Wood was ordered to lower the dam he had erected.
In addition, the irregularity of the river flow from natural causes was
also a problem. Shears' mill, Braithwaite went on, "*works day and night,
and being not infrequently short of water, there is an additional steam
engine of 40 H.P.*". Shears was not the only miller to resort to the use
of mechanical power as a back-up to the irregular and unreliable
flow of the river. Then, as now, lawyers no doubt tapped into a rich
vein with the continual disputes over water usage and expropriation.

The problems of water supply on the Wandle, and the direct
impact scarcity of water could have upon welfare and economic
well-being was highlighted as early as 1610. At this time a scheme
was proposed by one of the King's chaplains whereby water would
be diverted from the springs feeding the Wandle to supply London
with pure water via an underground pipe from Waddon. A set of
commissioners, in an early form of public inquiry, looked into the
proposals. Giuseppi in his 1908 paper records that a strong case for
the poor of Surrey was put to them:

THE PETITION OF THE YEOMEN AND FARMERS OF EAST SURREY
TO THE COMMISSIONERS. *Moste humblie sheweth unto your good
Lordships, your poor supplicants ye yeomen & farmers dwelling in ye
Este partes of ye Countie of Surrey that whereas it is intended by some to
convey to London a parte of ye river of Croydon, to raise thereby a private
gaine & benefitt: it may please your good Lordships to understand, if this
their purpose be brought to passe, it will turne to all our exceeding great
losse & hinderance, for whereas a great number of mealmen, badgers,
bakers & brewers doe grinde ye corne they buy of us in ye markettes at*

Croydon Kingston & Rigate at those milles which are erected upon ye streame comming from Croydon aforesaid, and imploy it afterwardes for ye use & service of his Majestie , ye Prince & Citie of London, ye worke of ye said milles decaying throughe ye decrease of water, ye said mealmen, badgers, bakers & brewers cannot have their usuall proportion of graine ground there, by reason whereof, not being able to utter soe muche as heretofore they have done, they will not buy ye quantitie of corne of us which now they doe, to ye great impoverishing of us, our wifes & children, ye cheifest meanes by which wee raise ye maintenaunce of our familes, & abilities to pay our rentes & performe ye services of ye King & cuntrie, proceeding cheiflie from ye benefite wee take by ye sale of our corne unto those said persons. Soe hereby wee shalbe driven either to keepe our corne upon our handes, or ells to sell it at farre lower rates then wee can live by, to our utter undoinge ; besides (if it may please your good Lordships) as ye water now is, wee are many times compelled to leave our corne at ye milles 2 or 3 dayes, they not being able throughe want of water to grinde it sooner, which stay of our corne there must be muche longer, if any water be taken away, to ye great want in ye meane time of our necessarie sustenance. In consideracion whereof wee moste humblie beseeche your good Lordships & ye rest of ye right honorable & right worshipfull commissioners to be pleased to weighe & consider our estate with your accustomed gratious care & love to ye cuntrie, this proceeding herein may be stayed & these inconveniences prevented, and wee may enjoye ye benefitt which God & nature throughe ye scituation of ye place hath bestowed upon us, in recompence of those many services which wee of necessitie are subject unto, throughe ye neerenes of or dwellinges to ye court & citie more then ye rest of ye Countie, for which wee shalbe bounde to pray to God for ye long contynuance of your Honors & Worshipps in all health & prosperitie.

The Commissioners duly reported back, and found in favour of the petitioners:

We therefore finde that if a tenth parte of the said River runnyng from Croydon to Waddon mill be taken away & carried to London That then it wilbe a very greate domage to our most gratious Soveraigne Lord the Kinges Majestie in respect of his milles … and wee finde that if the said water be carryed away either in pipes or channelles to the said Cittie That then it will be a greate domage to the cuntry of Surry in generall and to every private person thereof through whose groundes the said pipes and channelles shalbe convayed all which damages for the reasons before recited wee deeme so inestimable that wee cannot sett downe the true and certen value thereof.

So far as is known, this was the first important attempt to draw off a large portion of the water and it was very stoutly, and apparently successfully, resisted. But the Wandle has had others eyeing up its water too – at the end of the eighteenth century, pressure to improve transport of the goods produced on the river, and indeed beyond, led to calls to construct a waterway from London to Portsmouth, of which the river was to form a part. When this scheme was stillborn, a group of Wandle businessmen considered a scheme for a 'Grand Surrey Canal' and called in William Jessop, a leading canal engineer, to advise them. Jessop reported that the only source from which to draw the water would have to be the Wandle. In each case the interests of owners of the mills and other industrial concerns on the river were too great to render the scheme practicable. Jessop concluded: *"Strong objections would arise to taking water from the streams that feed the River Wandle, unless the owners of the mills can consent to the canal being supplied from some of the sources of the River Wandle, I am sorry to say that I must consider the scheme impracticable."* Thwarted by this to an extent, the industrialists of the river turned instead to alternative technology, and thus was born the plan for the Surrey Iron Railway (see p. 50). Moving into the nineteenth century, there appears to have been another attempt to use the Wandle as a water supply: 1849 plans show large reservoirs to be fed from it at Wandsworth and on Wimbledon Common, from where the water was to be conveyed to Lambeth and Newington via Clapham. These reservoirs were never constructed, so this scheme was apparently also fought off successfully. A few years later though the Croydon Board of Health was more successful in tapping the sources of the Wandle for water supply, although it led to a celebrated lawsuit in the House of Lords following an action brought by Mr Chasemore at Waddon Mill for damages, as he ascertained by gauges that the pumping of the Croydon Board from their deep chalk well had reduced his mill's power. A hierarchy of courts found in favour of Croydon Health Board. It was the turning of the tide in terms of demands on the river: the importance of maintaining a reliable water supply for a rapidly growing population was becoming top priority. Falling water tables and continued abstraction reduced the twentieth-century river to a fraction of its former strength, but this, of course, coincided with the decline in the use of the river as a source of power, so no doubt as the century wore on, the powerful voice of the milling interests was not there as before.

The Croydon Wandle became more unreliable despite temporary relief in 1908 when the Wandle Protection Act limited the amounts of water that Croydon Corporation could remove from boreholes in the Waddon area; and it was unceremoniously buried under Wandle Park in the 1930s, at a time when aesthetic considerations were lower on the agenda than today. In Carshalton the ponds dried up in 1922 and increasingly regularly thereafter. In 1935 the Carshalton Urban District Council commissioned a report on the future of the ponds and springs with a view to the possibility of artificially augmenting the supply, an outcome which eventually came to pass (see below). According to the records of the Distillers Company whose Mill Lane plant was directly downstream, a crop of grasses and weeds was cut by a reaping machine following another drought in 1947! As a result, the weir below the cascade had a recording notch (which is still visible today) installed in the same year. Nonetheless, the natural level of the water table had a continuing impact upon the springs in the Carshalton village area, and following several episodes of failure of the springs feeding Carshalton Ponds, and another proposal by the water company for a large new bore near the Oaks Park, the decision was taken in 1967 to install a concrete, waterproof floor to the ponds and the section of the river channel upstream of the cascade. Ironically, heavy rain during the proofing works the following summer flooded the drained ponds and filled up all the watercourses!

In addition, a water recirculation system was put in place, which in effect recycles water from Goat Bridge to Carshalton Ponds, and enables water levels to be maintained (in theory at least: the West Pond is often very low today as a result of this system not being used continuously). Residents of Carshalton will concur that today the feeder channels in Carshalton Park and Carshalton Place, and in Festival Walk, rarely carry water, whereas the author recalls as a child these channels being regularly full, as was the old Westcroft Canal alongside the modern sports centre, which today is almost always dry.

The regular section (with metal side gauges) on this weir in The Grove, Carshalton, enables discharge to be measured.

Carshalton Ponds now have a concrete bottom, following waterproofing in 1967–68.

Today at least, a strategy is in place to manage water in the river, balancing the needs of abstractors and other water users whilst leaving water in the environment to conserve aquatic habitats, especially during low river flows. This is part of a national scheme of Catchment Abstraction Management Strategies (CAMS) introduced by the Government in 1999. The cell containing the Wandle within the London CAMS is assessed as 'no water available'. This means that no further water is available for consumptive abstraction during low flows.

Flooding and flood management

Flooding of the river has been a problem for man ever since the Wandle Valley was first settled; orders to keep banks in good repair and ensure the river was free from obstructions crop up regularly in the records. As the catchment area became urbanised from the nineteenth century, the flood risk increased if anything, since much rainwater would now run directly over impervious surfaces and into the watercourses directly. Set against this, a comprehensive programme of flood protection works has been put in place along the river during the past 50 years; these have generally been successful in reducing the flood hazard. Some of these works are in the form of detention basins, which can be deliberately flooded when necessary and have had a biodiversity spin-off; the biggest example is Beddington Farmlands, although the smaller wetland at Carew Manor, Beddington, is easier to view.

The Environment Agency states that the Wandle catchment is extremely 'flashy' with the risk of surface water, sewer and fluvial flooding occurring within minutes of heavy rainfall. Typical of this type of catchment is rapid rise and fall of river levels, meaning the depth, speed and duration of the floodwater are not likely to be great, but the lag period between the rainfall and a flooding event will be relatively short. This can mean that a flood can be very disruptive. Typically, most documented Wandle flood events occur in summer during thunderstorms when rainfall intensity can be very high.

The Bournes, the intermittent headwater streams of the river, were referred to in Chapter 1. Their last disruptive appearance was in 2001 when serious flooding in the Whyteleafe area lasted for at least three weeks. Ironically, this was the year in which plans to resurrect the river in Wandle Park in Croydon also resurfaced.

There were severe floods in 1968 all along the Wandle with the Hackbridge area being particularly severely hit. Further flooding took place in 1977, 1982 and 1985 and one of the worst affected areas was at Beddington. In the area around Richmond Road damage was at its worst. In 1985 the Greater London Council installed computer monitoring of water levels in rivers around London including the Wandle linked to a weather radar station in Buckinghamshire. In 1990 work began on the excavation of a lake on nearby Beddington Farmlands as part of a relatively new flood defence strategy of storing floodwater; but in 1991 there was again a serious flooding incident in Beddington. Ironically, this took place just 3 months after the National Rivers Authority (NRA) had begun work on a flood relief scheme in the area. This scheme involved the widening and deepening of the river channel. The schemes in combination do appear, however, to have been successful because the following year in November 1992 during a very heavy downpour, the swollen river was contained within the new river banks. Now the work of the NRA has been taken over by the Environment Agency. They ran a flood awareness day in Mitcham in March 2009, aimed at raising awareness and informing residents as to what they can do to protect themselves.

The past 50 years have seen a change in thinking about dealing with flooding. Typical 'hard engineering' responses in the past were concrete revetments and straightening channels to speed water flow. These approaches, still very much in evidence along the Wandle, impoverished the bank side ecology, but also exacerbated flood risk in downstream areas. A 1950s magazine article in Sutton's Local Studies Centre extols the then new London County Council (LCC) scheme to line the Wandle at Earlsfield with concrete channels and steel sheet piles. Today, however, in Wandsworth the council's policy states:

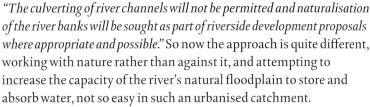

These concrete revetments on the Wandle at Morden are typical of a mid-twentieth century approach to urban river management.

"*The culverting of river channels will not be permitted and naturalisation of the river banks will be sought as part of riverside development proposals where appropriate and possible.*" So now the approach is quite different, working with nature rather than against it, and attempting to increase the capacity of the river's natural floodplain to store and absorb water, not so easy in such an urbanised catchment.

All four London Boroughs affected have detailed strategies for dealing with Wandle flooding. The starting point is the flood risk work undertaken by the Environment Agency, which assigns to three separate zones the likelihood of disruptive floods on a recurrence interval basis, but of course much of the Wandle floodplain had undergone development well before the advent of modern assessments and strategies. By and large, new development in flood risk areas has to satisfy a number of tests and to employ Sustainable Drainage Systems (SuDS). In Merton the strategy includes:

- Ensuring that flood storage capacity is enhanced
- Strengthening established flood defences
- De-culverting watercourses
- Ensuring any flooding impacts can be controlled.

Sutton's strategy specifically says: "*River channel restoration should be undertaken where possible to return the river to its natural state and restore floodplain to reduce the impact of flooding downstream.*" Examples of where this strategy is being implemented include Beddington Park: here, revetments have been removed from some stretches allowing the river to run freely through open parkland. In Merton, new wetland in Morden Hall Park acts as a flood storage basin, whilst enhancing biodiversity and habitat variety. The redevelopment of the BP Chemicals site in Mill Lane, Carshalton for housing presented an opportunity to give the river banks here a natural treatment, one which has been largely grasped with the banks now lined with vegetation and trees. Nonetheless, financial constraints on local authorities means that redevelopments often encroach closer to the river than ecological imperatives might dictate, so even at this site, and at an adjacent site immediately downstream of Butter Hill Bridge, which was developed a little later, new housing is very close to the river channel and the riverside margin is thin despite representations from conservation groups.

Interestingly, the Wandle has been part of a government-funded initiative looking into flood management. The *Long Term Initiatives for Flood Risk Environments* (LIFE) project was carried out in 2008 by the BRE Trust. Three sites were selected to represent typical UK flood risk locations along different rivers, and included the Wandle at Hackbridge as the instance of an upper catchment location (the other locations were on the Nene at Peterborough and the Arun at Littlehampton). The report informed Sutton Council's climate change adaptation strategy particularly insofar as it affected their proposals to develop Hackbridge into a 'sustainable suburb'. Recommendations formed part of a 'Blue Infrastructure Adaptation Toolkit', *"providing advice and guidance on the use of suitable measures to ensure that new developments within Hackbridge are fully adapted and resilient to the increased risks of flooding arising from climate change"*. This holistic approach (on paper, at least) is mirrored in the Flood Management Strategy of the new Regional Park blueprint, which makes the right noises about avoiding obstructions to flow, preventing *"inappropriate development"* on the floodplain, *"linking fragmented habitats within the river corridor"* and *"re-naturalising the riverbanks with the aim of increasing natural habitat and increasing flood storage"*.

Water quality: pollution then and now

The Wandle, as a chalk stream, had a reputation for its pure waters. This was one of the reasons why the calico bleaching industry developed along its banks, for pure water was required to wash out the chemicals at the last stage in the whitening process. Several other economic activities depended upon pure water for their wellbeing, chief among them brewing, and the widespread growth of watercress along the upper reaches of the valley. It was also the source of its rich fisheries.

The growth of the Wandle as an industrial area had an increasingly significant impact upon the water quality in the river. Many Wandle industries polluted the river directly – several of them were notoriously dirty, for example, the cloth printing processes that discharged a range of dyes and chemicals into the river. In addition of course, the growing population in the catchment area, particularly in Croydon precipitated a serious sewage problem as hundreds of privies emptied directly into the river. Braithwaite was writing at a time when there was precious little statutory regulation of water

The Wandle near Strathville Road, Earlsfield, in 1958. This was when the river was at about its worst.

pollution, and he pulled few punches about the impact of pollution on the river, which began at its very source in Croydon. Here the network of channels and ponds in the centre of the town had, by the mid nineteenth century, become little more than open sewers and was a major reason for the culverting of the river. It would be unfair to blame Croydon excessively, however, because in one respect the town had been progressive. In 1845 the Final Report of the Health of the Towns Commission led to the 1848 Public Health Act, which provided for local Boards of Health; and in 1849 Croydon was one of the first to establish such a Board under the auspices of this Act, and to build and operate a municipal sewage system. *"It was the object of the Local Board not merely to drain Croydon but also to purify the Wandle which was much esteemed as an ornamental and interesting feature of the neighbourhood",* Braithwaite noted.

Nonetheless, one impact of the local health boards was to externalise the pollution problems, to send them out of town. For example, Braithwaite noted of the river at Lambert's Mill, Beddington: *"The mill head, like that at Waddon, is full of mud; at times, the water does not exceed 4 inches in depth, and the stench is only kept in check, by a low temperature. The chief cause of this is the filth from Croydon, which finds its way through the wheel at Waddon Mill. It is seven years since the head was cleared, but the greater part of the deposit has accumulated recently..."*

Water pollution in Victorian Croydon

The population of the parish of Croydon in 1841 was 16,712, rising by 1851 to over 20,000. Although a board of Improvement Commissioners had been appointed in 1829, charged with 'lighting, watching and improving the Town of Croydon', by 1848 the population still had no piped water supply, drainage or sewerage. A questionnaire on the sanitary state of Croydon in 1848 described it as 'the worst of any district in the country, exclusive of the Metropolitan Districts'. Hundreds of privies overhung the tributary streams of the River Wandle, using them as open sewers, and the town's two large ponds, Laud's and Scarbrook, served as cesspools. As late as 1861, the ponds were found to be choked with black, evil-smelling mud to a depth of 5 feet. Early in 1849 two local reformers, Dr Edward Westall and Cuthbert William Johnson, secured a petition signed by ratepayers to have the Public Health Act applied to Croydon. A preliminary commission of inquiry was held in March 1849, which noted the relatively high level of mortality in Croydon. One in seven people died in infancy, compared to one in eight for the rest of Surrey; average life expectancy was only 30 years and 1 month, compared with 36 for the rest of Surrey. The inquiry also took place in the midst of a cholera epidemic, which killed 53 people in Croydon in 1849. As a result of the inquiry, it was resolved to create a local board by Provisional Order of the General Board of Health. The Order was published on 14 July 1849, and Croydon Local Board of Health came into being on 1 August, one of the first to be created under the 1848 Act.

Lambert himself brought several injunctions against the Croydon Local Board of Health during the 1850s, eventually receiving an out-of-court settlement in his favour. There were similar complaints from Wallington Mill, and in general mill owners seemed content to pass the buck back to the Board. Alfred Smee, who owned the garden at The Grange just above Wallington Bridge, also sued the Croydon Board and won. However, the Board is said to have 'resisted the law till a committal was signed to commit the members of the Board to prison' for contempt of court. This eventually led to the construction of Beddington Sewage Farm on a 96-acre area of flat land that had formerly been the northern part of the Carew family's Beddington deer park.

In contrast, Braithwaite commended the Carshalton branch of the river as being *'especially brilliant and pure'*; but things got steadily worse downsteam. The washing of skins in tanneries, and the dyes and chemicals used in the cloth printing and bleaching processes, were particular culprits. He also refers to privies directly overhanging the stream at some locations; no wonder he remarks further down in his paper that residents in the vicinity of Mitcham Bridge complained that the water was unfit to drink! Braithwaite goes into graphic detail about the pollutants entering the river at Merton: *"At Messrs. Littler's* [printing works] *in dry seasons, there is not sufficient water in the whole river, for washing purposes; twenty men are constantly employed in rinsing dyed goods... 13 cwt. of sulphuric acid, and 3 cwt. of alum are used weekly, ...*[and] *the equivalents of sulphuric acid and potash of the alum are washed out, and ...discharged into the stream. Prussiate of potash, muriate of tin, chloride of lime, and nitrate of iron, are also used, and a great proportion of these also pass into the stream by the washing process. The works require a constant flow, and this water runs off extremely foul... It may be generally remarked, that the water below all the print works was much coloured, when any print-washing was going on. The colour did not appear to settle, it only became largely diffused."*

There were other environmental impacts of the pollution identified in Braithwaite's paper. For example, there was concern over fish deaths, even though this was chiefly couched in financial terms: an 1884 petition stated that the Wandle fisheries were of great pecuniary value. Another direct impact of pollution relating

The river near Plough Lane, Wimbledon, in 1950.

Attempting to deal with the effluent in the river at the Merton Board Mills in 1976.

to sewage was foot rot in sheep, and negative impacts upon effects on timber and hedgerows.

Braithwaite also made a direct connection between the pollution from sewage and the death rate, in his discussion about the construction of the Beddington sewage works by the Croydon Board of Health: *"the sanitary condition of the town was greatly improved…the deaths were now only 16 per 1,000 per annum while the average for the previous ten years was 20 per 1,000 and before the operations of the Board it was 22 per 1,000".* He also notes approvingly that some 20 tons per week of rich manure *'consisting almost entirely of night soil'* fetched about one shilling per ton! Partial deodorisation of the sewage, which was then discharged back into the Wandle from the Beddington works was achieved by adding a fluid, 'McDougal's fluid' to the polluted water. This fluid was a by-product of coal tar distillation, and was added to raw sewage, which was then spread on fields as manure. The problem was that the fluid killed fish and other living organisms in the river, so was used sparingly with the outcome that a *'sickening odour'* arose from the fields.

George Parker Bidder, the President of the Institution of Civil Engineers, who presided over the gathering at which Braithwaite's paper was presented, had a vested interest in the river quality since he owned land along the river at Mitcham. He complained at the meeting that pollution was costing him some £100 per year, and went on to call for legislation to deal with river pollution since it was becoming endemic throughout the country. He took legal action against Croydon Board of Health, but there was little lasting impact although in the following year, 1862, Mr.Chasemore at Waddon Mill did in fact obtain an injunction prohibiting the Board from polluting the River Wandle, probably because of the impact of sewage pollution on his mill's operations. Bidder had to wait another 15 years for the first specific piece of legislation on industrial river emissions, the 1876 River Pollution Act, but his son, a Queen's Counsel, had more success, securing a permanent injunction specifically prohibiting the Authority from polluting the river. This was hardly the end of the matter though: there were continual problems with the Beddington works, and in any case any improvements in treatment were negated by the growing volume of sewage discharges as population increased. Added to this were industrial effluents from the new factories springing up along the banks of the Upper Wandle and replacing the water mills. Around the outbreak of the First World War in 1914, at a time when trout were rapidly expiring even in the cleaner upper reaches of the river, Bidder's grandson Harold tried in vain to re-stock the river at Ravensbury: a combination of insufficient oxygen in the water and pollution from surface runoff conspired to kill them off.

In 1929 a detailed report on the condition of the river by Wandsworth Trades Council painted a very sorry picture of an open sewer, which was a menace to health and a source of danger. The report referred to the cocktail of junk which littered the bed and banks of the stream:

> From the mils at Merton-Road bridge right to the place where the Wandle enters the Thames at Bell Lane Creek the whole stretch of the river runs through land which is alternately patches [of] factories, works, laundries, power stations, etc., and patches which are given over to sewage, rubbish dust shoots, industrial refuse dumps, where very imaginable kind of muck, filth and putrefying matter is heaped, and exposed to the open air.

Many of these factories continued to use the river to discharge their wastes well after the advent of the planning system in 1947. In fact, the use of synthetic detergents after the Second World War made things visually worse than ever. In the 1950's and 1960s when water quality in the river was generally considered to be at its worst, it was not uncommon to see banks of foam on the river, particularly on the grimmer stretches around Earlsfield, and dyes could still contaminate and colour the river. Ignominy reached new depths in the 1960s when the lower part of the river was officially declared a

The outfall from the Beddington Sewage Treatment Works crosses Mill Green before joining the river at Goat Bridge. Steady improvement in the processing of this effluent is responsible for the continued improvement in the Wandle's ecological quality.

sewer. In 1969 a disastrous discharge of sludge from the Beddington works marked perhaps the lowest point in water quality in the Wandle; even the National Trust complained at the stench emanating from the murky water.

In the last 50 years there have been steady improvements, although not without some setbacks in the quality of water in the river. Not only have most of the factories now closed but, of course, we do have at last a combination of public concern and legislation. The foam problem disappeared as manufacturers started using softer detergents, which could be broken down in the sewage works. Without doubt, steady improvements in the standards of treatment, and controls over the quality of effluent discharged have been the most important factors in improving overall water quality, given that the great majority of the river volume downstream of Goat Bridge consists of treated effluent from the Beddington Sewage Treatment Works operated by Thames Water. There have been several significant setbacks, the result of accidental discharges in the main, and the risk of these is never likely to completely recede. Examples of this occurred in 1973, 1995, and 2007 (see below). Despite this, the biological quality of the river downstream of the effluent outfall at Goat Bridge has been steadily improving, according to the Environment Agency (EA), from grade E (the poorest quality) in 1990 to grade C in 2007, although in keeping with other urban rivers phosphates are still a significant problem except in the upstream sections. In the upstream section (above the effluent outfall), the biological quality of the river has been '*consistently fair*' between 1995 and 2009 according to the EA.

This represents a river where there is an absence of some species that are sensitive to pollution and a rise in the number that tolerate it. The chemical water quality in the river has also been improving with the best stretches not surprisingly upstream where the river is fed by chalk springs. The Carshalton and Beddington stretches achieved a grade 'A' between 2000 and 2009, but the method of grading has been altered to remove oxygen demand, which is one measure of organic pollution.

The Water Framework Directive is European legislation under which rivers are graded, and this focuses particularly upon river ecology. Under this assessment the Wandle is still 'poor', with the Carshalton arm likely to improve to 'moderate' by 2015. A reasonable inference from all this is that, for a heavily urbanised catchment, the Wandle is making generally good progress and continuing to improve, but as the 2007 incident reminds us there is always the prospect of setbacks. Pollution from runoff and from illegal discharges from individuals or small businesses is a continued threat and one which is difficult to counter.

The 2007 pollution incident

Before the 2007 pollution incident, the Wandle had become well known as one of the best urban coarse fisheries in the country, supporting a wide a variety of species including Chub, Roach, Dace, Gudgeon and Barbel. These had been introduced into the river by the Environment Agency following a previous pollution incident in 1995. It was on 17 September 2007 that Environment Agency officers received reports from local residents and anglers of hundreds of dead or distressed fish in the River Wandle in the vicinity of Mitcham. There were also reports of a strong smell of chlorine, and milky water. It took three days for Environment Agency officers, helped by members of the Wandle Trust and local angling clubs, to remove some two tonnes of dead fish from the river. The culprit was sodium hypochlorite (chlorine), which had been carelessly released from Beddington Sewage Treatment Works during a cleaning operation in the plant. The fine handed down – £125,000 and some £21,000 in costs, represents less than 0.1% of the company's annual turnover, so will have done less damage to the company than the bad publicity, and in fairness Thames Water have since been active in a vigorous programme to bring the river back to life again, pledging some £500,000 in a five-year plan which is ongoing, and has included restocking the river with fish.

'Williamson's Dyeworks' (1861) by J E Nicholls. The works stood on Garratt Lane by Mapleton Road bridge, Wandsworth.

3 The industrial heritage

London's engine room

The Wandle had two key advantages that made it such a significant manufacturing centre. The most important was that the river was close to London, so there was a great market for industrial goods; and it's worth remembering that, at the height of Wandle output, there were no other sources of power available that came close to water power. The second asset was that the gradient of the river was relatively steep, certainly compared with potential competitors close to the capital. This was particularly true in the upper reaches of the Wandle. The whole river falls about 124 feet by the time it reaches Wandsworth, but using Braithwaite's calculations, the Wandle at Carshalton falls about 55 feet (approximately 16 metres) from the ponds in the village centre to Mitcham Bridge close to the northern boundary of the parish; this is a distance of about two miles. Along this stretch there were at least ten mill sites, most with more than one wheel. Even the larger Lea could not compare with the Wandle when it came to mills.

In 1086, the Domesday Book recorded 13 mills on estates known to have bordered the Wandle. Research by the Wandle Group suggests that no fewer than seven of these were in the ownership of Westminster Abbey! The power and influence of church and state at that time

Lower Mills Wandsworth, around 1885.

were pervasive, of course. The first use of Wandle mills other than as corn mills was the fulling of cloth. Fulling is a process of cleaning cloth or wool by hammering the fibres and scouring them with a cleaning material, notably Fuller's Earth whence the process derives its name. This material was available locally in Surrey. The machinery was operated by cams on the shaft of a waterwheel or on a tappet wheel, which lifted the hammer. Although fulling goes back to the time of the Romans who probably introduced the process to Britain, before the twelfth century it was a manual activity involving people in physically trampling the cloth in tubs and streams. Nonetheless, fulling was the first part of the cloth-making process to become mechanised. The first records of fulling on the Wandle were at Wandsworth in 1303 and later at Carshalton in 1361.

Technology, skills and enterprise

The Wandle did have its limitations; for example the river's gradient although steep in the London context hardly bears comparison with, for example, those running off the Pennines into Sheffield. And the area also had geographical shortcomings, for example lack of access to the hill sheep to encourage a textile industry to grow, or the absence of metal ores nearby. But before the Industrial Revolution saw manufacturing industry moving to coalfields, the Wandle Valley enjoyed a productive heyday, particularly as increasingly sophisticated technology enabled the power of running water to be adapted for a wider variety of uses. Of course, in some industries, for example paper and felt making, and textile printing, the water-wheel only

Lower Mill, Butter Hill, Carshalton, in late Victorian times when it was operating as Denyers Flour Mill.

did ancillary work and many of the processes were divorced from water power. Nonetheless, most of the major industrial trades came here in some form or other: metal working, textile finishing, papermaking, leather. The period between about 1640 and 1800 in particular was a boom period for industry, as reference to the industrial occupations in the Wandsworth parish registers testifies. Scarlet dyeing for example developed in the 1640s, rekindling an earlier dyewood grinding industry. A little later copper and iron working grew up along with gunpowder milling. Shortly afterwards the skilful Huguenots brought some sophisticated techniques to the Wandle Valley from France and the Low Countries. For example, refugees from Caudebec in Normandy brought hat making, keeping the secrets of their trade (which involved a liquid process to prepare the beaver and rabbit skins) well covered until they

Smith & Brownsmiths mills, Carshalton, in 1894. This mill, on the Westcroft Canal and later known as Grove Iron Mill, had the only overshot wheel on the river.

were leaked in 1730. Up until then, ironically even the Cardinals of Rome ordered their hats from the poor Protestant refugees in Wandsworth! Hat making continued at Wandsworth until the first half of the nineteenth century.

By 1680 more industrial skills had been developed, for example calico printing, which was to become a major Wandle industry, but also leather and felt. Bleaching itself had been brought to England by the Dutch and is first recorded on the Wandle at Mitcham in about 1620.

Wandle industries continued to grow during the eighteenth century, whilst elsewhere in the country engineers and industrialists were forging what would become the coal-based industrial revolution. Ironically, one of the men who was credited with being a leader in the transition from wind-and-water to steam power, John Smeaton, also turned his hand to improving water wheels, which of course in the mid-eighteenth century were still the chief source of power. Smeaton's tests proved that breastshot waterwheels were much more efficient than undershot because of the use made of gravity, and overshot wheels the most efficient of all. Smeaton, regarded by many as the father of modern civil engineering, was engaged by George Shepley at his Upper Mills in Wandsworth and at Carshalton where he rebuilt the Hackbridge oil mill in 1778. He also worked on Adkins Mill at Wandsworth, Waddon Mill and the paper mill at Carshalton, although it's not clear if his plans were consummated in these cases. In all, he built over 40 mills, the most significant probably being at the Carron Company Ironworks, Falkirk in 1769.

How many mills?

The reference to the Wandle being the hardest-worked river for its size in the world at the start of the nineteenth century is well known, along with the suggestion that some 90 mills were at work on the river at one time. Indeed, at least one source contends that the number of separate wheels might have been double that! All this seems excessive, yet many sites had more than one wheel at work, in more than one building. One observer wrote: *"Old maps do not do justice to the mill establishment, neither do the various investigators who seem to have charged up and down the stream missing more than they had seen."* It's certainly true that not all mills needed a complex arrangement of mill heads, leats and sluices. Some, like the Liberty Mill at Merton, for example, were simply undershot wheels using the normal flow of the river. In other locations, as at Middle Mill, Wandsworth, historical references suggest two mills on this site by the eighteenth century, along with a windmill as well.

Michael Wilks, a distinguished researcher and long-time chair of the *Carshalton Society*, produced in 1967 a checklist of Wandle water mills on the Carshalton river. Apart from the well-documented sites in the parish, Wilks suggested that there may well have been several other mills, for example, Doerr's Mill near the house known as *Culverside* (see Culvers map p. 164) *'shown on the Bowen map of 1755'* as a copper mill but later a leather mill tenanted by Louis Doerr. Peter McGow's research suggests the mill wasn't a mill proper, but a factory which continued in operation until the twentieth century, later than Wilks suggests. The mill referred to by Braithwaite as Hitchcocks Mill on the Westcroft Canal, near the junction of the main river was shown as Cressingham's Snuff Mill on the 1847 tithe map; Wilks thought there may have been two mills here which were eventually absorbed into the Grove Ironworks. There was possibly also a manorial mill in the grounds of *Carshalton House*, and another snuff mill alongside the manorial corn mill (Upper Mill). Below Goat Bridge was Gibbs Mill (the tannery and parchment manufactory and therefore probably not a mill at all in the strict sense) and both peppermint and gunpowder mills. Wilks says

Possibly the only surviving picture of the Wandle Tannery, also known as Gibbs Mill, which stood on the Carshalton bank of the river immediately downstream of Goat Bridge. This view dates from around 1906.

"*it is difficult to disentangle the references to mills here*", but suggests that half a dozen can be positively identified. It's certainly true that some mills come and go from early maps, which lends weight to the idea that early cartographers were not always too fastidious about including everything.

The modern consensus seems to be that the most likely maximum number of mill sites on the river was around 50,[1] although many of these would have been buildings housing more than one wheel.

Wandle entrepreneurs

The river also attracted numerous entrepreneurs who played an important part in developing the industrial capacity of the river, just as in later times and different areas when, for example, coal or engineering have been the key driving force for industry. Josias Dewye, for example, who was an eminent gunpowder manufacturer at Chilworth, Surrey, came to Carshalton in 1661. George Shepley is another such figure. A Yorkshireman, he came to London and when he acquired the Hackbridge Mills in 1765 he was described as a leather dresser from Southwark. He also acquired the lease on the Wandsworth Upper Mills at about the same time – his main uses of the river were the closely linked industries of oil, and leather dressing, but he also had interests at Walthamstow, for a late eighteenth-century court record mentions one Benjamin Parker who was indicted in that town for "*feloniously stealing, on the 4th of January, a peck of linseed, value 1s., an iron keep of a mill, value 1s. an iron hoop, value 1s. 6d. and eight new spikes, value 8d., the property of George Shepley*" (of Carshalton). He was sentenced to three months in Newgate and a public whipping.

George Ansell was another big name, on the upper reaches of the river. Originally a calico manufacturer in Wallington, he soon diversified into papermaking and by the 1780s had control of the entire Carshalton paper industry, although he was happy to leave others to run the mills while he continued to expand his calico interests. He had also converted one of the Butter Hill mills in Carshalton to snuff manufacture sometime in the 1780s, so he is a good example of a contemporary Richard Branson figure who tried his hand at several trades where money was to be made! He also had plenty of children. Four of George's sons each took on one of the Carshalton mills although none of them seems to have been a very good businessman with the exception of Robert, the youngest who with his own son continued to work the snuff mill until about 1892, when even they ended up bankrupt.

The river attracted men who became leaders in their field, notably, of course, William Morris who turned out his famous chintzes and much else besides at Merton in the last quarter of the nineteenth century; or indeed the Littlers nearby who developed such a close relationship with the Liberty empire, supplying them with their high-quality printed cloths. But there were lesser known figures such as Peter Mauvillain, a calico printer of French extraction, who claimed in 1719 to be employing over 200 people at Mitcham (almost certainly at Ravensbury) and at Wandsworth. This may not seem particularly noteworthy, but it's important to remember that at this time the factory system was still in the future.

In contrast to the production of woollen textiles, which at this time was still very much a domestic industry, the printing of calico, cotton and linen was in many respects a more complicated business. It required a good deal of capital investment before production could begin, in infrastructure (diversion/construction of water channels, bleaching/tentering grounds, etc) and the employment of a range of skilled craftsmen. Interestingly, the early eighteenth century was the time when water-powered factories were just being established, for example Thomas Lombe's silk mill at Derby (1720), often referred to as the first mechanised factory in the world. One difference, of course, was that the print works did not use water to power directly; nonetheless, the Wandle factories played an important role in the early development of the factory system. It's recorded that Henry Gardiner employed 250 people in 1792 (according to Lysons) in his calico printing works at Wandsworth, a very significant figure if correct.

Industrial case studies
Calico and other textiles

Of all the Wandle industries, textile printing, and in particular the colourful printed cotton cloth known as calico, was perhaps the most widely represented in the valley, particularly when one considers the associated cloth bleaching grounds that abounded close to the river. Although distance from raw materials meant that the textile spinning and weaving trades were poorly represented here, textile finishing was quite a different matter. The river was able to tick all the boxes of the factors of production: clean water for bleaching and other processes, access to high-quality dyes made on the river, plenty of capital and a ready market in London (both numerically and in terms of the affluence of customers) and, significantly, the skills to develop the techniques. We can thank the Huguenots for much of the development of textile skills in the Wandle Valley: French Protestants who were subject to intense persecution in France after 1685 when Louis XIV declared Protestantism illegal, many Huguenots fled to Britain and a substantial enclave settled in the valley especially around Merton and Wandsworth. They helped to develop industries like hat making, felt, silk weaving and printing, and above all, calico. The name comes from Calicut (now Kozhikode), the chief city of the Malabar region of Kerala, India. During the seventeenth century the East India Company imported calico, which when bleached, then dyed or printed, was known as 'chintz'. Although very expensive, it became very popular in well-connected circles. This innovation was seen as a threat by established weavers elsewhere in the country and, although the Wandle never saw the sort of Luddite scenes perpetrated by machine breakers in the Pennines, the English woollen industrialists obtained an Act of Parliament in 1700 banning imported printed fabrics. This despite representations from important printers like Peter Mauvillain, one of the most successful of the Huguenot refugees, who occupied the Ravensbury Print Works at Mitcham. These restrictions, although later eased, remained in some form for 75 years, and even after that, calico was taxed. As a result, merchants imported plain cotton and developed the techniques of printing here in Britain, although the skills were brought across from the Low Countries by the Huguenots using wood blocks and rollers. Wandle water was regarded as pure and clean, an important attraction both for bleaching and printing the cloth. Despite the graphic accounts of pollution described particularly by Braithwaite in the 1850s, it's worth remembering that the discharge of the river was high and pollutants were able to be diluted during this period.

Bennett and Leach at Merton

Daniel Lysons in his 'Environs of London' written in 1792 discusses the development of calico at Merton: "*In the year 1724 a manufactory for printing calicoes was established on the site of Merton Abbey which still exists upon the same spot, being at present in the occupation of Mssrs Newton, Hodgson and Leach who…have brought the art to a great degree of perfection*". Within the abbey walls he refers to another calico printing firm, which had been opened in 1752 on the west bank of the river close to Merton High Street. These were the works that eventually would be bought by William Morris in 1881. Lysons quotes what seems a remarkable employment figure for the time, although this included Thoyts copper mill… "*Upon a moderate computation there are 1000 persons employed within the walls in different manufactories, a pleasing contrast to the monastic indolence which reigned there in former times!*"

John Leach, son of the managing partner of the firm, was born in 1742 and carried on the business in the Abbey grounds, residing in one of the houses shown in the old print on p. 203. Factories at Merton used a lot of coal and this is how Leach came to know Thomas Bennett, also born the same year into a well-established family of coal merchants in Wandsworth. Whilst John's eldest son died tragically in a Thames accident in 1794, Thomas's son, also Thomas, who was born in 1775, courted and married John's eldest daughter Sarah-Jane in 1797, cementing the two families closer together. Meanwhile John Leach had dissolved the partnership referred to above and left Merton Abbey print works to set up an extensive new works on both sides of the river. He was in need of younger blood, and his second son was still young; so his son-in-law Thomas, with the blessing of his own father, left the coal wharf at Wandsworth and went into partnership with Leach. The old man retired in 1812, whereafter Thomas developed a process of printing black and white patterns in calico which earned the business a high reputation throughout Europe. The large range of buildings which Leach had built became known as Bennett's Mill (map p.200), but on his own retirement in 1825, Thomas's only son John Leach Bennett was faced with an industry in decline; and he resigned the lease to one Edmund Litter, a silk printer, who had arrived at Merton Abbey print works two years earlier and who, of course, went on to develop Merton's association with high-quality textiles (see chapter on Merton in the walks section).

The Bennett family house which Thomas had built stood in extensive grounds close to the modern junction of Haydons Road and Merton High Street. It was named *Hotham House* after the fragmented estate of Sir Richard Hotham, a knight and one-time MP for Southwark. Sir Richard it was who until 1792 owned and occupied Merton Place, prior to its later acquisition by Emma Hamilton and Horatio, Lord Nelson.

All along the Wandle the industry took hold, and the distinctive bleaching fields with their parallel water channels became part of the Wandle Valley scene for about 150 years. The bleaching of the cloth was a necessary preliminary to the actual printing, and they were two quite separate activities (although sometimes found close together on the river). The cloth was washed in a lye solution (potassium hydroxide) made from wood ash, continually wetted and dried by men (or more likely, according to surviving images of the bleaching process, women) who walked along the narrow ditches and scooped water over the cloth. Sunlight took over and the process of oxidation bleached the cloth, but this took at least a month even in favourable conditions. There were grounds all along the river, at Croydon, Wallington, Carshalton, Mitcham, Merton and Wandsworth. The bleaching grounds were quite extensive – one large one occupied part of the modern industrial estate between Deen City Farm and Merton Abbey Mills; another, owned by the Reynolds family on Culvers Island, Carshalton, was referred to as the 'most extensive in the kingdom'.

Other calico printing mills were established along the river from Croydon (where within the old Archbishop's Palace, part of which remains, a mill used the river before it was buried underground) all the way down to Wandsworth. Textile printing had been established at Merton in the early eighteenth century in the old Priory grounds (box p. 36), although the site is perhaps associated more with the famous fashion and design firm of Arthur Liberty, established in Regent Street in 1875. In fact it was the previous occupiers, Edmund Littler & Co., who developed the works as a site of high-quality output using wood block printing. When Liberty set up shop, he was attracted by Littler's craftsmanship, and as one of the few firms able to meet Liberty's high standards, Littlers soon ended up sending almost all their printed silks to Liberty's. It was a natural development when Liberty took over the works in 1904. Liberty's continued on the site until well after the Second World War, only ceasing production in 1972, although textile printing on the site continued for another decade thereafter. It was the long-established tradition of textile printing at Merton from the early eighteenth century which was one factor attracting William Morris to Merton in the late nineteenth century.[2]

2. For more on Morris at Merton, see the Merton section of the Trail Guide, pp. 202–203.

Further upstream, William Kilburn, one of the most celebrated of textile designers, had a factory on a branch of the river at Wallington until his death in 1818, although he also had earlier connections with the industry at Merton Abbey Print Works. The whole printing process was complex. Hardwoods like pear or sycamore were used in the cutting of the design; they might be a couple of inches thick and in 'plates' of 10 inches. The ink was transferred to the calico in a complex process made the more so by the fact that each colour had to be applied separately and, on a large tableau, a block of say, 10" x 6" would need to be applied many hundreds of times, each with great accuracy. Kilburn's designs would typically have had maybe five or six colours. Even some of the dyes for printing the cloth were produced on the river, in the log-wood and madder dye mills which ground tropical wood and roots to produce rich red dyes. This industry collapsed, however, after synthetic bleaches were invented in the early nineteenth century and competition from the Lancashire mills stimulated the geographical shift of cloth manufacture. For some time after that, however, in a Wandle form of 'industrial inertia', the bleaching grounds with their distinctive channels survived, many being taken over for the growing of watercress.

Snuff
Until Queen Victoria's time from the seventeenth century, inhaling the ground powder of tobacco was very much in fashion. It appears to have been brought back to Europe from South America by the Spanish and was credited with therapeutic properties, it being thought that sneezing induced by the inhalation cleared the body. Despite hostility from some authorities and even the Catholic Church, it caught on, particularly in high society – George IV for example had a huge stock of snuff – and it was produced in a bewildering variety of blends and flavours. Snuff was so popular that the writer Jonathan Swift claimed that its production employed "*by far the greatest number of hands of any manufacturer in the kingdom*". Although the parallel vice of smoking tobacco leaf in a pipe, for which we can credit the Elizabethan English who introduced it from North America, was also popular, it was the arrival of the cigarette in the mid-nineteenth century that marked the beginning of the end for snuff. Interestingly, English snuff still occupies a small niche market, and is made by a couple of old firms in Sheffield and Kendal, and there are even signs of a small revival.

It is hardly surprising then, that the water wheels of the Wandle were turned to this industry, so suited to the use of grinding stones, particularly in the faster flowing upper reaches of the river from Beddington and Carshalton down to Mitcham and Morden. Also, unlike the large textile factories, snuff mills required few workers and relatively little capital.

The popularity of snuff increased apace in the seventeenth century and the mills took over and produced large quantities. Before grinding, the tobacco had to be dried in a kiln or oven, not unlike the way in which hops were dried in an oast house. It was quite skilled work, turning and exposing different parts of the leaves in turn. There are no remains of ovens now on the river, save for a filled-in brick arch in the wall of Ravensbury Mill. Close to the entrance to Ravensbury Park, a reconstruction of a milling arrangement has been installed. A large shallow bowl built up of elm and sometimes lined with copper held the ground snuff, one or more vertical stone wheel(s) grinding with their edges. This, of course, was in contrast to corn mills where the sides of the stones did the work. Later on, a more sophisticated set-up was employed, for example, at Lambert's

Hackbridge snuff mill, whereby a series of pestles were turned in bowls.

Although snuff was manufactured right along the Wandle, Morden was arguably the centre of the Wandle snuff industry, between the Ravensbury Mill and the two adjacent mills in Morden Hall Park. In 1914 an historian wrote: "*Leaving the village (Mitcham) by the path across the marshes west of the church, the low rumble of a water wheel betokens a mill at work, and the fragrance shows that it is snuff.*" Nonetheless, for the employees, working in a snuff mill was not pleasant: like much factory work in the past, shifts were long, commonly 12 hours, in a hot and dusty environment with little light and in a confined space. The dust problem was there every day for the millers and for anyone else whose duties took them into the mill. Workers wore wet sponge respirators and found conditions very trying. The snuff was sifted, weighed and frequently blended, for there was an astonishing range of varieties, before being packed in barrels for shipment.

Ravensbury Mill, Morden photographed in 1983

The Morden snuff mills were large and had a high output, turning out about 6000 lb of snuff each month, working day and night. We know that John Hatfeild, whose great grandson Gilliat Edward was eventually to bequeath the Morden Hall estate to the National Trust, married into the Taddy family, noted snuff grinders; and his son Alexander became a partner in the City firm Taddy, Tomlin and Hatfeild (later, simply 'Taddy & Co.'). The business did well and opened extensive premises in the Minories, in the City of London. Some time around 1835 the firm leased Morden Mills to supply snuff. It was a job for girls at the Minories factory to sort the tobacco, the good leaves going for smoking whilst the stalks and veiny parts ended up going for snuff grinding. Records suggest that up to 70 employees worked at the Minories. Snuff making continued at the Morden mills until 1922, when following a strike at the Minories, Gilliat Edward who ostensibly had no real enthusiasm for what was by then an industry in decline, closed the factory and mills. To be fair to him and his name as a philanthropist, however, he did offer displaced workers from the mills the opportunity to work on his estate. A kiln for drying the tobacco leaves survives in the mill.

Ravensbury Mill is associated with the Rutter family, who were in occupation from 1805 until it ceased manufacturing tobacco and snuff in 1926. Ravensbury was the home of Rutter's 'Mitcham Shag', a popular smoking tobacco.

Paper

Paper-making is another industry in which, unlikely as it might seem today, the Wandle was pre-eminent for a time. Before wood pulp was used in paper making (about 1850), the major raw material was simply old rags and, of course, London was an important source of these. Clean water was an essential ingredient as well, of course, as the power provided by the stream. The earliest Wandle paper mill seems to be the one owned by the Scawens, an important Carshalton family, in a lane known at the time as Paper Mill Lane. This mill was later leased by William Curteis and later his sons John and Thomas. Nearby in an adjacent mill, like Curteis's leased from Carshalton industrialist George Ansell, Christopher Patch was one of the first to use chlorine to bleach the rags for his paper. According to his 1792 obituary in *The Gentleman's Magazine,* he was "*one of the best paper-makers this country has yet produced*", and the two mills together made Carshalton a centre of national significance for paper making. Even as late as 1895, when the bulk of the industry had moved elsewhere, C. Barrett (in *Surrey Highways, Byways and Waterways, 1895*) claimed Ansell's 'noted' paper mill produced 'the finest handmade foolscap' in the Kingdom. Further down the river paper was made at several locations; we have records from 1860 of the Royal Paper Mills at Wandsworth, which were on a far larger scale than the Carshalton mills. 'News and plate papers, lithos, cream laids, writings, fine printings and super-calendered' were among the range of output. There were two machines, 76" and 84" wide and the output increased from about 60 tons per week in 1889 to 90 in 1901, according to the annual paper mills directories. In late Victorian times newsprint from the Royal Paper Mills in Wandsworth supplied *The Times* and the *Illustrated London News.* The raw material used was a kind of rush grass known as 'esparto' imported from estates owned by the proprietor, William McMurray, in Spain and North Africa. It was brought into Wandsworth via the former Surrey Iron Railway basin which became known as McMurray's canal. The manufacturing process at Wandsworth was interesting: the esparto was dusted by beating, boiled in caustic soda, passed into washers and breakers to produce a brown pulp, then bleached and strained to make a kind of thick blotting paper termed 'half-made'. This material was then again passed through the beaters, washed and broken to give a thin milky liquid, which was passed to the large vats above the papermaking machine and made into paper in rolls from five to eight miles long (!) and weighing 10 to 15 cwt (about ½ to ¾ of a ton).

Brewing

The pure chalk waters of the Wandle and the area's proximity to London made it an obvious place for brewing. Numerically, Croydon was the centre of the Wandle brewing industry. Crowleys stemmed from a Quaker brewing family who started brewing in the late eighteenth century at nearby Waddon, but went on to become something of a swallower of smaller breweries themselves. Throughout several acquisitions, including the Alton Brewery, the company continued to trade as Crowleys, their one claim to fame being the acquisition in 1901 of the business of William Garton, patentee of the invert sugar subsequently used in the brewing industry. Crowleys, in turn, were bought, along with their sizeable estate of 248 licensed houses, by Watney Combe Reid in 1948. It's interesting *en passant* that the Watney brewing family had several connections to the Wandle Valley, although their Stag brewery was sited in Pimlico and later moved to Mortlake. James Watney lived in Haling Park, Croydon, whilst the large family had links with Beddington, Mitcham and Wimbledon; and inherited property in Merton and in Morden. Watneys it was who produced the first 'keg' beer, *Red Barrel*, and became the *bête noire* of the real ale movement.

Nalder & Collyers was sited on land now occupied by Leon House in the High Street. It was acquired by Fulham's Swan brewery in 1919, then transferred to Hoares in the mid 1920s before being, in turn, absorbed by Ind Coope a decade later, in a story typical of the dog-eat-dog history of brewing. Page & Overton stood off Surrey Street, close to the engine house which survives. Page & Overton's Brewery, the third of Croydon's ale brewers, was formed in 1892 when Nathaniel Page joined forces with Frederick Overton, owner of the Royal Oak Brewery in Surrey Street. £100,000 was spent in 1929 on enlarging the brewery premises and installing additional plant. A report compiled in 1932 outlines the improvements made to the plant, the bottling machine being described as a 'real marvel', filling and crowning bottles at a rate of 300 dozen per hour. The Page & Overton Company became one of the oldest and largest industries in Croydon, before being closed in 1954. It had its own maltings in Church Road and its own wells for extracting brewing liquor (water to you and me). The malthouses survived until the early 1970s, but today all that remains is the brick granary at No 8 Overton's Yard. Built in 1880, this has been restored as Granaries Nightclub and is still commemorated in the street name of Overtons Yard. The *Swan & Sugar Loaf* pub in South Croydon retains a striking Page & Overton

Detail from the Swan & Sugar Loaf, *Croydon, showing now rare Page & Overton brewery signage*

Bottle labels from the Boornes brewery at Wallington.

exterior frontage. There was also a large works at Croydon, Whites, making ginger beer and other mineral waters.

At Wallington, Boorne's brewery was established in 1809. It took its name from one Thomas Boorne, a former Deptford dockyard foreman. Brewing ceased in the 1930s, but the buildings survived until 1968 when they were destroyed by fire. The site is now occupied by a block of sheltered housing, *Old Brewery House*. The handsome brewhouse fronted the London Road just north of the pond between it and the former brewery tap, the *Rose & Crown*, which survives. It too was absorbed by Ind Coope.

A brewery stood close to the river at Mitcham. The first reference to it appears to be in 1789 when it was Hughes Brewery, and went through several name changes including the 'Surrey Brewery' before it was acquired by Thunder & Little in 1884, when the place was known as the Eagle Brewery. A photograph survives of one of the company's wagons delivering their well-known 'Mitcham Ales'. In 1898 T & L

Boorne's brewery, Wallington, photographed in 1908.

took over the Cheam brewery and changed the name to Mitcham & Cheam brewery. However, following the usual fashion in the industry, they in turn were bought out in 1912, by Page & Overton of Croydon who promptly shut the Cheam site. Brewing at Mitcham ceased between the wars, but like Boorne's, the buildings survived until the early 1970s. And so to Wandsworth and to Young's brewery: this is the largest, longest lived and by far the most successful of Wandle breweries. Much has been written about Young's, but brewing on the riverside site of the Ram brewery seems to date back as far as the sixteenth century. Young's themselves were founded in 1831 when the brewery was purchased by Charles Young and Anthony Bainbridge. Until its closure in 2006, the company claimed with some justification that the Ram Brewery in Wandsworth was the oldest brewing site in continuous operation, and it still had a steam engine which had been installed in 1835 and had been in regular use until the 1980s.

In a modern twist, which again mirrors the recent history of British brewing, the name of the river has been resurrected and commemorated in the beers brewed by a new microbrewery, Sambrook's, which is based at Battersea. Their first brew, which is still going strong, was launched in early 2009 and called 'Wandle Ale' after the river which is only a ten-minute walk from the brewery. In many ways it is an apt symbol of the regenesis of the river!

Dyeworks

Dyeing was another well-represented industry along the river, produced by grinding either plant or insect matter, or from wood, principally logwood (a species of flowering tree giving dark dyes including black) and Brazil wood which produced a reddish-brown dye. Incidentally, the name Brazil is assumed to derive from the Portuguese word for the red colour of brazil wood, which was found in abundance during the Portuguese colonisation of the Americas. In Wandsworth, according to Gerhold, dyeworks were introduced by Nicholas Plume to take advantage of the river's clean water. In addition to the Brazil Mill (the Middle Mill), there were several other dyeworks. Between Middle Mill and the High Street, on a site later absorbed into Young's Ram Brewery, was the Barchard family's dyeworks, whilst further south stood the Williamson works where the famous Wandsworth scarlet dyes were produced using cochineal and kermes, both derived from insects. It is said that these fast dyes were highly prized by Catholic Cardinals for their hats! The other significant dyeworks belonged to the Dubuissons (a prominent

Wandsworth family); the location of their dyeworks is uncertain, but it could have been at the Duntshill Flock Mill site. There were other dye mills along the river, for example, the madder mill at Merton and the seventeenth-century logwood mill on the river near Mitcham.

Leather working

Reference to a leather mill is first recorded at Goat Bridge, Carshalton in 1644, on a site which continued an association with leather skins for almost 300 years. The distinct processes in leather treatment were all represented on the river. First of these were the tanneries (see, for example, the Beddington Corner map, p. 170) where the skins were chemically treated, originally with tannin, to turn them into leather, which does not decompose. Softening the leather to make it workable was usually achieved with oils, particularly linseed oil, hence the close association with this industry and the leather mills, for example at Hackbridge (see p. 162–163). Skins were placed in a trough of linseed oil and pounded by hammers to soften them.

But leather working continued at numerous locations on the Wandle until well into the twentieth century, often closely associated with linseed oil mills; a variant was budge or lamb skin, which was used as a type of fur to decorate the edges of gowns; this took place at Mitcham Mill, Carshalton for a while in the eighteenth century. This site, including the former logwood mill nearby, was acquired by Deed & Sons of London in 1875, and operated as the Eagle Leather Works. Deed's turned out high-quality soft leathers such as buckskin, and while the mill building survived until 1965,

Deed's Leather Mill and tannery stood downstream from Goat Bridge. It survived until the mid 1960s.

the firm continued in operation in other nearby buildings until as late as 1989. The long association of this Beddington Corner area with the leather industry was kept alive in the name of the nearby pub, the *Skinners Arms*, which itself met its demise some ten years ago.

Finally, mention should be made of the Connollys' leather mill at Merton: Samuel and John Connolly had long experience as leather dressers before they acquired a former calico works just downstream of the mill in the final years of the nineteenth century. This was the 'patent leather works' shown on the 1894 map. The brothers then took over Merton Mill nearby in 1919, and the corn mill, and converted it to leather. Their reputation for high quality leathers was unrivalled, and they came to specialise in leather for use in vehicles, particularly in Rolls Royce and Jaguar cars and in ocean liners. The firm continued in operation until 1994.

Other industries

At the other end of the river, Wandsworth developed a range of industries, not all of which used the river directly, although they were often good examples of what geographers would now call industrial linkage. For example, Blackmore's bolting cloth factory in Wandsworth Plain (1814–1919) turned out material for sifting flour, in an industry which goes back to Roman times when wheat was sifted into several grades using, for the most part, woven horse hair. This was a very important activity since ground grains from the mill come in a variety of sizes, and the finest particles are generally the best quality and most sought after. Later, this industry became mechanised and wire replaced textiles, which were prone to wearing out. Other industries in Wandsworth area which have been briefly referred to already included hat-making and metal working. In the eighteenth century, the valley lost its copper and iron manufacture, but gained malting and distilling, oil pressing and chemicals, linked to textiles. According to local historian Dorian Gerhold, the town had a greater range of industry than almost any other parish in the country. This all declined in the nineteenth century, of course, when steam engines replaced water power and the river became polluted

A 1950s view of Wandleside Cable Works, near Mapleton Road, Wandsworth.

by the remaining industries, although new industries, not necessarily with direct dependence on the river, moved in as the nearby population continued to swell. An old press cutting of around 1919 refers to the new industries in the valley, although many water wheels were still in business at that time. *"...One part of the [Royal] paper mills makes varnishes now and the other ... is a gas mantle factory ... a little higher up is a gramophone workshop. At Earlsfield, street lamps are made in an old factory that still has memories of silk."*

Reference to gunpowder has already been made; the Wandle became a leading supplier for about a 50-year period from the late seventeenth century. The ingredients, chiefly charcoal, saltpetre (potassium nitrate) and brimstone (sulphur) were ground by edge runners (vertical millstones) in a similar fashion to snuff, and compacted before being packed into barrels for sale. Older readers will remember the Pain's fireworks factory in Mitcham, which was a geographical successor to the industry until its own demise in 1965.

Industrial change and decline

As the use of the water to power industry directly declined, industrial sites along the river became used for new industries, many of which may have had little direct link to the river other than geographical proximity. The continuation of industries on sites of former water mills can be seen by studying the map of the area around Lower Mill, Carshalton, in 1933. Compare this map with that from 20 years earlier on p. 148. The paper mill, which briefly became a chocolate factory between 1908 and about 1915, and then a pencil works until 1922, is no more, having being replaced by Distillers chemical works.

There are other chemical works, later the home of Vinyl Products Ltd., on a large site adjacent to a linoleum works on the river itself, dwarfing the old Snuff Mill which still stands alongside the river. Even this, however, had new uses: R. Thurston Hopkins, author of *Old watermills and windmills* visited the mill in 1930 and offered the following description: *"[an] old snuff mill, a plain weatherboarded building, with a roof of warm red tiles … inside, the building shows every sign of respectable old age, the oak framework being solid and not less than two hundred years old. The waterwheel has been dismantled, and nothing of the old snuff-grinding machinery remains, if we except one or two of the mill-stones which are now displayed in odd corners … Although the mill is no longer working, it is still the home of an ancient craft carried on by John Boughton, who manufactures parchment and vellum … Mr. Boughton informed me that the vogue for the jazz band gave a new lease of life to his business, owing to the fact that the heads of bass drums required the best vellum…".* Mr Boughton had previously worked at the Hackbridge leather mill a few hundred yards downstream. He clearly stayed some time at the snuff mill since Hillier writing in 1951 made a passing reference to *"the snuff mill (now Broughton's* (sic) *parchment works)"*. Interestingly, the snuff mill, much altered, is still in industrial use today by a lithographic printer, and is known as the vellum mill.

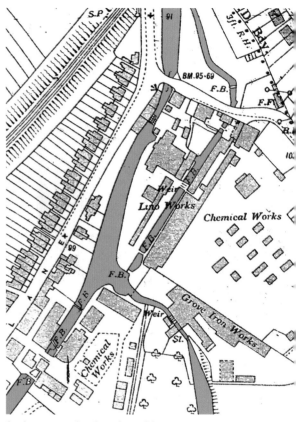

Ordnance map of the Mill Lane area, Carshalton, 1933.

In general, more recent industrial use of the riverside was related more to what geographers call locational inertia than to any direct draw of the river as a raw material or power source. That's to say, the sites remained in industrial use, often zoned as such in local plans. This applied both to many of the larger employers on the river in the mid twentieth century like Mullard's at Mitcham or the Merton

Mullards factory at Hackbridge in 1983. The view is taken upstream from the foot of Buckhurst Avenue, Carshalton.

Board Mills, but also to the industrial estates on the riverside today as at Earlsfield, Mitcham and Hackbridge. Other industrial sites have gone, changing to retailing (at Merton, for example), or housing. Significant new residential developments took place on both the Mullards site and BP Chemicals/Vinyl Products site (Carshalton) during the 1990s. Access issues, land values and pollution have all led to such locations no longer being favourable ones for large industries. Another clear trend over the past 40 years has been in the direction of developing the river's amenity and biodiversity value at the expense of industry; given how grim it was formerly, the stretch between Connolly's Mill and Summerstown is perhaps as good an example as any.

Demolition underway on the site of Vinyl Products Ltd., at Mill Lane/Butter Hill, Carshalton, September 1986

The Surrey Iron Railway

The rapid growth of industry along the Wandle, particularly during the eighteenth century, was hampered by the inadequacy of the available transport. Horse and wagon was about the only option, but needless to say roads were generally very poor and journeys both slow and laborious. As noted in chapter 2 (see p. 15), this prompted local businessmen to engage William Jessop in 1799 to advise them as to the feasibility of a canal. He was unenthusiastic, as we have already seen, but he went on to suggest an iron railway on which goods could be carried in wagons drawn by horses along iron rails. Horse-drawn plateways were still a relatively new technology, but the businessmen reacted favourably. The Surrey Iron Railway Company was formed by the great and good of the river including Henry Hoare of Mitcham Grove, a prominent banker; James Perry of *Wandle Bank House* who owned Merton Flour Mill, and George Shepley, who had mills at either end of the river in Wandsworth and Hackbridge, and thus had a particular interest. Indeed, it is quite likely that he originated the idea. Certainly, his sons Richard, Hugh and Michael were all named in the eventual Act as shareholders in the company. In fact, the scheme as conceived was part of a wider plan to secure a railway to Portsmouth from the Thames, to enable year-round transport of goods. There were fears of invasion at this time, so there were strategic reasons for wanting to improve communications, but these receded within a few years following Nelson's success at Trafalgar. In 1801 a Bill was presented to Parliament for the construction of a two-track plateway from Wandsworth to Croydon. It received royal assent on 21 May 1801 as "*an Act for making and maintaining a Railway from the town of Wandsworth to the town of Croydon, with a collateral branch into the Parish of Carshalton, and a navigable communication between the River Thames and the Railway at Wandsworth, all in the County of Surrey*". This Act allowed the Surrey Iron Railway to raise £35,000 in shares of £100, and a further £15,000 by shares or mortgage. In the event it cost £60,000, so cost overruns are not a new thing! The Surrey Iron Railway became the first public railway, which any individual or company could use for a set toll. It was also the first company to use

A montage display of Surrey Iron Railway rails at Wandsworth Museum. Note that the flanges were on the inner sides of the rails and not on the wheels.

SURREY
Iron Railway.

The COMMITTEE of the SURREY IRON RAILWAY COMPANY,

HEREBY, GIVE NOTICE,. That the BASON at *Wandsworth*, and the Railway therefrom up to *Croydon* and *Carfhalton*, is now open for the Ufe of the Public, on Payment of the following Tolls, *viz.*

For all Coals entering into or going out of their Bason at Wandsworth, — *per Chaldron,* 3d.

For all other Goods entering into or going out of their Bason at Wandsworth — *per Ton,* 3d.

For all GOODS carried on the said RAILWAY, as follows, viz.

For Dung, - - *per Ton, per Mile,* 1d.
For Lime, and all Manures, (except Dung,) Lime-ftone, Chalk, Clay, Breeze, Afhes, Sand, Bricks, Stone, Flints, and Fuller's Earth, — *per Ton, per Mile,* 2d.
For Coals, - - *per Chald. per Mile,* 3d.
And, For all other Goods, - *per Ton, per Mile,* 3d.

By ORDER of the COMMITTEE.
W. B. LUTTLY,
Clerk of the Company.

Wendsworth, June 1, 1804.

BROOKE, PRINTER, No. 35, PATERNOSTER-ROW, LONDON.

Poster of toll charges on the Surrey Iron Railway.

the word 'railway' in its title. On 26 July 1803 the line opened to the public from the Ram Field in Wandsworth to Pitlake Meadow in Croydon. In Wandsworth the line crossed the River Wandle on two wooden bridges. The track was based on a cast iron plate rail, and the joins between the plates were supported by stone blocks, about 14" square by 9" thick. The use of stone blocks to support the rails ensured that the horses had a clear walkway between the rails. The bed of the track was gravelled, and the gauge was 4' 2" (127 cm). The wagons were approximately 8' long, carrying a maximum load of over two tons. Jessop calculated that one horse could pull 5 tons at 3 miles per hour for 10 miles.

The short Carshalton branch, doubtless promoted by George Shepley to serve his Hackbridge Mills, opened on 1 June 1804. Shepley's siding terminated at a 'wagon house' just south of the oil mill, according to a contemporary historian, although Shepley did not enjoy the advantages of the railway for very long: he died in February 1807 aged 69. A second line, the Croydon, Merstham & Godstone Railway was added by 1805, extending the route from the Croydon Canal basin (now the site of West Croydon station) and on to the Merstham chalk and limestone quarries. In fact, ironically this part of the line, carefully engineered for gentle gradients, was more of a financial success. On the original section, the low tolls meant that the Railway hardly ever paid a dividend, and its life was short; the advent of steam engines, followed by stronger iron (and later steel) rails from the 1820s rendered the line obsolete. The Merstham section closed in 1838 and the Surrey Iron Railway went by 1846. Nonetheless, William Jessop's engineering expertise was borne out when new lines for the steam trains were laid along much of the Surrey Iron Railway route and are still used today.

Detail from 'The Culvers' (1847) by George Harley (1791–1871).

4 The houses of the river

The Wandle's role as an industrial river is an important part of its biography; but alongside this is the story of its great houses and even today it is still possible along the river upstream of Wimbledon to recognise the legacy of the ancient demesnes and the big houses built by the wealthy on the river's banks. These two facets of the Wandle story overlapped to a considerable extent in later years since the industrialists assumed the mantle of the feudal lords in using the waterside for their pleasure even as they were exploiting it for their gain.

Church, gentlemen and businessmen

It was unsurprisingly the church, which as a great landowner had a big influence on the shaping of Wandle settlements and houses. For example, at Morden and at Merton the villages were dominated by ecclesiastical foundations, Westminster Abbey and Merton Priory, respectively.

Croydon's early history is closely tied to the Archbishops. The wonderful and yet somehow understated collection of buildings in Croydon known as the *Old Palace* is a good place to begin a modern survey of Wandle buildings, since when the Archbishops developed the site it was virtually surrounded by Wandle headwaters and ponds. There may have been earlier buildings on the site, but Croydon's Palace as we know it started life as a twelfth century manor house used by the Archbishops (as Lords of the Manor) as a staging post on journeys between London and Canterbury. The visitors' book included an impressive list of monarchs from Henry III onwards, although at least one, James I of Scotland, was here as a prisoner rather than a guest. William Laud (Archbishop 1633–1645) spent much time in Croydon, and was

Croydon: the Archbishop's Palace, overshadowed by Croydon Minster.

responsible for refurbishing the chapel of Croydon Palace. His name lived on in the pond that was a feature of this part of Croydon until the mid-nineteenth century. Croydon is the only one of the residences owned by the medieval and Tudor archbishops to have survived with its Great Hall intact; during and after the Civil War, and after the execution of Archbishop Laud, the post of Archbishop was abolished and thereafter halls at many other residences were sacked or even demolished. The Grade I listed Great Hall at Croydon, built by Archbishop Stafford around 1450, still has its original oak roof under walls of flint rubble with ashlar buttresses. Also exceptional is the survival of the private rooms used by the Archbishops. These include the Guard Room, originally the Great Chamber, built in about 1400. Even at Lambeth, the Archbishops' main home for more than 800 years, these rooms survived only until the 1820s. Croydon was also the only palace used by the Archbishops after the Restoration. The place fell from favour as the town grew, and the site was considered unhealthy. Their graces eventually decamped in the eighteenth century to nearby Addington, but remarkably the buildings survived, although they successively became, fittingly for Wandle-side buildings, a textile printers, a bleaching works, then later a laundry; and for the last 120 years, a school. Tours are offered on some days: check the website at www.friendsofoldpalace.org for details. The place is well worth a visit and is one of London's architectural gems, which would probably be far more well known and loved were it not in brash, modern Croydon!

Before leaving Croydon and on the subject of buildings, one should mention Archbishop John Whitgift, who of all the Archbishops has left the biggest impact on the town he was so fond of. Among his very rich legacy, the remarkable *Whitgift Hospital*, the almshouses in the very centre of the main shopping street, is an amazing survival, although to call it a Wandle house is perhaps pushing the boundaries. It has probably survived as many municipal demolition attempts by Croydon Corporation as Fidel Castro did assassination attempts by the Americans!

The first recreational use of riverside lands was by the aristocracy, and favoured government servants who enjoyed their country retreats within striking distance of the capital. Relatively few of these estates retain anything approaching their medieval form, but there are significant remnants of them which have survived the onslaught of suburban development, and one or two still have the old parish churches attached to them. The best example is *Beddington Park House*, usually known as *Carew Manor*, with its great Tudor Hall embedded in

Beddington: Carew Manor, properly Beddington Park House, has been much altered but survives in its parkland setting.

a nineteenth-century building. Quite a number, including Ravensbury and Waddon, have left us parks, although little trace of the succession of manor houses that once stood in them. In the case of Ravensbury, nearby stood one of the finest houses on the whole river, *Mitcham Grove* (see p. 183), probably built for one of Elizabeth's court officials. *Merton Place* is a fine example of the use of the riverside location to enhance the location of the house. Originally built in about 1750, it had several mercantile owners before it was acquired for Nelson by

Merton Place. A print from c. 1805.

Lady Hamilton. The gardens made full use of the Wandle, notably in the so-called 'moat', which was later dubbed 'The Nile' in recollection of Nelson's famous naval battle. Merton was clearly a prestigious address since just across the road at this time in *Wandle Bank House* lived Nelson's friend James Perry, the proprietor of the influential *Morning Chronicle*.

Down at Morden, until the Dissolution, the area which is now Morden Hall Park was owned by the Abbey of Westminster. In the mid sixteenth century the estate was brought by Richard Garth, a London clerk and son of a successful lawyer; the house he acquired was called *Growtes*, described in sales particulars of the time as 'recently built'. *Growtes* was a spacious two-storey mansion, which stood in the grounds of what is now *Morden Lodge*, and served as the manor house for Morden until the Hall was built, reputedly by the fifth Richard Garth between 1750 and 1765. In all, the land remained in the stewardship of the Garth family for some three centuries.

The next major wave of riverside colonists consisted of prosperous merchants, lawyers and military types who could afford to build substantial retreats and lead a sort of double life as an *ersatz* country squire! This process was particularly true, of course, of the more attractive southern half of the river, upstream of Colliers Wood. Consider *Morden Lodge*: the original building was the home of Abraham Goldsmid, a senior partner in one of London's largest brokerage firms. His social circle included Nelson, William Pitt, the then Prime Minister, as well as the Prince Regent and the playwright Sheridan. Following his suicide (another case of money problems), the present house is said to have been built by a John Tyrell, of the Mitcham Steam Washing Factory (see p. 196) and occupied by the proprietor of the Ravensbury Print Works. The house still survives, thanks to its acquisition by the Hatfeilds of Morden Hall, although it's well hidden – the best view is from the top deck of a bus on Morden Hall Road!

One of the most famous names to settle on the banks of the Wandle in the nineteenth century was probably George Parker Bidder. It's not a name that rolls off the tongue today, but Bidder, born in Devon in 1806, was a child mathematical prodigy who later became a celebrated engineer. He worked with Robert Stephenson on the London & Birmingham Railway, planned the Victoria Docks in London and did much else besides, including founding the Electric Telegraph Company. His skill and experience also led to much work abroad, for example in Scandinavia and India. In 1860 he was elected 10th President of the Institution of Civil Engineers, and in January of the following year he chaired the meeting at which Frederick Braithwaite

SITE OF WANDLEBANK HOUSE
THIS IS THE SITE OF WANDLEBANK HOUSE, FROM 1791 TO 1821 THE HOME OF JAMES PERRY, OWNER OF THE NEARBY MERTON CORN MILL. PERRY WAS EDITOR AND PROPRIETOR OF THE MORNING CHRONICLE, FOUNDED IN 1770. HE WAS ALSO A CLOSE FRIEND OF ADMIRAL LORD NELSON. WANDLE PARK ONCE FORMED THE GROUNDS OF THE HOUSE.
mer moving life

Wandle Bank House, Merton, in the 1860s.

presented his paper *'On the Rise and Fall of the River Wandle; its Springs, Tributaries, and Pollution'* (see Chapter 2). His connection with the area began in 1846 when he and his wife bought Mitcham Hall (which stood close to Mitcham station[1] on the London Road). Here, most of their children were born. They later sold this and bought the nearby Ravensbury estate, which at that time was very extensive and lay on both sides of the river. On it, he built *Ravensbury Park House* into which the family moved in 1864 (see p. 181). He also found time to intercede to help save Mitcham Common from development, and he fought a rearguard action to stop the Wandle's waters from being polluted and damaging his fisheries. His son, George Parker Bidder QC, took over the house, and one of his grandsons built the far more attractive *Ravensbury Manor* right on the river in 1912.

Perhaps the largest number of substantial houses lay, not surprisingly, on the clean waters around the springs at Carshalton and Wallington. Carshalton itself was a favoured retreat of the wealthy merchants of London during the eighteenth century and probably owes its finest building, *Carshalton House*, to a snuff and tobacco merchant, Edward Carleton. The exact date of the house is not known for certain, but it was probably soon after 1700; certainly the style is of the Queen Anne Period (1702–1714). Sir John Fellows acquired the house in 1714, thereby socially emulating the Lord of the Manor, Sir William Scawen, another rich city merchant. Sir William had acquired the manor in 1696 and had started to lay plans for a grand house in his estate, Carshalton Park. He engaged the Italian architect Leoni to design a great 'palace' (drawings survive), but died in 1722 before the scheme could be put in place, and his heir and nephew Thomas started but never consummated the project. Instead, he bought the Stone Court estate a little distance down the

1. The station building at Mitcham, now a private residential block, has a claim to be the oldest railway station in the world. It was built for the Surrey Iron Railway very early in the nineteenth century.

Carshalton House.

river, which came with a house, rebuilt around 1710 and since demolished, which stood a stone's throw from the ornamental cascade and the Upper Mill. The surviving house across the river known as *The Grove* is later, first appearing in the record in 1847. It is possible that stone from the stillborn Carshalton Park 'palace' ended up in another fine house built close to the Wandle around 1780, *Bramblehaw*. Both the Grove and Carshalton Park estates survive as public parks, thanks in part to an unusually enlightened Urban District Council. Older than all these houses, however, is *Strawberry Lodge*, half a mile downstream, which dates back as far as 1685 and was built by Josias Dewye, a gunpowder maker, who had acquired a mill nearby at Hackbridge. He also owned a larger house known as *Bacons,* which was close to the site of the later *Shepley House* (see below). We know that in the early nineteenth century *Strawberry Lodge* had an estate of some 45 acres of land with a river frontage. As the map (p. 153) shows, George Shepley later built *Shepley House* very close by, although unlike Strawberry Lodge it's no longer with us.

The Water Tower or Bagnio, *Carshalton House.*

Given all this riverside building, it's no surprise that the artist Dewey Bates, writing in the *English Illustrated Magazine* in 1889, remarked that the river was becoming less industrialised and more the preserve of the wealthy: "…[it] *now winds through lovely gardens* [with] *rustic bridges, glens, glades and varied vegetation*". The picture painted above is one of an almost continuous ribbon of gardens and parks along the upper part of the river, many surrounding one or more country houses and retreats.

The beginning of the end

Their demise, however, was faster than anyone might have imagined; London's advancing tide spread south during the nineteenth century and engulfed much of riverside Wimbledon and Merton, whilst around village centres like Carshalton the speculators were at work too. The railway arrived here in 1868 and just four years later, for example, the grounds of *Strawberry Lodge* (above), which had already been truncated by the new line, were acquired by a property developer and

CARSHALTON, SURREY,

One of the healthiest Villages in England, is situate on Gravel soil, about 250 feet above High Water at London Bridge; 3½ Miles from Croydon, 6 from Epsom, and 10 from London.

That part of the Village through which flows the clear rapid Water of the RIVER WANDLE is a Locality held in high estimation, not only on account of its great natural beauty and the excellent Trout Fishing the River affords, but also as being particularly healthy, owing to the influence of the River itself, which, always flowing at about 48 degrees, causes the Temperature to be mild and genial throughout the year.

Residences on the Banks of the Wandle are few in number, and it is seldom one can be purchased.

At HACKBRIDGE, the prettiest part that is intersected by the River, and near where it is crossed by the Road from Carshalton to Mitcham and London, is

"HACKBRIDGE LODGE"

Delightfully situate on the Banks of the

RIVER WANDLE,

Which forms the Boundary on the North, having the Grounds of HACKBRIDGE HOUSE on the opposite Bank, and of

THE CULVERS AND HACKBRIDGE COTTAGE

On the South and East.

It is approached by a PRIVATE CARRIAGE DRIVE by the side of the River,

Coloured Brown on the annexed Plan,

AND COMPRISES

A FREEHOLD COTTAGE RESIDENCE,

SUBSTANTIALLY BUILT of BRICK, SLATED, and TILED,

HAVING

Eight Bed Rooms, One Dressing Room, Box and Store Rooms.

Verandah Entrance with Steps to Hall; a Library, which is a very pleasant Apartment, opening to a Paved CONSERVATORY, heated with Hot Water, and having Tesselated Flower Boxes all round, and back Wall covered with Plumbago and Geraniums.

Also, Dining and Drawing Rooms with Marble Chimney Pieces, and Bay Windows opening on to the Verandah.

The OFFICES, which are on a level with the Ground at the back, comprise—

Housekeeper's Room with Range and Cupboards; Kitchen with close Range and Dresser; Butler's Pantry with Stove; Larder; Scullery; and 2 Water Closets.

Capital Wine and other Cellars. Paved and Glazed Enclosure for cleaning Boots, &c.

The Gas is laid on, and there is an abundant supply of good Water from a Well, with Pump in Butler's Pantry.

THE GARDENS & GROUNDS

Are well laid out and enriched with fine Forest and other Trees, Coniferæ, and Shrubs.

The Frontage to the River is about 450-ft, part of which is a Beautiful

TERRACE WALK

Of 40 Yards, by the side of the RIVER WANDLE.

1879 Particulars of sale bill, Blake, Son and Haddock, Auctioneers.

divided into building plots. Moving into the twentieth century the development of first the suburban rail network and later the opening of the Underground railhead at Morden enabled estates to fall like ripe plums into the hands of developers. A good case in point is Harold Bidder's *Ravensbury Manor,* which he built in a lovely riverside location as late as 1912, making it the last significant Wandle-side mansion to go up. He could never have foreseen that in less than 20 years the area would become overwhelmed by the tsunami of suburbia; the coming of the Underground in 1926 prompted the construction of the St Helier Estate, which transformed the fields between Morden and Carshalton, and private speculative builders were quick to match this with middle-class housing around its edges. Again, we have to thank the foresight of the local councils in Morden and Mitcham for saving a rump of the estate as parkland.

Across the parish boundary in Carshalton, *Bishopsford* was another large house standing in semi-rural isolation well away from the old village. It would have commanded fine views across a sweep of the river near Bennett's Hole and the Watermeads. It was built around 1865 for Alfred Attwood, a drug merchant. The house survived in altered form until fairly recently thanks to the purchase of its extensive grounds as a public park, and the footprint of the house is now occupied by modern flats within Poulter Park.

In fact, although many of the houses have gone, we are left with a surprising number of substantial riverside open spaces along the Wandle Valley, which make the riverside ribbon so rewarding a walk even today.

Case study – the Wandle riverside at Hackbridge

Leaving aside the extensive estates at Morden Hall Park and at Beddington Park, perhaps one of the most favoured stretches of the whole river for the eighteenth- and nineteenth-century man of means was the area around Hackbridge (see map, and also more detailed map of Culvers Island on p. 164). Indeed, this stretch of the river was probably unequalled for the number of fine detached houses that once stood on its banks. For those who could afford it these riverside houses with estates varying in size between one and 77 acres, offered an enviable lifestyle in well-appointed houses with servants, each with its surrounding gardens and lawns sloping down to the river. There were orchards and vines, stables and rustic bridges crossing the divided waterways to secluded wooded islands. Some of the houses had boathouses and exclusive fishing rights.

Apart from *Strawberry Lodge* and *Shepley House* (and its predecessor, *Bacons*), which were older, the other houses here all dated back to the period from the late eighteenth to the mid nineteenth century.

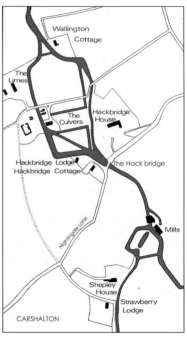

Hackbridge 1870 showing the riverside houses.

As is noted in the walk section to this part of the route (see p. 165ff), much of the land on the Carshalton (west) side of the river and even some on the east bank was part of the substantial 280-acre Culvers Estate, which had been acquired by the Quaker Reynolds family, owners of one of the world's largest calico firms. It is very likely that the house that gave the bleaching estate its name was an old one, possibly early seventeenth century, but we do know for certain that the house was enlarged and substantially rebuilt in 1850 by which time the great banking family of the Gurneys had married into the estate. Foster Reynolds himself had almost certainly built *The Limes* in 1786, described as an "*elegant house* [of] *grey stock bricks*" by Manning & Bray (in their *History of Surrey*).

The Culvers, Carshalton in 1913. The site of banker Samuel Gurney's lovely country seat is now occupied by the houses of Culvers Retreat.

The Limes, a substantial house dating from 1786 on the Culvers Estate, Carshalton. It was demolished in 1913.

It was indeed on an elevated site as they say, overlooking the floodplain of the river. *Culverside* stood where Mullards was later built, and was formerly known as *Wallington Cottage*. Photographs suggest it was anything but a cottage, more a very substantial house. The same is true of *Hackbridge Lodge*, which despite having just one acre of grounds, was a lavishly decorated eight-bedroomed house with butler's pantry and cellars as well as 'copious stabling'. From photographic evidence it was a fine double-fronted house with a sweeping driveway and conservatory to the side. It was right on the river where the inter-war semis of Hackbridge Park Gardens now stand. Nearby, *Hackbridge Cottage* was as large, standing in four acres of land. They both appear on the 1933 map (p. 62), but had been demolished a few years later (around 1936 and 1941 respectively).

Hackbridge House first appears on the 1808 map of Culvers Estate, but the date of construction may be earlier. It became the home of the Goad family, who had industrial interests connected with the river. When the 27-acre estate and house was put up for auction in 1908 there were no fewer than 20 bed and dressing rooms including seven for the servants; four 'elegant' entertaining rooms, a billiard room, domestic offices and numerous outbuildings. The river frontage boasted 'fine trees' with 'rustic bridges'. Interestingly, the sales particulars at that time also gave a foretaste of things to come: "*City Men – for occupation and ultimate development, the valuable and improving residential and building estate…*" boasting of the proximity to Hackbridge and Carshalton stations with their "*express trains to London in under half an hour*". The auctioneers went on to say "*although [the house is] in every way desirable for private occupation… [we] beg to draw special attention to the considerable present and prospective building value*" of the property. It seems the new owner, a Mr Salmon, immediately began to realise some of this potential, for all the land to the east of the house was soon divided into building plots and sold. He himself, having made his money, apparently moved on within a couple of years and the house became known as *Hackbridge Park* and operated as an hotel, apparently with some success since it acquired the nickname of the 'abode of love'! This lasted until around 1936 when it was acquired by the War Office and became a base for the Royal Engineers. The poor old house was knocked around substantially thereafter; searchlights and guns were installed in 1938 and a drill hall was built on the old kitchen garden. After the war, the military function continued with the Territorial Army and cadet training, and the building survived until the TA vacated the place in 1969 and it was put up for auction for the last time. A year later, the house and its now densely overgrown land was bought by developers and the high-density flats of Corbet Close went up, marking the end of the last chapter in the story of the Wandle-side houses of Hackbridge.

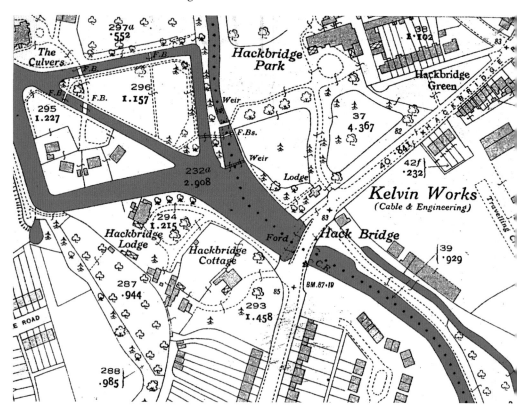

1933 and the tide of suburbia laps at the door of the riverside houses. Just north of this area The Limes *and* Culverside *have already disappeared, the latter buried under the new Mullards factory. Hackbridge Park is still a hotel with its lodge intact, although the eastern part of the estate is now sold off for houses. The Culvers still enjoys a pleasant riverside location although four detached houses have been put up on one of the little islets in the river (these survived until the 1960s when in turn the area was redeveloped again). In the south-east of the map extract the new homes on the former Shepley Estate are visible, and more new houses line the Nightingale Road just yards from* Hackbridge Cottage. *Just a few years later, this and* Hackbridge Lodge *would be gone.*

Gazeteer: surviving Wandle houses

Apart from minor domestic buildings such as the various lodges to have survived, the following is a list of some of the more significant Wandle houses that have survived today:

Beddington Park House (Carew Manor), Beddington.
Wandle Bank, London Road, Wallington
Carshalton House, The Old Rectory, Honeywood, The Lodge,
    and The Grove, all in Carshalton village
Strawberry Lodge, Mill Lane, Carshalton
Crieff Villas, Mill Green, Mitcham
Morden Lodge, Morden Hall Park
Morden Hall, Morden Hall Park
Wandle Villa, Phipps Bridge Road

A former mill owner's house, Goat Bridge, Beddington Corner.

Wandle Bank, London Road, Wallington.

Crieff Villas facing Mill Green. These handsome houses are probably named by the mid nineteenth-century lessee of the nearby leather mill, William McRae, after his home town.

Several Lodges to some of the big riverside houses survive.
The following pages present a photo-montage of most of them.

Gatehouse to the Lodge, *Carshalton. This is one of the smallest and among the most attractive of the surviving lodge buildings, lying a stone's throw from the ponds at Carshalton. Its parent house, The Lodge, still stands, close by.*

East Lodge, *Beddington Park. The largest and surely the loveliest of the surviving lodges, occupying a prominent position close to Carew Manor. It is dated 1872.*

Lodge to the Grange, *Wallington. A large lodge house of flint at the edge of Alfed's Smee's former house and garden. Sadly, the parent house was destroyed by a fire in 1960.*

Lodge to the Culvers, *Hackbridge. This stands at what was the eastern opening of Culvers Avenue, now named Medland Close at this point. Note the new BedZed Eco-homes beyond.*

Lodge to the Grove, *Carshalton. At the opposite end of the ponds to the lodge gatehouse, this red brick lodge stands at the entrance drive to the Grove.*

West Lodge, Beddington Park. A far more humble building than the East Lodge, it stands close to busy London Road at the end of a path that crosses the park from east to west. Despite its small size, it has an impressive chimney and unusual windows, although it has suffered from some unsympathetic modernisation.

Lodge to the former Wallington Manor House (Manor Cottage), R.I.P.? This handsome little cottage, surrounded on two sides by water, and close to Wallington Bridge, is the former gatehouse to the Wallington Manor House. Sadly, at the time of writing it is in a sorry state – its owners have stripped the windows and roof, although an application to demolish it and replace with a larger house has been refused. The Manor House itself and the grounds are long gone, buried under the houses of Derek Avenue and Quinton Close.

Morden Hall Lodges and Gatehouse. The two very similar lodges at each end of the park survive, whilst the attractive gatehouse, shaded heavily by a large cedar, stands at the entrance nearest the Hall itself. Note the initials 'GH' set into a stone in the front elevation.

Carshalton in the year 1820. The artist is unknown, but the painting predates 1828 when the carriageway across the pond was widened. Note also *Dame Duffin's Cottage*, and *Queen's Well*, at the right hand edge of the view.

5   **The wild river**

This chapter considers the fauna and flora along the river. Despite the urban setting, there is a wealth of plant and animal life along the Wandle, and whatever the season a naturalist can always find something of interest.

As far as the past is concerned, information is patchy. Alfred Smee lived at The Grange, Wallington and in 1872 published *My Garden*, a 650-page book that included the wildlife in his garden. Later in 1924, Dr John Hobson published *The Book of the Wandle*. His book dealt with the whole Wandle catchment rather than just the river itself, so it is often impossible to tell if a species referred to by Hobson occurred on the river itself. Other sources of information include publications from the London Natural History Society, Surrey Wildlife Trust and Wandle Group.

Flora

The river provides three habitats for plants: the river itself, the waterside and the banks. Each has it own distinct flora, albeit they have all been greatly influenced by man. In the past, water meadows would have abutted the river where flooding would have been controlled for calico bleaching and watercress growing. No meadows survive; rather, along many stretches the banks have been raised as a result of the disposal of debris from bomb damage after the Second World War. The raising of the banks suppresses waterside vegetation; furthermore, often the material was rich in nitrate leading to colonisation by nettle, bramble and other plants that favour such conditions. One of the motives for disposal may have been to prevent flooding; however, with the increase in housing close to the river, it was still necessary to build revetments along much of the river. The revetments are particularly high where they coincide with the raised banks. In general, the number of different species of plant decreases as one progresses downstream, chiefly because more of the river is revetted and the revetments tend to be higher. There is almost undoubtedly no natural habitat remaining along the river. The oldest habitat is probably at Wilderness Island, Carshalton, and even that is man-made, originating in the eighteenth century when ponds were used for some kind of fishing operation. Of the four ponds, one has been lost, one colonised by Greater Pond Sedge and the other two survive to the present day.

In recent years, revetments have been removed to create more natural margins and enable more waterside plants to thrive. Unfortunately, the opportunities for such schemes are few because the risk of flooding remains but revetments have been removed from stretches in Beddington Park and Morden Hall Park. However, there have been many initiatives to improve the habitat adjacent to the river. The wetland at Carew Manor, Beddington was created as a flood alleviation scheme; a large area of wetland has been created in Morden Hall Park; new channels and a reed bed have been created in Wandle Park, Colliers Wood; the former Wandle Valley sewage works at Colliers Wood has been sympathetically converted (see p. 104) and is now managed for wildlife, being renamed Wandle Meadow Nature Park. All these initiatives have led to increases in the flora.

The Wandle is considered to be a chalk river since it derives its water from springs in Carshalton and Croydon where the chalk dips below the London Clay. Chalk rivers are base-rich with little nitrate and phosphate and are particularly good for plants. However, the water quality of the river is influenced by rainwater run-off and effluent from Beddington Sewage Treatment Works that enters the river at Goat Bridge, Mitcham. The effluent is rich in nitrate and phosphate, so changes in the flora might be expected where the effluent enters the river with species characteristic of chalk rivers being less abundant downstream of the inflow. Stream Water-crowfoot is an indicator species of chalk rivers where the water quality is good:

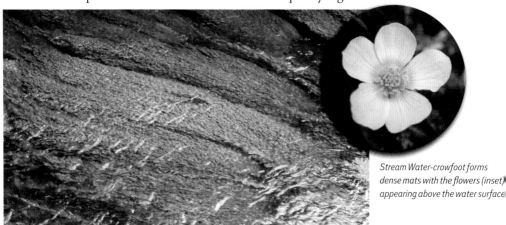

Stream Water-crowfoot forms dense mats with the flowers (inset) appearing above the water surface

a member of the buttercup family having finely divided leaves and white flowers with a yellow centre that protrude above the water surface. It occurs abundantly upstream but surprisingly is nearly as abundant downstream of Goat Bridge. Unbranched Bur-reed will grow in more nitrate-rich water; it has long grass-like leaves reaching the surface that sway with the current. The globular spiky heads with the male flowers above the female flowers can occasionally be seen poking above the water surface. It is abundant downstream of Morden Hall Park, but is rare upstream. Fennel Pondweed may become dominant in rivers rich in nitrate and phosphate, but is relatively uncommon along the Wandle. The plants growing in the river are important in that they deflect and concentrate water flows keeping the gravel stream bed free from silt and provide shelter and food for invertebrates. They are in effect the Wandle's own 'kelp forests'.

Where there are no revetments, plants of the waterside (emergents) can grow. Each species requires a different depth of water to grow in and can tolerate different speeds of current. Several species grow in dense patches and have tall sword-like leaves making them difficult to distinguish until they flower. The flower spikes are held well above the water surface so that they can cope with any sudden changes in water level. Once the flowers of Yellow Flag appear, they cannot be confused with any other emergent. Branched Bur-reed has similar flowers to Unbranched Bur-reed but bears them, as the name suggests, on more than one stem. Reedmace produces brown sausage-shaped seed heads, which gradually break down to release

Unbranched Bur-reed is a component of the 'kelp forests' of the Wandle. Its flowers (inset) can occasionally be seen poking above the water surface.

Yellow Flag is one of several emergent species with sword-shaped leaves; its flowers (inset) make it unmistakable.

the seeds. Common Reed (the tallest of all the emergents), Reed Canary-grass and Reed Sweet-grass have characteristic grass-like flowering heads. Other emergents do not have sword-like leaves. Fool's Watercress, as the name suggests, is easily confused with Watercress, despite being in different families, carrot and cabbage, respectively. They have similar leaves and both have small white flowers arranged in a flat top but can be told apart by their fruit: Fool's Watercress is egg-shaped while Watercress has a long seed pod.

On the damp banks, many more plants occur. Gypsywort, Water Figwort, Great Willowherb and the highly poisonous Hemlock Water-dropwort are particularly widespread. Early in the year, Marsh-marigold with its large bright yellow flower adds colour to a late winter's day. It can be found growing at Hackbridge, Mitcham (Bennett's Hole and Watermeads) and Morden Hall Park. Pendulous Sedge is difficult to miss since it can grow up to 6' high with its flowering heads rising above the leaves. In Surrey, it is usually found growing in damp woods on clay so might not be expected to occur on the river. It is possible that Alfred Smee planted it in his garden, from where it may have colonised the river. Cuckooflower, named because it flowers at the same time as Cuckoos call, has an attractive flower with pale lilac petals, which can be seen at several places along the river. Ragged Robin with its irregularly dissected pink petals flowers occurs at Watermeads, Ravensbury Park and Wandle Meadow Nature Park. Trifids in the form of Trifid Bur-marigold appear sporadically in muddy patches along the river.

Watercress (right) occurs along the river and is possibly a remnant of the once flourishing industry. But Fool's Watercress (left) is just as common and is often mistaken for Watercress.

The yellow flowers of Marsh-marigold bring colour to an overcast spring day.

For the avid plant hunter, there are a number of plants that are rare in London. Already mentioned are Stream Water-crowfoot, both species of Bur-reed, Marsh-marigold and Ragged Robin. Others include Marsh Arrowgrass and Great Burnet in Beddington Park; Lesser Water-parsnip at The Grange and Spencer Road Wetland, Hackbridge; Ivy Broomrape at Ravensbury Park; Pink Water-speedwell at Waddon Ponds; and Butterbur (see p. 133).

There have been concerns over declines in the flora of European rivers. These declines have been attributed to nitrate enrichment, siltation, low flows and unsuitable management practices. Siltation and low flows are probably applicable to the Wandle, but improvements to the sewage treatment works have led to a reduction in nitrate levels, while management practices have improved. In Poulter Park, Broad-leaved Pondweed used to be very abundant but

The flowers of Butterbur appear in March before the rhubarb-like leaves that by autumn can attain a diameter of 3'.

has declined drastically; Branched Bur-reed is now restricted to far fewer patches than in the past.

Of the trees, several species of willow and sallow grow along the river, including a fast-growing form of White Willow that was planted at Watermeads for the manufacture of cricket bats. They were harvested at intervals, the last time being in 1987. Alder is also common along the river. One tree that is especially associated with rivers and their floodplains is Black Poplar, which is now considered to be our rarest native tree. There are many Black Poplars along the river; however, they are nearly all hybrids of European and North American poplars that are planted for their faster growth rate. Our native tree has declined because the damp conditions required by their seed to germinate rarely occur due to widespread drainage. Telling native and hybrid trees apart is not easy, but thanks to recent advances in technology, DNA fingerprinting is now a practical proposition. Many trees in London have been tested and three poplars on Mill Green, Mitcham were found to be native. Two native trees were planted at Spencer Road Wetland in 1993 and one tree is now over 50' tall.

There are many magnificent London Plane trees along the river. The best known tree is in Festival Walk, Carshalton, which has a plaque commemorating it as the tallest London Plane in Britain (taller ones have been found since it was surveyed in 1964). London Plane is neither native to this country nor a pure species: rather they are hybrids of Oriental and American Plane. London Plane is by no means the only non-native tree; the owners of the estates would often plant exotic trees in their grounds, some for their fruit (Mulberry and Medlar) others for their aesthetic value, particularly the avenues of Lime and Horse Chestnut in Beddington Park and Morden Hall Park. Other trees have been planted more recently, including Dawn Redwood, which was thought to be extinct, being only known from the fossil record until it was discovered growing in a remote area of China in 1945. There are many other trees worth looking out for. There are several Tulip Trees with their distinctive lobed leaves and attractive yellow tulip-like flowers. The one in Festival Walk can be viewed with best effect when flowering in May and June from the top of the Water Tower. The Gingko or Maidenhair Tree is one of the oldest trees on an evolutionary scale; male trees are usually planted, but there is a female tree in the rose garden of Morden Hall Park that produces fruit every year (Gingko is Japanese for silver apricot). Swamp Cypress as its name suggests can tolerate

The Tulip Tree derives its name from the yellowish flowers (inset) that resemble tulips. This tree was photographed from the top of the Water Tower in the grounds of Carshalton House.

flooding and produces specialised roots that arch up into the air to form knees that act as aerating organs. There are some particularly good examples of trees with knees at Waddon Ponds. As well as the commonly planted trees, there are a few very special ones. Pride of place must go to Ravensbury Park, where east meets west as a Chinese Plum-Yew grows very close to a Californian Laurel! Both species are rarely planted and can be found along the channel by the children's playing area. The park has a fine collection of trees including Foxglove Tree, Persian Ironwood and Ponderosa Pine. The Grange, Wallington also has a fine collection, started by Alfred Smee, that includes Caucasian Wing-nut (also at Waddon), Red Snake-bark Maple and Wellingtonia, a giant redwood from California.

The storm of October 1987 had a devastating effect on the trees along the river. Several large London Plane trees, along with many other trees, were blown over. Watermeads was the most badly affected stretch where the poplar plantation was almost totally felled. As a result, the National Trust took the opportunity to create a water meadow. The loss of so many trees may well have been of benefit to other plants, since the dense shade cast by trees inhibits their growth. However, nature has been quick to recover and shade from trees along many sections of the river is again preventing the development of a rich flora.

Probably the tallest Swamp Cypress on the river can be found at Wallington Bridge. They form characteristic 'knees' like these good examples at Waddon Ponds.

Trees are not the only plants to have been introduced along the river. In Ravensbury Park, there is a small colony of Snake's Head Fritillary, a species associated with flood-plain meadows along the upper stretches of the Thames. Others including Cornflower and Corncockle have escaped from gardens or been introduced with a wild flower seed mixture. These introductions of native plants pose little threat; however, non-native plants may cause problems. They are mostly garden pond plants that have been intentionally or unintentionally introduced into the river, where they grow rapidly and displace native plants by smothering them or out-competing them for resources. They are termed invasive and the worst offenders are covered by Schedule 9 of the Wildlife and Countryside Act 1981, which lists plants that are illegal to plant or cause to grow in the wild. The Canadian Waterweed is a North American species that was introduced to Britain in 1842 and by 1860 was so serious in choking rivers that a Minister for Waterweed was appointed! It is abundant in the river, along with Nuttall's Waterweed that has colonised more recently. Large patches of Japanese Knotweed are rampant on the river banks in places. More recently two other species have colonised the river: Floating Pennywort and Indian Balsam. Floating Pennywort originates from North America forming dense mats that float on the surface and if allowed will spread from one bank to the other. Indian Balsam is an annual originating from the Himalayas and its rapid growth can shade out even nettle. It has pink hooded flowers that give rise to another name – Policemen's Helmet. After flowering, the seed pods burst open to release the seeds, you can hear them popping or you can induce explosion by touching them that give rise to another name – Touch-me-not! These two plants present a serious problem along the river and the Environment Agency has drawn up action plans to eradicate them with control

The Wellingtonia is also known as Giant Sequoia. This tree can be seen in The Grange, Wallington, but it grows in the wild in California where the largest individual, Giant Sherman, is the world's largest living creature.

Floating Pennywort is very invasive and if unchecked will spread across the river. Here it is seen growing on Jack's Pond in Watermeads.

Indian Balsam is another invasive species with attractive flowers resembling a policemen's helmet (inset). Here it has nearly closed the channel at Wallington Bridge.

measures already costing several thousand pounds each year. There are other invasive plants along the river that could become a problem, but are still limited to a few locations where they are easier to eradicate. They include Giant Hogweed, Parrot's Feather and Water Fern. Giant Hogweed can grow up to 12' and is very striking as it towers over the other vegetation; however, be careful not to touch it, since the sap produces an allergic blistering when exposed to the sun. Since 2010, all of these species are on Schedule 9. If you buy plants for your garden pond and they grow so quickly that they take over the pond, please do not discard them into the river. Better still, before buying find out if they are on Schedule 9 and if so leave well alone.

Fish

In the seventeenth century, the Wandle had a reputation as a trout stream, and fishing was so good that in 1606 the river was declared a 'Royal Preserve' between Wandsworth and Merton, extended to Croydon in 1634, with bailiffs being employed to prevent poaching. At this time, only the native Brown Trout occurred, but in the late 1800s, Rainbow Trout, which is a native of North America, was introduced. Large catches of both species were recorded: Mr Dingwall, the owner of Shepley House, Carshalton caught 60 trout on 1st April 1899 and around 500 a year between between his home and Butter Hill Bridge. Some fish ended up as trophies and survive

Brown Trout have been re-introduced into the river and some are now over a foot long.

to the current day: a Rainbow Trout caught in 1898 can be seen in Honeywood Museum, Carshalton.

Several famous anglers have connections to the Wandle. It is often asserted that Izaak Walton (1593–1683) mentioned the Wandle in *The Compleat Angler*, one of the earliest books on fishing; however, it is only in notes to later editions that references to the Wandle can be found. Admiral Lord Nelson (1758–1805) is reputed to have fished the river while not engaged in naval battles. Frederick Halford (1844–1914) watched anglers false casting with flies on the Wandle, the 'Carshalton dodge', and went onto develop the method, which inspired his writings on fly-fishing.

In *My Garden* of 1872, Smee considered Eel and Brown Trout to be the most abundant fish with Bullhead and Three-spined Stickleback common. River Lamprey visited in January and February, presumably to breed, while Dace were occasional visitors. His attempts to establish Tench, Salmon, Charr, Grayling and Burbot were unsuccessful. Away from his garden on the river, Smee knew of Roach, Stone Loach, Pike and Perch and claimed that Bleak, Carp, Gudgeon, Chub, Minnow, Roach and Ruffe did not occur. Unfortunately, the fish listed in Hobson's book refer to the county of Surrey rather than the Wandle.

Pollution had become a threat to fish by the time Frederick Braithwaite presented his famous paper in 1861 (see p. 11). He raised serious concerns over the impact of deteriorating water quality on fish, particularly trout. Attempts were made to save the trout in the river but these were always likely to fail because of poor water quality. Around 1895, the owners of the fishing rights between Willow Lane, Mitcham and Ravensbury Mill formed the Wandle Fisheries

Association. They appointed a bailiff and established a trout hatchery at Watermeads. For ten years, trout were released into the river but water quality continued to decline and survival was poor. At the termination of their lease, a dispute arose over water quality and the Association dissolved. Captain Harold Bidder, the son of one of the founders of the Association, made another attempt to restore trout to Ravensbury Park in 1912, but his attempt was cut short when he rejoined his regiment at the outbreak of war. There are many claims that the last trout was caught on the river around 1914, which given the poor water quality and cessation of stocking seems eminently reasonable; however, there is a later claim for 1934.

Trout was not the only species to become extinct, other species met a similar fate. In the 1970s, electric fish surveys by Thames Water found only Three-spined Stickleback. Electric fishing entails passing a current through the water that stuns any fish in the vicinity whereupon they float to the surface where they can be netted (picture p. 107). The fish are measured, weighed and a sample of scales taken to determine their age and growth rate. The fish are released back into the river none the worse for the ordeal. In addition to electric fishing, Thames Water also conducted surveys on the invertebrates and monitored the water quality, which suggested that the river was capable of supporting fish. As a result of these surveys, a stocking programme commenced with Brown Trout and Grayling followed by Barbel, Gudgeon, Chub, Dace, Roach and Perch. Subsequent electric fishing found that the fish had survived, except the Grayling and Perch, which suffered heavy mortality. Growth rates were good due to two features of the water from the sewage treatment works: relatively high temperatures and high nitrate levels. However, there was little evidence for successful breeding since fry were rarely seen. Habitat management to create breeding places and continuing improvements in water quality have led to successful breeding, but the fry suffer heavy mortality such that the populations are not self-sustaining and the river continues to be stocked on a regular basis. Over the years, the programme has been set back by large fish kills as a result of pollution incidents: an oil spill in 1979 led to the death of nearly all the recently introduced Brown

Bullheads are found commonly along the river downstream of Goat Bridge.

Trout. Each incident is investigated and the culprits fined, including paying for restocking. Unfortunately, the river still suffers occasional serious pollution, the most recent incident being in 2007 (see p. 27); fortunately, the river seems to have great powers of recovery. We do not fully understand the effects on the other fauna and flora, but do know that it takes time for the restocked fish to grow to the size they were before the pollution incident.

Apart from pollution, the other problem facing fish, particularly Brown Trout and Eel, is the many weirs that hinder their movement. The European Water Framework Directive of 2000 requires free passage for fish, which has given greater momentum to the Environment Agency to remove weirs. Passes are another solution and in 2011, a fish pass was installed at Butter Hill Bridge, Carshalton (picture p. 156) and an eel pass at Merton Abbey Mills.

The loss of the iconic Brown Trout led to another re-introduction attempt, which it was hoped with improved water quality would be more successful than the attempts at the turn of the century. In 2001, the Wandle Trust (see p. 107) initiated 'Trout in the Classroom' whereby trout eggs are delivered to local schools in January and children, under supervision, oversee the hatching, nurturing and feeding of the fry for up to 12 weeks prior to release into the river with great ceremony. Their enterprise has been rewarded and it is quite common to see anglers fly fishing, better still, trout were seen spawning in 2008 and fry were found in March 2010.

The smaller fish are not monitored so well by electric fishing: Three-spined Stickleback and Stone Loach are common and Bullhead occur upstream of Goat Bridge, Mitcham. The Wandle was the only river in London where the Environment Agency found Ten-spined Stickleback in the 1990s, although they were suspected to be more widespread. The return of fish to the Thames, with nearly 120 species recorded, is one of conservation's success stories. Flounder and Smelt are now found on the tidal reaches of the Wandle. Flounder breed in seawater and migrate into rivers during the summer months, while Smelt live in seawater and migrate into freshwater in spring to breed. Smelt do not spawn in the mouth, as some have claimed, but in the tidal Thames around the mouth. The increase in tidal fish does not apply to Eel, which have declined throughout Europe. They are now more common on the Wandle than many other London rivers; in 2010, the Environment Agency specifically electric fished the river for Eels, recording nearly 700. In the past, numbers would have been much higher and their long migration to and from their breeding haunt in the Sargasso Sea may make them susceptible to climate change. Other more exotic fish have found their way into the river as they grow too big for the garden pond, particularly Carp, sometimes Koi Carp. But the most remarkable catch from an electric fishing session was a Piranha; this fish did not find its way back into the river!

Birds

The chapter on birds in Hobson's *Book of the Wandle* lists 104 species in the river catchment, including several species that no longer breed in Surrey: Corncrake (last bred 1946), Red-backed Shrike (1973) and Cirl Bunting (1979). He does not mention Wryneck that bred in Smee's garden and last bred in Surrey in 1984. Hobson mentions Grasshopper Warbler at Walton Heath and Hawfinch at Caterham while Smee saw both these species in his garden with the latter occasionally breeding. Nightingale was seen each year by Smee in his garden and Hobson considered it 'common near the Wandle'; it is likely to have given rise to the name of Nightingale Road in Carshalton.

A Kingfisher sitting on a branch (right) with the artificial bank built at Spencer Road Wetland (left top) and abandoned Kingfisher holes in a root plate at Morden Hall Park (left bottom).

Other sources of information include *The Birds of Beddington Park* by Chambers that cover the period 1925–1930 after it was first opened to the public, and surveys conducted for the British Trust for Ornithology by the author (see boxes below).

The bird that we all want to see on the river is the Kingfisher with its iridescent blue flash; the key is to learn their high pitched call since they are nearly always heard before being seen. Today, sightings

Winter on the Wandle

Each year in late December, the waterway birds on the river between Carshalton Ponds and the mouth at Wandsworth are counted as part of the BTO/RSPB/JNCC* Wetland Bird Survey. The counts for three winters are shown in the table. The counts of Moorhen are of particular significance exceeding the threshold of 100 for inclusion in the annual report of the Survey.

	2004	2007	2010
Mute Swan	2	6	3
Canada Goose	44	65	85
Egyptian Goose			2
Gadwall	3	14	104
Teal	53	32	156
Mallard	269	297	429
Shoveler			18
Pochard			3
Tufted Duck	17	34	30
Little Grebe	12	7	18
Great Crested Grebe	1		
Cormorant	1	1	19
Little Egret		2	3
Grey Heron	4	9	13
Water Rail	3	2	
Moorhen	179	186	248
Coot	70	72	93
Snipe	2	1	
Redshank			1
Kingfisher	4	4	2
Grey Wagtail	11	11	13

*British Trust for Ornithology (BTO),
Royal Society for the Protection of Birds (RSPB),
Joint Nature Conservation Committee (JNCC).

Summer on the Wandle

Between 1983 and 2007, a Waterways Bird Survey was conducted as part of a national survey organized by the British Trust for Ornithology to determine trends in abundance of waterway birds. It entailed making nine visits during the breeding season when the river was walked between Butter Hill Bridge, Carshalton and the tramline in Morden Hall Park. An estimate of the number of breeding pairs for five years are shown in the table.

	1983	1990	1995	2000	2007
Mute Swan			1	2	1
Canada Goose	1	2	1	14	9
Mallard	43	41	51	55	79
Tufted Duck		2	2	11	7
Little Grebe			3	1	3
Grey Heron				3	12
Moorhen	15	39	52	46	62
Coot	12	24	23	23	28
Kingfisher			2	5	4
Grey Wagtail	2	6	6	3	6
Pied Wagtail	1	1			
Reed Warbler				2	
Reed Bunting				1	1

are much more likely than in the past. Smee, Hobson and Chambers considered that they bred along the river, which is consistent with the London Natural History Society, who found them breeding between 1900 and 1935. However, the Society did not find them breeding between 1936 and 1971, which they attributed to increased pollution. Kingfishers are vulnerable to cold weather when fish become less active, which leads to many birds dying from starvation. In the summer following the extremely cold winter of 1962/63 only one pair was found in London. From the early 1980s, birds were occasionally seen in the winter months but never bred, although there were enough small fish to support a nesting pair. The Wandle lacks soft vertical banks where Kingfishers can excavate a tunnel with a nesting chamber at the end, but all was to change following the storm of October 1987. The exposed root plates of fallen trees provided nesting opportunities where, amazingly, Kingfishers could burrow through the tangle of roots. There is one root plate with over ten holes, which presumably are abandoned efforts where the tunnel was impeded by a tree root. At least two pairs are still using root plates of trees that fell in the storm. Other 'man-made' nest sites support breeding pairs. An artificial bank composed of layers of sand for the Kingfishers to burrow into and layers of concrete for stability has been built at Spencer Road Wetland, Hackbridge. Old drainage pipes may be used: a pair at the mouth of the river, which must be the closest breeding pair to central London, use a pipe.

Grey Herons are a common sight along the Wandle, thanks to the river supporting a good fish population.

After Kingfisher, the other bird that demands our attention is the Grey Heron. Like Kingfisher, they suffer heavy mortality in cold winters, so the spell of warmer winters has led to a rising population and the formation of many new heronries. Herons nest in colonies building large nests at the top of tall trees, preferring islands in large water bodies where there is little disturbance. There are no such sites on the Wandle and there were no heronries in the past. However, the river has a plentiful food supply since the stocking of fish in the 1980s, so perhaps it was not such a surprise when herons nested at Morden Hall Park in 1999. Since then, another two heronries have been established; at Watermeads, Mitcham in 2002 and Beddington Park in 2006. They nest early in the year, sometimes laying their eggs before Christmas and may be sitting on eggs when snow is on the ground! They incubate their eggs for eight weeks and spend a further eight weeks feeding their young in the nest. Outside the breeding season, they tend to congregate together at 'day roosts' where they stand around making little attempt to feed, departing in the evening to fish along the river sometimes with the help of street lights but at other times in almost total darkness. There was a day roost at the mouth where 28 birds were counted in 1995 but this roost has been lost to developments along the Thames. Another day roost is found on Beddington Farmlands where 85 were counted in 2010.

The Grey Heron is not the only heron that you can see on the river; you may see a smaller pure white heron, if so it is a Little Egret. They were very rare in this country being restricted to southern Europe but, during the 1980s, they started to spread northwards and it was only a matter of time before they reached England. In 1989, there was a large influx and in 1996, they started breeding. The colonisation of this country has undoubtedly been helped by milder winters. On the Wandle in winter, they are a regular sight, often shaking their yellow feet to disturb fish and invertebrates. They usually nest amongst Grey Heron colonies and it is possible that they may start breeding.

Feeding ducks on a family outing is a pastime that most of us have enjoyed. The Wandle provides many places for such activities since, Mallard can be found along the length of the river. However, Mallard is not the only duck to be found on the Wandle; for such a small river, it may come as a surprise that at least 17 different

Little Egret have colonised the river in recent years. They have yet to breed, but are a common sight in winter.

A drake Tufted Duck named after the tuft on its head.

species of duck have been seen. So the river is not just a good place for feeding ducks, but for birdwatchers too! After Mallard, the duck most likely to be encountered is Tufted Duck. The drake is black and white with a bright yellow eye and a tuft on its head. They have adapted to urban life and can be seen diving amongst Mallard to retrieve bread. They breed late in the year with ducklings being seen in July and August; breeding was intermittent in the past, but since the 1980s has become regular. The only other duck that has bred on the river is Shelduck. A brood of nine juveniles was seen battling against the current at Watermeads in 1993, but they were not seen again and it is suspected that they spent too much time fighting the current and not enough time feeding.

Winter, especially during cold spells, is the best time to see ducks on the river. The resident Tufted Ducks are augmented by birds from further afield. Another winter visitor, Pochard can often be seen at Waddon Ponds but their numbers have declined in recent years both nationally and on the Wandle. In contrast, Teal and Gadwall have become frequent, especially at Poulter Park, Watermeads and at the mouth of the river. During cold spells, still waters freeze forcing ducks to move onto ice-free rivers. Many of the ducks that feed on Beddington Farmlands move onto the river and are joined by others from more distant waters. February 1991 was exceptional when Pintail, Scaup, Goldeneye and Smew were all seen after a heavy snowfall.

Wading birds (or waders) with their long legs also take refuge on the river in cold spells. Snipe is the wader that you are most likely to see, but Woodcock, Ruff and Redshank have all been spotted. Green Sandpiper may also be seen and is likely to have come from

A family of Mute Swans. Cygnets are a popular sight along the river.

Beddington Farmlands, which is one of the premier wintering sites in the country for this species. There is little habitat for waders to breed, along the river; however, Little Ringed Plover are opportunistic, breeding in gravelly areas. In 1995, when the BP Chemicals site in Mill Lane, Carshalton was demolished, a pair of Little Ringed Plover were watched incubating eggs for over a week but then deserted.

Mute Swan appear on the lists of Smee, Hobson and Chambers. They still breed along the river, but unfortunately are too often subject to malicious attacks; several birds have ended up in a wildlife hospital after being attacked by a dog or even by people. We regard Canada Goose as commonplace so it may come as a surprise to hear that up until the 1950s they were a scarce breeding bird in London and did not breed on the Wandle until 1978. Today, they are so common that they are considered a nuisance from the fouling that their droppings cause. Canada Goose is one of a number of species that have established feral breeding populations after escaping from collections. Both Canada and Egyptian Goose were in the collection of Charles II in St James's Park in the late sixteenth century. Egyptian Goose was seen on the river in 2008 from the recently established London population (an earlier introduction at Wandle Park, Colliers Wood in 1910 failed). The male has a loud call that some consider to resemble a steam engine, which may alert you to his presence. They nest in tree holes but no youngsters have been seen so far. The very attractive Mandarin Duck from China is established in Surrey and is occasionally seen on the river. Samuel Gurney MP introduced Black Swans from Australasia to his estate at *The Culvers*, Carshalton. It seems that there was only one pair, but they were very prolific, raising 73 cygnets between 1854 and 1859. More recently, a pair sat on a nest at Waddon Ponds during the summers of 2005 and 2006, but the eggs were infertile.

Moorhen and Coot (members of the rail family of birds) are often confused, but can easily be told apart. Moorhen has a red bill and white under the tail while Coot has a white bill with a bald white patch extending up the forehead. Being common, they are both taken for granted, so there is little information on their abundance in the past, being just mentioned by Hobson and Chambers. Smee does say that Moorhen was more numerous than Coot at The Grange, Wallington. Moorhen remain the more numerous, mainly

A pair of Egyptian Geese. These are recent colonists; and it cannot be long before they start to breed on the river.

The leucistic Coot that frequented Ravensbury Park between 2007 and 2010.

because they occur along the entire length of the river while Coots are restricted to stretches where the river is deep enough to dive for food. Moorhen have shown a large increase on the stretch covered by the Waterways Bird Survey (Box, p. 80) such that there is a pair about every 100 metres, one of the highest densities in the country. Coot have also increased on the Survey. Waddon Ponds has always had an unusually high concentration of Coot and these are dependent on food from the public. There are around 20 breeding pairs and a non-breeding flock of up to 100 birds. Occasionally, a leucistic Coot is reported. Leucism is a genetic mutation that leads to aberrant

On the bridge at Waddon Ponds, you can overlook Little Grebes and can even watch them as they dive underwater.

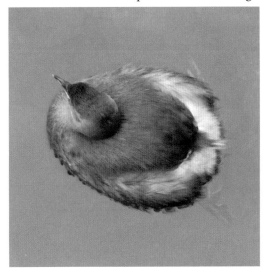

plumage, usually pale or white; it is different from albinism that affects body parts as well as the feathers. There was a fawn individual at Waddon Ponds in 1998 and a white individual at Ravensbury Park between 2007 and 2010. The other member of the rail family to occur is Water Rail. They are very secretive but give themselves away by their squealing calls. In winter, they occur at several sites notably Morden Hall Park (where they have bred) and Spencer Road Wetland.

Little Grebe, the smallest of our grebes, tends to hide amongst vegetation and dive underwater at any disturbance. However, they give their presence away with a loud vibrant trilling sound and can be remarkably approachable at times. Little Grebe were seen by both Smee and Hobson but they do not say whether they were breeding or wintering. They are more common in winter, but suffer heavy mortality in cold winters and no birds were recorded breeding after the cold winter of 1963. Since then they have gradually increased in

Cormorants can be seen in the tops of tall trees, drying their wings.

numbers and breeding occurs regularly where the river is deeper. You will know if they have bred since you will hear the begging cries of the youngsters as they constantly demand food from their parents.

They may have as many as three broods in a long breeding season and have been seen sitting on eggs in December! These very late or early nests are nearly always abandoned.

One bird that did not occur in the past is Cormorant. They have become a much more frequent visitor to inland waters, reflecting the declining fish stocks in coastal waters. They are more common in winter, but can still be seen during the summer. They are not popular with anglers, but do indicate that there are plenty of fish in the river. Fishing must be easy for them since it is common to see several birds perched in the top of tall trees where they are sometimes mistaken for herons. Make sure you look up otherwise you are likely to miss them!

One group of birds that you cannot miss are gulls. They used to occur only in winter, but thanks to the landfill at Beddington Farmlands, Herring and Lesser Black-backed Gull can be seen throughout the year. In winter, the commonest gull is the Black-headed Gull, albeit without the chocolate brown head that only develops during the breeding season. The landfill at Beddington attracts thousands of gulls in winter: estimates of 20,000 have been made. With so many gulls, it is not surprising that there have been reports of rare species. In April 2007, a visitor from the north Pacific, a Glaucous-winged Gull was seen. The same bird (identified by its colour ring) had been sighted previously in Gloucestershire and Carmarthenshire and was the first to be seen in the country. Another rare gull that occurred even before the landfill started is Mediterranean Gull, which has been seen at Carshalton Ponds and Beddington Park. Surprisingly, there have been no reports of gulls breeding on the industrial sites surrounding the landfill, but the first Great Black-backed Gull to breed in London was on a barge on the Thames by Wandsworth Park in 2008. The barges were moored and covered with gravel to try to establish a day roost for Grey Heron in compensation for the one that had disappeared under a Thames-side development. Herons use the barges, but not in large numbers.

Grey Wagtail (left) is often incorrectly identified as a Yellow Wagtail (right).

Wagtails, in particular Grey Wagtail, are often associated with running water. Wagtails characteristically wag their tail up and down seemingly in harmony with the movement of the water, and one of the theories for the wagging is that it may reduce the chance of being spotted by a predator. Grey Wagtail occur along the river but are frequently misidentified as Yellow Wagtail. However, if you were to see a Yellow Wagtail you would immediately see why they deserve the name yellow. Males are more colourful: Yellow Wagtail has green upperparts and yellow underparts, while Grey Wagtail has grey upperparts and yellow restricted to the rump and breast. Smee and Hobson only saw Grey Wagtails in winter and it was considered to be a bird of fast-flowing, rocky upland streams. There have been intermittent reports of breeding, but in the 1950s they started colonising London's rivers, and a survey by the London Natural History Society between 1979 and 1981 found nine breeding pairs on the Wandle. In 2002, eight pairs were recorded on the section of

How are waterway birds faring on the Wandle compared with the national picture?

The British Trust for Ornithology conducts many surveys monitoring the fortunes of Britain's birds. For rivers and canals, the Waterways Breeding Bird Survey (WBBS) has replaced the Waterways Bird Survey (WBS) as the national scheme. The chart shows data from the River Wandle WBS with national data from the WBS and WBBS for five species (Mallard, Moorhen, Coot, Kingfisher and Grey Wagtail). The vertical scale is an index of the size of the populations: the average percentage change between consecutive years of the five species scaled such that it is one in the first year.

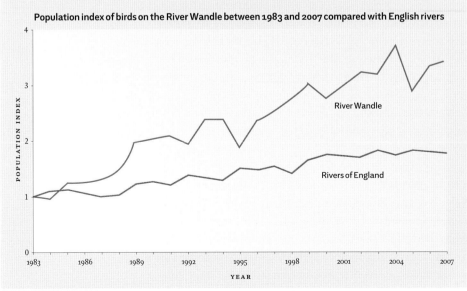

Population index of birds on the River Wandle between 1983 and 2007 compared with English rivers

the river covered by the Waterways Bird Survey, so the increase has continued. The weirs and mill races mimic the fast-flowing water of upland streams and holes in these structures provide suitable nesting sites. The spread has continued into the high streets of many shopping centres along the river where they find food for their young in puddles on flat roofs. In winter, they have started coming into gardens to feed, so they may no longer qualify solely as river birds!

Reed Warbler and Reed Bunting require reed to different extents. Reed Warbler is very dependent on large stands of reed but those along the river are on the small side. Reed Bunting is not so dependent on reed, but is still scarce along the river. Both species have bred at Morden Hall Park and Spencer Road Wetland.

An emerging theme throughout has been that all the waterway birds are doing better now than they were in the past. Surveys conducted by the British Trust for Ornithology show that waterway birds are doing well nationally, but it is also clear that the increases on the Wandle are larger than those found nationally (see box on p. 87). What are the reasons behind this increase? Changes that might be responsible include water quality and waterway management. The river beyond Goat Bridge is dominated by the discharge from Beddington Sewage Treatment Works and the quality of the water is very much dependent on the sewage treatment process, which has improved considerably over the years. Water quality upstream of the discharge is better still, although since the 1980s this has had no marked effect on the abundance of birds either side of the discharge. In the 1960s, however, very poor water quality downstream of the discharge would have in all probability affected bird numbers adversely. Since the 1980s, there has been a big change in bankside management. Until that time, management practice was savage clearance along the river to keep the banks tidy; but the frequency of this practice declined thereafter due to local and national policy changes towards more sympathetic management for wildlife. Nearly all species would be expected to increase with less intensive bankside management.

Many other non-waterway birds may be seen along the river; however, they have not fared as well as the waterway birds. Pied Wagtail, Mistle Thrush, Spotted Flycatcher, Tree Creeper, Nuthatch, Bullfinch and Linnet have all declined. Smee considered Lesser Spotted Woodpecker to be the commonest woodpecker in his garden. It was still common in the 1980s but has shown a strong decline and is now very scarce. In contrast, Great Spotted

Woodpecker and Green Woodpecker have increased. Kestrel still breed in some of the larger parks along the river, yet they used to be able to find enough small mammals to breed where the river corridor was narrow. While Kestrel has decreased, Sparrowhawk, which feeds on small birds, has increased. At Wilderness Island and Spencer Road Wetland, Kestrel bred in the 1980s while Sparrowhawk breed there today. The warblers have fared better; Blackcap is the

Beddington – from sewage farm to farmlands

Beddington Sewage Farm has treated sewage since the 1860s with the end products being water and a residual sludge. The water is diverted to the River Wandle forming up to 90% of the flow downstream of Goat Bridge, Mitcham so the water quality of the river is very dependent on the sewage treatment process. The disposal of sludge has changed over the years. Up until the 1970s, fields were flooded with sludge where it was left to dry, since then sludge has been pumped into small embanked drying beds. This disposal method is gradually being phased out with the modern practice being to reduce the water content via a mechanical clam-press, which does not require land for drying allowing the site to be developed for other uses. Thames Water gained planning permission for gravel extraction and landfill followed by restoration for wildlife and people. Viridor Waste Management run the landfill and are responsible for the restoration. The site, now known as Beddington Farmlands, will become a major nature reserve open to the public and part of the Wandle Valley Regional Park.

Beddington is one of the best birdwatching sites in London (www.beddingtonfarmlands.org.uk) with over 250 species recorded and about 150 species seen each year.

The flooded fields used to support up to 1000 Snipe in winter with a record count of 5000 in a cold spell in December 1962. Snipe, Lapwing and Redshank used to breed but only Lapwing breeds today. Over 30 pairs of Yellow Wagtail bred in the 1950s, but they slowly declined and last bred in 1997. A flood alleviation lake was created in the early 1990s that has added to the diversity of the site and attracts wildfowl, waders and terns. Many species are seen as they migrate to and from their breeding grounds so, when favourable weather conditions occur, spring and autumn can be exciting times. Osprey, Red Kite, Avocet and Short-eared Owl are regular visitors. Over the years, many rarities have been seen including Killdeer and Lesser Yellowlegs from America, Crane and Rustic Bunting from northern Europe, Alpine Swift and Ortolan Bunting from southern Europe. It is for Tree Sparrows that the site is most important, having one of the largest breeding colonies in the country. Tree Sparrows have shown one of the largest declines of farmland birds. In 1992, 100 nest boxes were erected for Tree Sparrows, with further boxes erected in later years. Each year, many of them are used with 2007 being the best year when 143 boxes were used, producing over 1100 young.

commonest warbler along the river and has increased along with Chiffchaff and Whitethroat. In winter, the resident species are joined by winter visitors. Redwing and occasionally Fieldfare can be seen, being more numerous in cold spells. Siskin and Redpoll can sometimes be seen feeding on the seeds of Alder. Most Blackcap and Chiffchaff migrate, but a few remain during the winter months.

One species that attracts attention with its bright green plumage and raucous cries is the Rose-ringed Parakeet. There was a small colony in Beddington Park in the early 1980s that died out. Since 2000, however, they have spread from other sites in London and are now very common. There is a large roost on Mitcham Common that held nearly 3000 birds in 2011. They nest early in the year in holes in trees so may displace other hole-nesting species and may be considered an invasive species.

Reference has been made to the sewage farm and landfill at Beddington and the influence it plays on the birds of the Wandle. It is one of the most important sites in London for birds and is due to become a major nature reserve (see box on p. 89).

Mammals

The commonest mammal along the Wandle today is the Brown Rat; but at the time of Smee and Hobson, it may have been the Water Vole, which is strongly associated with rivers. Water Vole have declined more than any other mammal in the country and are now considered extinct on the Wandle being last reliably reported from Wilderness Island, Carshalton in the early 1980s. It is possible that they are still present, since there are occasional claims; however, Brown Rat is

Water Voles are now considered extinct on the river, but there are plans to reintroduce them.

One of many Mink traps along the river; no footprints of Mink have been found so far.

easily mistaken for Water Vole. The main differences are in the face, ears and tail. The Brown Rat has a pointed face, prominent ears and a long pink scaly tail, while the Water Vole has a blunt face, concealed ears and a short furry tail. The London Wildlife Trust working with various partners began a London Water Vole Project in 2001 with the aim to reintroduce Water Vole onto the Wandle. Before reintroducing any animals, the Trust wants to ensure that there is sufficient suitable habitat along the river and such work has been carried out along several stretches of the river (see pp. 110–11). In other parts of the country, Mink has been implicated as a major cause of the decline in Water Vole. So, as part of the Project, the Trust has placed a number of Mink 'traps' along the river. They are not really traps but an open-ended tunnel on a floating board with a soft clay base. Mink, being inquisitive, investigate the tunnel leaving footprints in the clay. So far no footprints have been found. The increase in waterway birds is not consistent with a resident population of Mink, since they feed on both adult and young birds. It is intriguing that waterway birds have increased, while Water Vole has declined.

Otter and Water Shrew are also associated with rivers. Otters are increasing nationally and are now found in Surrey, but it is unlikely that they will ever colonise the Wandle. Smee occasionally saw Water Shrew in his garden at The Grange, Wallington and they are known to favour watercress beds, so may well have been more widespread. A national survey was conducted by the Mammal Society in 2004–5 when Wilderness Island and Spencer Road Wetland, Hackbridge were surveyed, but no sign of their presence was found.

Fox and Grey Squirrel are the mammals you are most likely to see along the river. If you are lucky, you may spot an albino squirrel, which have been reported from Beddington and Carshalton since at least 1960. Grey Squirrels were introduced from North America and some were imported because of unusual features such as a black or white coat. It is thought that a number of squirrels with an albino gene were introduced into Kent, Surrey and Sussex. There was a small colony of Rabbits at Summerstown, which seems to have died out; it must have been one of the closest colonies to central London.

Several species of bat can be found along the river. Daubenton's Bat, sometimes called the Water Bat, flies just above the water surface hunting for insects, dangling its feet in the water at times. It does not emerge until well after dark, but can be heard with the aid of a bat detector at several stretches along the river. Serotine is a large bat that emerges soon after sunset, so there is a better chance of seeing one, particularly as they tend to fly out in the open. It is rare in London, but there is a colony in Beddington and Carshalton, which feeds in the area, including Beddington Park. The river provides an important feeding area for Pipistrelles, now recognised to be two species: Common and Soprano. Beddington Farmlands is one of the best sites in London for bats with Noctule, Leisler's Bat and Nathusius' Pipistrelle being seen in addition to those already mentioned.

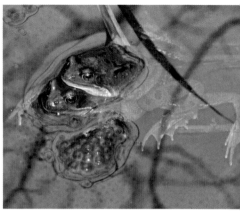

Frogs can be seen in the pools and ditches along the river in early spring.

Amphibians and reptiles

The Common Frog and Common Toad are both found along the Wandle, not in the river itself but rather in the pools and ditches along the river. Any spawn laid in the river would be washed away by the current and end up in the Thames! Frogs tend to spawn in late February, but may be later depending on the weather. While tadpoles, they are eaten by many predators including dragonfly larvae, water beetles, water boatmen, newts and fish. Toads spawn slightly later, laying their eggs in strings rather than in clumps; after hatching they form aggregations of many thousands of tadpoles. They can afford to advertise themselves in such a way because, unlike frog tadpoles, the skin of a toad tadpole contains a distasteful toxin. If a predator attacks a toad tadpole, it quickly learns to leave the others alone.

Smooth Newt also occur in the pools and ditches along the river. In the late 1980s, they were very numerous at Spencer Road Wetland, Hackbridge, but are nowhere near so numerous today. Light-coloured/unpigmented Smooth Newts were reputed to be at the old sewage pools at Wandle Meadow Nature Park. There are records of Great Crested Newt from the past, but it has disappeared in recent decades. In the early 1980s, the London Wildlife Trust undertook the management of the pond in the grounds of St Philomena's School, Carshalton. The pond was made waterproof so that it retained water throughout the year. A few years later, a pond in Sutton Water Works was being developed for housing when it was found to have Great Crested Newt. Many newts were rescued and relocated to St Philomena's by the British Herpetological Society Conservation Committee. The reintroduction was initially successful, but lowering of the water table caused by over-abstraction led to the pond drying out in the late 1980s. Newts are long-lived and a male was seen nearby in the channel along Festival Walk in April 1995. It is perhaps surprising that they did not colonise the pond in the Ecology Centre.

Terrapins are popular as pets but when they become too large they may be released into the wild. Red-eared Terrapin, a native of the southern United States, has been seen at several places along the river. They are omnivorous being more carnivorous when young and more herbivorous when adult. They can live for up to 30 years attaining a length of 1', but fortunately, do not seem able to breed, probably because the water is too cold.

Dragonflies and damselflies

Dragonflies and damselflies are associated with water because the larval stage is spent entirely under water. Most species lay their eggs in the pools and ditches along the river rather than in the river itself. There are a few river specialists including the spectacular Banded Demoiselle, which is probably the commonest species along the river. The male has a broad iridescent blue band in the middle of the wing, while the female has greenish wings; they are so different that they could easily be mistaken for different species. Males are strongly territorial attracting females with a graceful butterfly-like flight, which shows off the blue band on the wings. Once mated, the male and female fly in tandem with the female laying eggs, frequently being pushed under water by the male; she can continue to breathe

Male (right) Beautiful Demoiselle is so different from the female (left) that they could easily be mistaken for different species.

on a layer of trapped air between her wings. The larvae are active predators during the summer, but spend the winter in the muddy bottom. They usually overwinter twice before emerging as an adult. They are very abundant along the deeper water downstream of Goat Bridge, Mitcham where it is muddy, but since about 2000 have spread upstream, perhaps an indication that the river is silting up. The pollution incidents seem to have little effect on their numbers.

The earliest damselfly to appear in the year is the Large Red Damselfly, which can be seen from early April. Before 2000, they had not been seen along the river but have colonised and are spreading downstream. You are more likely to see one of the small blue and black damselflies. Blue-tailed Damselfly is easily identified since the blue is limited to the tip of the abdomen; Common Blue and Azure Damselflies are more difficult to separate.

Dragonflies tend to be on the wing later in the year than damselflies. Of the hawker dragonflies, Southern, Brown, Migrant Hawker and Emperor can be seen. The easiest to identify is the Brown Hawker because of its amber tinged wings, and the largest is the Emperor having a blue abdomen with a black stripe. Broad-bodied Chaser is the only chaser to be seen. Of the darters, the Common Darter emerges in July and may still be flying in November. It is worth looking out for the similar-looking Ruddy Darter, which used to be very rare in Surrey, but has increased and has been seen on the Wandle where there is plenty of Reedmace. The blood-red abdomen of the Ruddy Darter distinguishes it from the orange-red abdomen of the Common Darter.

A Comma that derives its name from the white comma-like mark on the hind wing that is clearly visible in this picture.

Butterflies and moths

There are no butterflies specifically associated with water; however, there are several species that occur along the river. First to appear in the year, having spent the winter as adults, are Brimstone, Comma, Peacock and Small Tortoiseshell. The Orange-tip spends the winter as a chrysalis and the attractive male can be seen in spring. Speckled Wood is unique amongst British butterflies spending the winter as either a caterpillar or chrysalis and may be seen from spring until autumn. As summer progresses, more species emerge. A blue butterfly flying high amongst bushes is likely to be a Holly Blue, while one flying in grassland is likely to be a Common Blue. The

Wasp or Moth? The Hornet Moth is a very convincing mimic.

Hairstreaks are difficult to see because they fly around the tops of trees, only occasionally coming down to flowers to drink nectar. Both Purple and White-letter Hairstreak have been seen at Wilderness Island, Carshalton. Meadow Brown is common but in recent years, two other browns, Gatekeeper and Ringlet, have been spreading downstream.

There are many more species of moth than butterfly, so it is not surprising to learn that there are several species associated with wetland. There are even a few species where the caterpillars feed under water. At Spencer Road Wetland, Hackbridge where recording has been carried out since 1989 by the author, 240 species of larger moth have been identified that include several wetland specialists, which are rare in London. Further recording along the river has found these wetland species to be present at several sites. Another wetland moth, Dotted Fanfoot, which had not previously been seen in Surrey since the nineteenth century, was seen at Morden Hall Park in 2009. In July, it is very common and can be seen flying above vegetation in the early evening. It is interesting to speculate on the origin of these moths: are they survivors from the past or more recent colonists? None of these wetland species were amongst the list in Hobson's book. Whatever their origin, they have undoubtedly benefited from habitat creation along the river. Another moth worthy of mention is the day-flying Hornet Moth that is common along the

Wandle, but rare in south-east England. The caterpillars feed on the roots of Black Poplar taking two to three years before they emerge as adults. The holes where they exit can be seen at the base of the tree and you may even see a pupal case, resembling a cigar, sticking out. The adult moth quickly loses the scales on its wing to leave transparent wings and mimics a hornet to gain protection from predators.

Other fauna

Pond dipping is a popular activity at the environmental centres at Carshalton and Morden Hall Park where children are always amazed at the variety of creatures they catch. Other more scientific studies are conducted by the Environment Agency and Wandle Piscators. Since the pollution incident in 2007, the Wandle Piscators have made monthly surveys at a number of sites along the river as part of the Anglers' Monitoring Initiative of the Riverfly Partnership. They look for invertebrates that are indicators of good water quality. In the past, when the river was heavily polluted, it would have held little but blood worms (midge larvae) and sludge worms (true worms); both are red from haemoglobin that enable them to live at low oxygen levels. In recent years, water quality has improved, leading to more invertebrates being found. In particular, freshwater shrimps, may and caddis flies are recorded by the Anglers' Monitoring Initiative. Any abrupt declines in abundance would indicate that there has been a pollution incident and the Environment Agency would be alerted for further investigation. The Environment Agency itself conducts more thorough surveys, but at longer intervals.

Although pollution over the years has led to an impoverished fauna, many insects that spend their larval stage in the river have free-flying adults, which enable recolonisation providing they do not live too far away. In addition, the Wandle Piscators are introducing Green Drake (*Ephemera danica*), a mayfly. They collect eggs from female mayflies as they return to the river to lay their eggs. The harvested eggs are kept in a tank of water until they are ready to hatch, when they are released into the river. The larvae may spend up to two years in their burrows in the river bed before becoming an adult fly. The project started in 2010 when 600,000 eggs were introduced, and will run for three years.

Species that live underwater are not readily visible to us, but we can see species that live on the surface. Such species prefer the pools and ditches to avoid being swept away by currents. Commonly seen skating jerkily across the surface are pond skaters searching out any

Chinese Mitten Crab have colonised the river and pose a threat due to their burrowing activity undermining the banks.

insect that gets trapped in the surface film to provide its next meal. The front legs are used to grab prey, the middle legs act as oars and the hind legs act as a rudder. Whirligig beetles are glossy black oval beetles and live up to their name by whirling around chaotically together. They have a special adaptation for living on the water surface; they have four eyes enabling them to see above and below the surface. The wingless Water-Cricket can be seen skimming along the surface of the ditches in Beddington Park and Spencer Road Wetland, Hackbridge.

Another invasive species, the Chinese Mitten Crab, can grow up to 3" and derives its name from the large claws that are covered by soft bristles resembling mittens. They have been spread via the ballast tanks of ships, where water is pumped into vast tanks to stabilise the vessel and later discharged. They spend much of their life in freshwater but must return to the sea to breed. They were first seen on the River Thames in 1935, but numbers remained extremely low until the late 1980s when the population dramatically increased, they were first seen on the Wandle in 1995. They have the potential to undermine banks with their burrowing activities.

'Mills at Butter Hill' (1890) by John Fitz Marshall RBA (1859–1932).

6 The river reborn: the story of the reclamation of the Wandle

The Seers

The seeds of conservation along the river were sown through the commitment of pioneers like Octavia Hill, (1838–1912), social reformer and co-founder of The National Trust. With her encouragement, and that of Richardson Evans, a leader writer for the *Pall Mall Gazette* at the time, the River Wandle Open Spaces Committee was set up in 1904, with the objectives of acquiring or encouraging local authorities to acquire open spaces along the river to "*aid in the purification of the river*". It was intended that these open spaces should be linked together by broad green walks to "*form a protective zone against the building encroachments which have already marred ...the lower reaches of the river*". Later, this body became the Wandle Protection Association, who railed against 'municipal marauders'. This was the time when societies with civic values were being formed, for example the John Evelyn Society in 1903 which had also been founded by Richardson Evans (it later became the Wimbledon Society); but in the absence of planning controls it was either down to benefactors to donate land or to local councils to acquire it. In this respect the Wandle Valley has had relatively good fortune.

Wandle Meadows Nature Reserve, Colliers Wood, occupies a reclaimed former sewage works today.

An early success was the acquisition by Wandsworth of an area which is now Garrett Park. Magdalen College, Oxford, donated a small piece of land at Earlsfield to Wandsworth for use as a recreational ground, and in 1907 Wimbledon Corporation bought *Wandle Bank House* and its 9-acre grounds for £6000. This became, and remains to this day, a public park. Nonetheless, the best examples of benevolent patronage and municipal endeavour respectively relate to what are surely the two foremost jewels of the river, Morden Hall Park and

Beddington Park. The former was bequeathed to the National Trust in 1941 by Gilliat Hatfeild, and the latter was acquired piecemeal (but mostly in 1935) by Beddington & Wallington Borough Council.

When it came to the acquisition of riverside land for public benefit, Carshalton Urban District Council set a gleaming example, which would put modern local authorities to shame. For example, they bought a rump of the once-extensive Carshalton Park estate around the source of the river from the jaws of the developers in 1913, and the Grove Park in 1924 (see p. 155). They also bought what we now know as Wilderness Island (together with other small areas of river frontage) when the Shepley estate was developed in 1932,[1] but they blotted their copybook here by failing to enable public access. Nonetheless, in an era of continued industrial pollution and in the absence of a planning framework to rein in property developers, strategic thinking was all but impossible even though public concern was evident: in 1929 the report on the condition of the river by Wandsworth Trades Council (see Chapter 2) sparked a lively debate in the pages of the *Wandsworth Borough News*. The inter-war years saw rapid residential development along the southern half of the river, and developers did not always consider the possibilities of public access. Indeed, gardens with a direct river frontage would sell at a premium. The stretch of the Croydon river between Wallington Bridge and Wilderness Island remains inaccessible to this day for this reason.

Reclaiming the riverbanks: the birth of the Wandle Trail
The formal idea of a walkway along the length of the river goes back at least to 1969, when in a letter to the Greater London Council (GLC) from Sutton's planning department a co-ordinated approach to a riverside walkway was proposed. Later that year, the GLC created the River Wandle Liaison Group which comprised representatives from Sutton, Merton and Wandsworth boroughs with a remit of co-ordinating riverside work, redevelopments and environmental improvements. It could also purchase land for the creation of additional sections of riverside footpath. An early success was the transformation of derelict watercress beds at Guy Road, Beddington in 1972, which included re-routing of the river and new access to the riverbank. In 1973 the Wandle Group was formed to co-ordinate the activities of the various local voluntary societies interested in the river; they got straight to work producing a guide and handbook to the river which appeared in the following year. This little publication did much to raise public awareness of the river.

1. For a lengthier discussion of this see 'Wilderness Island: [An] Historical Review' (Bibliography)

It was in the 1980s that things really got moving, however: the Wandsworth Society, which had long campaigned to turn the river into an asset for Wandsworth rather than a liability, published an article in 1983 ('A Wandle for the Wendles?') reminding readers that for centuries the river was at 'the centre of town's work and life' and had only been shut in and forgotten in the nineteenth century. It was still true that very little of the river in the borough was accessible; and much of the article was devoted to practical suggestions as to how to 'open up as much of the Wandle as possible to the people of Wandsworth'. The mouth of the Wandle, downstream of the High Street, had long been a problematic area – there was little public access and The Causeway was at this time a virtual dead end. Plans for a boatyard/marina got off the ground in the mid 1980s but foundered partly, it seems, on the problem of the tidal nature of the river here – without some sort of lock gates to retain water at low tide, the place became ugly and muddy, with little prospect of a viable boatyard. Wandsworth Council withdrew support for the scheme in 1988 and it finally collapsed – although ironically a half tide weir was built in 1991 to impound water at low tide to aid recreational boating (see box p.227).

Good progress further upstream occurred when the London Borough of Sutton, in partnership with the Manpower Services Commission (MSC), oversaw a £600,000 Wandle facelift during 1983–4. This initiative was designed to assist the long-term unemployed by placing them in Local Authority initiated schemes. 132 full and part-time jobs were created over the 12 months, all financed by the MSC. Several projects involved establishing new walkways and paths, and there was a programme of tree planting. Perhaps the single biggest success was to unlock the dormant plans for what became the Wilderness Island Nature Reserve in Carshalton. This was a site of great potential from which the public had long been excluded for no good reason other than lack of cash. Work begun here in December 1983 and, following several years of further work, much by local volunteers, the site, now with full public access, was leased to the London Wildlife Trust. Leading on from this MSC scheme there was an integrated study of the whole valley in 1985. The 'Wandle Valley Area of Opportunity' envisaged opportunities created by floodwater storage in the valley. The document makes an early reference to the concept of a regional park, with at its core the 'Beddington & Mitcham Area of Opportunity' (BMAO, see box); it's clear to see the favoured terminology of the time! Like many grand designs it all went rather flat, but the floodwater lakes did eventually arrive; not until the 1990s, however. Piecemeal improvements in access continued along the valley, matched by increased concern and public involvement in cleaning up the river. Annual Wandle clean-up days started in about 1987, often attended by large numbers at points along the river. These were locally co-ordinated, for example by voluntary groups such as the Beddington Society, with local councils providing skips for the rich haul of junk hauled from the water.

In the Borough of Merton the banks of the Wandle were to change drastically during the 1980s. Plans to redevelop the Morris/ Liberty site went to a Public Inquiry with local campaigners strongly opposed to the vast new so-called 'Savacentre' to be built partly on the site of Merton Priory and William Morris's old works. This was

The Beddington & Mitcham Area of Opportunity

In the early 1980s, a study was conducted by the Thames Water Authority, the Greater London Council, and the London Boroughs of Sutton, Merton and Croydon into the future of Beddington Sewage Farm, Beddington Park and Mitcham Common. It became known as the Beddington and Mitcham Area of Opportunity (BMAO). The plan was to extract gravel and create a series of lakes on Beddington Sewage Farm that would offer extensive recreational facilities. The impetus for the study was the completion of a new sewage treatment works such that the land would no longer be required for sludge drying; nor would land now need to be safeguarded for the M23 extension since this had by now been abandoned. The end use of the lakes would be recreational; however, their main functions were flood alleviation and more importantly to improve the quality of the effluent from the sewage treatment works. The effluent accounts for up to 90% of the flow of the river downstream of Goat Bridge and this plan was a once in a lifetime opportunity to clean up the river. The effluent was to pass through a series of lakes where water quality would gradually improve. The initial lakes were to be used for bird-watching, later lakes for angling and the last lakes for sailing and other water sports. Unfortunately, the finance for the plan never materialised and the opportunity for the river was lost. It is hoped that the current regional park proposals do not meet a similar fate. Instead, a flood alleviation lake was created in the early 1990s and the then recently privatised Thames Water submitted a proposal for gravel extraction and landfill with restoration for wildlife and people. Unlike the BMAO plan, which was well received, the new proposal was vigorously opposed. Planning permission was granted after a Public Inquiry in 1995 with work commencing in 1998 and due to finish in 2023.

the first major battle joined by the Wandle Industrial Museum Trust, which had been founded in 1983. They had their hands full: apart from the wheel house, all the (admittedly derelict) buildings on the Liberty site were under threat of demolition. In 1987 the plans were largely approved: one plus was the retention and eventual rehabilitation of all the Liberty buildings (the site at this time was owned by Sainsbury's, the developers of the retail centre). Another was a riverside walkway from the new Merton High Street Relief Road (Merantun Way as it became known) to the High Street itself.

However, the original line of this road, approved by Merton Council back in 1980, was accepted, obliterating most of the Merton Priory ruins, after the archaeologists had moved out?[2] There was better news south of here however: a riverside walkway was opened up all the way to Morden Hall Park, where the awkward old railway bridge was replaced by a level tramway crossing in 1990.

2. See also the Merton section of the Wandle Trail guide, p. 199.

Several new bridges have been installed to improve access along the river as the Wandle Trail has been developed, like this one near Watercress Park, Hackbridge.

It was in 1988 that the Wandle Trail was finally born as an official entity, following co-operation between the Wandle Group and the Wandle Industrial Museum. Two hundred people attended the inaugural walk. The Wandle Group produced the first guide to the Trail, sponsored by Young's brewery. Despite this milestone, there were still some long 'no-go' stretches where the river was inaccessible, especially in and around Summerstown and Earlsfield.

In Merton the popular Deen City Farm moved to its current site alongside Bunce's Meadow in 1994; it is an ideal companion to the Trail. Another very sizeable opportunity presented itself to Merton at this time, and it was another one that was nearly thrown away. The old sewage works astride of the railway line from Tooting to Haydons Road had become redundant in 1975; and following clearance of the standing structures on the northern section of the disused works, the land was sold in 1984 for commercial and industrial development. The remaining land to the south of the railway lay within an area designated as open space, but it was lying in gentle decay in 1986 when the Council approved outline plans for the land to be used for the new stadium for Wimbledon Football Club, whose ground at Plough Lane was coming up for redevelopment. Many local residents were incensed at this and began a spirited campaign against the proposals, which culminated three years later in victory when Merton Council abandoned the plan. After some delay, in 1991 the Council resolved that this southern part of the former works should be rehabilitated as a park for the local community. In 1992 a feasibility study was carried out, putting forward various proposals for the site and a working party set up involving the National Trust, London Wildlife Trust, London Ecology Unit and officers of Merton Leisure Services. Most above-ground structures had been removed leaving subsurface tanks filled with hard-core and other rubbish, along with the concrete bases of the filter beds. There were also localised dumps of fly tipping and spoil; however a number of habitats had developed on the site in the 20 years it had been derelict. To the credit of those involved, the site was designated as a Local Nature Reserve, Wandle Meadow Nature Park. It has become a valuable informal park with a wide variety of habitats, including temporary water bodies, wet grassland and woodland, drier grassland developing over the old concrete surfaces, and scrub and woodland on debris mounds and beside the river. The area now sports a wide flora and fauna, including some species rare on the river as a whole.

*River bankside planting
to improve habitat and
biodiversity, Morden
Hall Park.*

Even Morden Hall Park was not immune from the 1980s Merton 'wind of change', although here too the changes were positive. The arrival of Peter Creasey in 1988 saw a transformation in the management of the park, much-needed investment and development of the estate as a community resource. The former regime of gang mowing the park was replaced by, more varied and sensitive approach, including the development of meadows and wetland areas. Over the following few years the Garden Centre and café were opened, with improved access into the park, and the western snuff mill was opened as an Environmental Centre, to the great benefit of local children in particular.

In Wandsworth Borough, meanwhile, the Wandsworth Society published a 'ten-point plan' to open up the river in December 1988. The following year in 1989 a document published by Wandsworth Council set out a 'vision' for improved riverside access in the borough, where public access was still patchy. A new walkway and cycle route had been installed in Merton to the south upon the development of the Weir Road/Wimbledon FC stadium area, opening up a previously inaccessible stretch. However, in Wandsworth the conclusion was that further access would be difficult either from a practical viewpoint, or on the grounds of cost. Wandsworth did, however, condemn proposals in the 1989 'South London Assessment Study' for a new road along the Wandle Valley! This fortunately stillborn highway would have done enormous damage to the river and the natural environment throughout South London: the proposed route would have skirted Mitcham Common and Morden Hall Park on its way to accompany the river in its lower reaches.

An article in the *South-Eastern Rambler* in 1990 considered that access to the banks of the Wandle was patchy but improving. At this time they estimated that about half its distance was accessible, although in fact the figure was probably higher than this by then.

In Carshalton some welcome progress was being made around 1990 – David Bellamy opened the Ecology Centre adjacent to the ponds in July 1989, on land which almost became a housing estate – and nearby the Carshalton House Water Tower was opened to the public on a regular basis for the first time a few months later. Unfortunately, leaks in the pond within the grounds of Carshalton House meant that by this time it was nearly always dry. Just downstream, the redevelopment of the industrial site in Mill Lane over several years from 1986 enabled a previously inaccessible stretch of the river to be added to the Wandle Trail – but the Wandle Group criticised Sutton Council for summarily condemning the attractive old paper mill buildings and allowing no proper consultation. The excuse – contaminated land – looked like a cover to add some valuable extra flats, which now occupy the footprint of the old buildings.

National Cycle Route milestone, Ravensbury Park.

The Wandle Trail itself has developed as a concept since the late 1980s; particularly significant has been the involvement of *Groundwork*, the federation of environmental and social charities, and *Sustrans*, who have developed the National Cycle Network (NCN).

The Wandle Trail is also part of the London Cycle Network.

Together, from the early 1990s they moved the Trail towards a shared-use path and this inevitably caused tensions as routes of this kind have done elsewhere; but also because of an apparent change of ownership of the concept of the Trail, conceived originally as a route for a quiet stroll rather than as a traffic-free route from A to B. The distinctive Wandle Trail waterwheel logo dates from this time. *Sustrans* have adopted the Trail as Route 20 in the NCN. *Groundwork's* funding also resulted in the publication of an updated Wandle Trail guide and map from the mid 1990s, as well as a programme of artwork along the river.

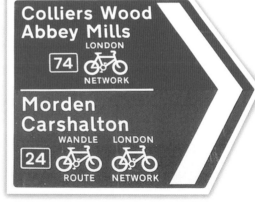

The Wandle Trust

The Trust was founded in 2000 as the Jet Set Club with a mission to restore the Wandle to full health and biodiversity as the very best sustainable urban showcase chalkstream in the world. It assumed the name Wandle Trust five years later. The Trust's work has three main thrusts:

- *River clean–ups*. The Trust holds well-attended community river cleanups every month somewhere on the river and, thanks to these, enormous quantities of rubbish are removed.

- *Trout in the Classroom*. A project launched in 2002 and running in around 20 schools. Tanks are set up, eggs are hatched into fry and schoolchildren help release the young fish into the river. In 2010 the first Wandle-born trout for 100 years were found.

- *Habitat restoration*. It was the Trust who commissioned a report in 2005, which assessed the river habitats in some depth and put forward recommendations for improvement. Armed with bursaries from the Wild Trout Trust, a national charity, which the Wandle Trust has secured, work has been undertaken to implement some of these recommendations. These include habitat enhancement works on the river, especially at Carshalton, designed to provide better river bed, flow and migration conditions for fish.

Ironically, the 2007 pollution incident has had a silver lining for the Wandle: part of Thames Water's £500,000 donation enabled the Wandle Trust to appoint a full-time Development Officer and thereby to assume a higher profile. In turn, the Wild Trout Trust bestowed its coveted Bernard Venables Award in 2008 upon the Chair of the Wandle Trust, Theo Pike, for his work on the river.

The Environment Agency conduct a fish survey. An electric pulse is used to temporarily stun the fish.

Towards a Regional Park?

The past 15 years have undoubtedly been the era of visions, grand designs and strategies designed to meet prevailing favoured criteria such as 'sustainability'. The Wandle has seen its share of these. The 1996 *Wandle Strategy and Action Plan* (WSAP) was prepared under the aegis of the *Sutton Regeneration Partnership*, with initial funding from the *Single Regeneration Budget.* The 'vision statement' to use the contemporary jargon, makes noises in favour of enhancing the environment and increasing pride in the Wandle 'brand' as poorer quality areas close to the river were regenerated (basically, old industrial land to be replaced by housing with some enhancement of open spaces).

In 1999 the *Wandle Valley Country Park* initiative, encompassing proposals affecting Mitcham Common in the north to Beddington Park in the south, including the restored Beddington Farmlands was drawn up to attract Millennium funding. The Millennium bid was unsuccessful, but the concept of the Country Park was developed in the next major strategy, the 2005 *Wandle Valley Green Ribbon Initiative*, a wider strategy aimed at realising the full potential of the River Wandle as an asset for the locality and London as whole. It envisaged taking forward the Country Park proposals from the WSAP: essentially the idea was to amalgamate the open spaces in and around Mitcham Common to form the Park. In addition, it proposed a programme of infrastructure, environmental and educational initiatives to regenerate the corridor and foster a sense of ownership.

Hard revetments are giving way to more natural planted edges, as here at Carshalton, close to the site of the former Mullards factory.

Also in 2005 the *South London Partnership*, an amalgam of several London Boroughs, and assisted by *Groundwork*, produced a discussion document laying out suggested opportunities and challenges along the Wandle Valley. In June a workshop attended by a wide range of organisations with an interest in the Wandle established a voluntary stakeholder consultative group called the *Wandle Forum*. Alongside this,

Early example of a Wandle Valley Regional Park information board from Culvers Island, Carshalton, 2011.

the *Wandle Valley Regional Park* (WVRP) *Management Board*, the executive arm, includes councillors, institution reps and the Chair of the Forum itself. The Forum and Board have met regularly ever since to further regeneration proposals along the Wandle corridor. They report to the *WVRP Development Board*, which consists of the officers of the riparian councils who hold the purse strings and release the monies! The existence of the Forum facilitates other bodies, such as *Natural England*, the *Environment Agency* and the *London Wildlife Trust* to contribute or seek funding and define project initiatives. Alongside these formal structures, the independent annual Wandle Festival, co-ordinating a series of events and activities along the whole river, which began in 2004, is just the sort of project that has helped to deliver the awareness-raising among the valley's residents, which all interested parties agree is important.

The Wandle Valley Regional Park is therefore best seen as a progression from these earlier initiatives. Once again, *Groundwork* is steering the project, but input is from a wide range of diverse groups and organisations representing a range of interests in the valley. These include the four local Boroughs, the Greater London Authority, local businesses, statutory agencies and third sector organisations. These and others come together in the Wandle Forum and in working groups who are currently trying to move the project and concept forward in a time of uncertainty over future funding. The 'vision statement' is very pious as usual:

> *An innovative, sustainable and high quality Regional Park in the Wandle Valley that is easily accessible, with a rich and thriving biodiversity, offering recreational, landscape, heritage, cultural and resource management benefits in which local people and businesses can take pride and ownership.*

A series of new WVRP information boards has started appearing in early 2011 which certainly should raise awareness of the 'brand' but at the time of writing it remains to be seen whether this project is more successful than its predecessors.

Water quality and habitat enhancement

Reference has been made (Chapter 2) to the steady improvement in water quality during the past 50 years, after the river status was officially described as akin to an open sewer in the 1960s.

Whilst water quality remained poor it was difficult to increase biodiversity, but now a good deal of work is under way on habitat restoration. There are always risks of setbacks to water quality from pollution in a river running through an intensely urban area; but following the Thames Water pollution incident in 2007, in December the company announced a £500,000 plan to revive and revitalise the Wandle over the following five years. The Environment Agency reintroduced 5000 young fish back into the river, the first step in a sustained restocking programme for the Wandle. Theo Pike, Chair of the Wandle Trust stated that the aim of the Wandle Trust was 'restoring the Wandle to its rightful status as the best urban chalkstream in the world'.

Trout fry being released into the Wandle at Hackbridge in 2011 as part of the Trout in the Classroom *initiative.*

Historically, chalk streams like the Wandle contained a unique habitat for wildlife on account of clear and fast-flowing water over clean gravel; but unsympathetic engineering works and poor water quality reduced the speed and clarity of the water which, in turn, affected the type of habitats and wildlife that can exist there. To combat these changes, chalk stream restoration measures have been put into place: one example is at Poulter Park. The river channel has been narrowed by measures including the construction of islands and the insertion of brushwood mattresses along the riverbed.

The stable block, Morden Hall Park, following its recent conversion into a 'Living Green' centre. Note the solar panels on the roof.

Wandle Trust volunteers carry out habitat enhancement in the Upper Wandle at Carshalton to encourage trout.

New gateway entry treatment on the Wandle Trail, installed in 2011 at Culvers Island.

This is intended to improve the rivers gravel beds and allow aquatic vegetation to establish which, in turn, will create improved spawning grounds for fish. Additional benefits provided by a faster and clearer river include the establishment of riverside plants, providing shelter for young fish during high river flows, and the blossoming of aquatic invertebrates. Wetland plants also provide food, shelter and resting grounds for birds, fish and insects. In late 2005, the Wandle Trust (box p.107) commissioned a full-river habitat survey from the Wild Trout Trust.

Although the focus was very much upon conditions favourable for fish, the detailed report focused upon the impact of river bank and river bed conditions and the impact of vegetation and shading upon habitat; and contained numerous recommendations, many of which are being implemented, the latest being on a stretch of river upstream of Butter Hill weir, Carshalton, in 2011. Here techniques including the installation of brash bundles to provide cover for fish, and the stapling of logs to the river bed to increase bed scour, are intended to enhance what is already a promising river bed for trout and other fish. To enable fish to reach this stretch of the river, a new Lariner fish pass was installed at the Butter Hill weir in March 2011.

Running in tandem is the ongoing project aimed at reintroducing Water Voles along a mile long stretch of the river near the Watermeads, Mitcham, spearheaded by the River Restoration Centre, The National Trust and the London Wildlife Trust. At Watermeads, half a mile of new channels have been dug, in which water levels can be controlled, to assist the creation of a habitat suitable for the endangered mammals.

Recognition for the Wandle

The momentum which has built up behind the drive to enhance the Wandle Valley is bearing fruit in numerous ways as we move into the second decade of the 21st century.

There was a fillip for the river late in 2010 when in a widely publicised national poll organised by the campaign group *Our Rivers*, the Wandle came in fifth place in the 'best rivers' category, behind more illustrious names like the Wye, Thames and Dart. Top reasons cited by people voting for their favourite river include a place to relax, ease of access, and opportunities to view wildlife. As a yardstick of the significance of this admittedly unscientific poll, the River Lea in North London was voted one of Britain's worst five rivers.

Volunteers on a Wandle Trust clean-up haul junk out of the river.

This was followed in September 2011 when the Environment Agency named the Wandle as one of the ten most improved rivers in the country. The BBC commented "*The list* [of rivers that had shrugged off their industrial past to become havens for wildlife and walkers again] *included the River Wandle in London which was officially declared a sewer in the 1960s...*"

2011 also saw some of the best news yet for the rehabilitation of the river, in the form of a high profile grant from the Heritage Lottery Fund (HLF) under its Landscape Partnership programme. The HLF has awarded £78,000 to a consortium of the four riverside London boroughs, and also set aside a further £1.9m to develop the project further in the coming years, if the next round of proposals meets the HLF's funding criteria. The money will be used to draw up plans to protect the valley's open spaces and diverse natural environment and encourage greater involvement in the life of the river by its neighbouring communities through volunteering and education. It will also aim to maximise the area's potential for sustainable transport, health, tourism and leisure. The *Guardian* newspaper noted on 1st August that of the eleven areas receiving grants, the Wandle Valley was "*distinctive by being the first urban landscape to get money from the HLF through this scheme*".

This new river bank treatment at Butter Hill Bridge, Carshalton will enhance the habitat for fish.

Get involved in the regeneration of the river and the wider Wandle Valley

Wandle Trust
The Wandle Trust clean ups are now a regular feature of the river calendar. As this book went to press the latest clean-up, in Wandsworth, saw around forty volunteers remove over two tonnes of detritus, including fourteen shopping trolleys, from the river. With the active help of volunteers the Trust is also engaged in regular rehabilitation work on the river. To get involved with the Wandle Trust, visit their web site at www.wandletrust.org, telephone 0845 092 0110 or write to PO Box 56545, London SW18 9DY

London Wildlife Trust
The London Wildlife Trust (LWT) lease the local nature reserves at Wilderness Island, Carshalton, and Spencer Road Wetlands, Hackbridge; whilst Merton Council manage the Bennett's Hole reserve at Mitcham aided by the Merton Group of LWT. Visit the LWT website at www.wildlondon.org.uk, or telephone 020 7261 0447.

Sutton Nature Conservation Volunteers
The Sutton Nature Conservation Volunteers (SNCV) offer volunteering opportunities, particularly at Carew Manor Wetland, Beddington, and Wandle Valley Wetland, Carshalton. There is information on the internet at www.sutton.gov.uk/index.aspx?articleid=1964. Alternatively, email sncv@sutton.gov.uk or telephone 020 8770 5821

The National Trust
The Trust are always looking for volunteers at Morden Hall Park. Contact them at The Stable Yard, Morden Hall Park, Morden Hall Road, Morden, SM4 5JD, telephone 020 8545 6856
Or visit www.nationaltrust.org.uk/get-involved/volunteer

Additionally other societies along the river take an active interest in various aspects of the environment of areas along the river valley. Prominent among these are:

Croydon Natural History & Scientific Society has a large membership and an active programme. The best way of making contact is via the Society's registered office, 96a Brighton Road, South Croydon, CR2 6AD

Carshalton & District History & Archaeology Society which also covers the area of the Wandle Valley in Beddington & Wallington. Their publications include some detailed material on Carew Manor and the Carew family. Write to the president at 32A Benhill Wood Road, Sutton SM1 3SL, or visit online at www.cadhas.org.uk where there are links to other local Friends' groups

The **Carshalton Society** campaigns to protect the heritage and amenities of Carshalton village. Contact via the Hon. Secretary at 25 Lavender Road, Carshalton, Surrey SM5 3EF, or visit www.carshaltonsociety.org.uk

Ecolocal Long-established, environment-focused sustainability charity which offers volunteering opportunities in the Upper Wandle Valley area. www.ecolocal.org, or Telephone 020 8770 6611. The Old School House, Mill Lane, Carshalton SM5 2JY.

Merton Historical Society is a very active group covering the Mitcham Morden and Merton reaches of the valley. They can be contacted via the local libraries in Merton, or online, find them at www.mertonhistoricalsociety.org.uk where there is also a link to the Wimbledon Society.

The **Wandsworth Society** has a long history of active campaigns in that borough, some of which are referred to elsewhere in this book. Contact via Studio 8, Royal Victoria Patriotic Building, Fitzhugh Grove, London SW18 3SX, or visit wandsworthsociety.org.uk

Many of the parks, open spaces and heritage sites along the river have Friends' groups who are active to varying extents. Space prevents naming them all, many of which can be accessed via local library sources; two of the most active are: The **Friends of Beddington Park** (www.friendsofbeddingtonpark.co.uk) and The **Friends of Carshalton Water Tower** (write to 136 West Street, Carshalton, Surrey, SM5 2NR or visit www.carshaltonwatertower.co.uk)

WANDLE LOCALITIES AND MAP OF HERITAGE SITES

The map shows the location of the more significant sites of heritage interest along the river, although it lays no claim to be exhaustive. Also shown are the approximate boundaries of the former parishes and districts bordering the river before they were subsumed into their respective London Boroughs in 1965.

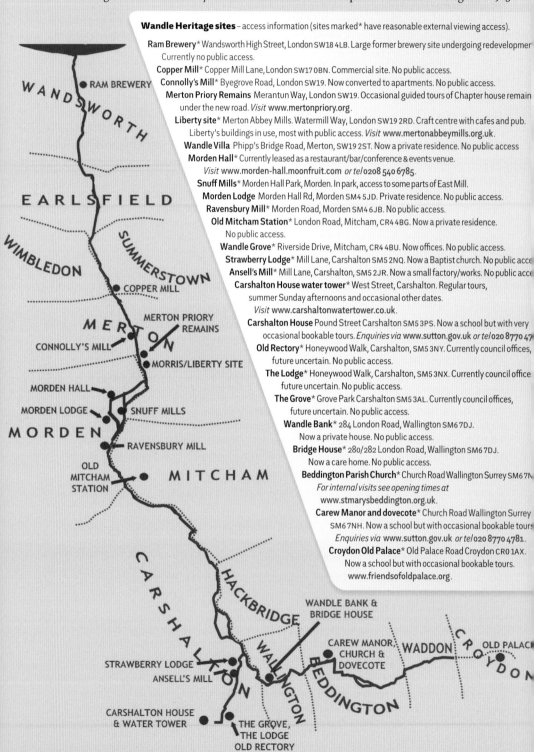

Wandle Heritage sites – access information (sites marked* have reasonable external viewing access).

Ram Brewery* Wandsworth High Street, London SW18 4LB. Large former brewery site undergoing redevelopment. Currently no public access.

Copper Mill* Copper Mill Lane, London SW17 0BN. Commercial site. No public access.

Connolly's Mill* Byegrove Road, London SW19. Now converted to apartments. No public access.

Merton Priory Remains Merantun Way, London SW19. Occasional guided tours of Chapter house remains under the new road. *Visit* www.mertonpriory.org.

Liberty site* Merton Abbey Mills. Watermill Way, London SW19 2RD. Craft centre with cafes and pub. Liberty's buildings in use, most with public access. *Visit* www.mertonabbeymills.org.uk.

Wandle Villa Phipp's Bridge Road, Merton, SW19 2ST. Now a private residence. No public access

Morden Hall* Currently leased as a restaurant/bar/conference & events venue. *Visit* www.morden-hall.moonfruit.com *or tel* 0208 540 6785.

Snuff Mills* Morden Hall Park, Morden. In park, access to some parts of East Mill.

Morden Lodge Morden Hall Rd, Morden SM4 5JD. Private residence. No public access.

Ravensbury Mill* Morden Road, Morden SM4 6JB. No public access.

Old Mitcham Station* London Road, Mitcham, CR4 4BG. Now a private residence. No public access.

Wandle Grove* Riverside Drive, Mitcham, CR4 4BU. Now offices. No public access.

Strawberry Lodge* Mill Lane, Carshalton SM5 2NQ. Now a Baptist church. No public access

Ansell's Mill* Mill Lane, Carshalton, SM5 2JR. Now a small factory/works. No public access

Carshalton House water tower* West Street, Carshalton. Regular tours, summer Sunday afternoons and occasional other dates. *Visit* www.carshaltonwatertower.co.uk.

Carshalton House Pound Street Carshalton SM5 3PS. Now a school but with very occasional bookable tours. *Enquiries via* www.sutton.gov.uk *or tel* 020 8770 47

Old Rectory* Honeywood Walk, Carshalton, SM5 3NY. Currently council offices, future uncertain. No public access.

The Lodge* Honeywood Walk, Carshalton, SM5 3NX. Currently council office future uncertain. No public access.

The Grove* Grove Park Carshalton SM5 3AL. Currently council offices, future uncertain. No public access.

Wandle Bank* 284 London Road, Wallington SM6 7DJ. Now a private house. No public access.

Bridge House* 280/282 London Road, Wallington SM6 7DJ. Now a care home. No public access.

Beddington Parish Church* Church Road Wallington Surrey SM6 7N *For internal visits see opening times at* www.stmarysbeddington.org.uk.

Carew Manor and dovecote* Church Road Wallington Surrey SM6 7NH. Now a school but with occasional bookable tours *Enquiries via* www.sutton.gov.uk *or tel* 020 8770 4781.

Croydon Old Palace* Old Palace Road Croydon CR0 1AX. Now a school but with occasional bookable tours. www.friendsofoldpalace.org.

WANDSWORTH

RAM BREWERY

EARLSFIELD

WIMBLEDON

SUMMERSTOWN

COPPER MILL

MERTON

MERTON PRIORY REMAINS

CONNOLLY'S MILL

MORRIS/LIBERTY SITE

MORDEN HALL

MORDEN LODGE

SNUFF MILLS

MORDEN

RAVENSBURY MILL

OLD MITCHAM STATION

MITCHAM

CARSHALTON

HACKBRIDGE

WALLINGTON

BEDDINGTON

WADDON

CROYDON

OLD PALACE

WANDLE BANK & BRIDGE HOUSE

CAREW MANOR, CHURCH & DOVECOTE

STRAWBERRY LODGE

ANSELL'S MILL

CARSHALTON HOUSE & WATER TOWER

THE GROVE, THE LODGE OLD RECTORY

Walking
the river

Morden ⊖ ¼
Deen City Farm ¾
Abbey Mills 1
Colliers Wood 1¼
🚲 20 ⚙

Phipps Bridge ▣ ½
Hackbridge 2½
Carshalton 3
⚙ 20 🚲

Wetlands

✿ National Trust
Snuff Mill ¼
Cafe, Shop

The Wandle Trail guide

The following section of the book is designed for those walking the Wandle Trail on foot (or from their armchair). The route is divided into sections, assuming a start from the upper end of the river in Croydon and/or Carshalton.

A note on maps used

The variety of maps employed should enable the reader to get the most from following the Trail. At the start of each of the walk sections, and with kind permission of the Wandle Valley Regional Park Development Board, is reproduced an extract from the contemporary map in the Wandle Trail leaflet covering the respective section. These maps have been updated where appropriate. No systematic attempt has been made to provide a key to all the symbols, most of which are self-explanatory. Yellow sections of the Trail (as opposed to red) are where the right of way is on foot only, as opposed to foot and cycle for the red sections. This fold-out leaflet and guide is still available for purchase, although the route as shown in the original is now outdated in places.

The remainder of the maps can be more easily identified by referring to the overview maps, which follow on from this introduction: they are designed to show the location of the more detailed maps found in each walk section. These 11 overview maps show the length of the river at a smaller scale. Much of the river, but not all of it, is covered by the larger-scale maps designed to show in greater detail the location of historic sites of interest.

The reader will notice that the maps employed are older versions of the Ordnance Survey map, reproduced from editions between 1867 and 1919. The reason for this is that these, superimposed in colour with more contemporary features, enable the location of features of historic interest to be located more easily as the Trail is being followed. For example, using these maps it should be possible to locate fairly precisely the former position of mills, historic houses and other buildings along the river, many of these referred to not just in the text in this section, but elsewhere in the book.

Notes to the overview maps (in source to mouth order)

The Croydon Wandle

On this 1911 map, Waddon was still a semi-rural hamlet at the edge of the encroaching Croydon with the lake and Waddon Court House largely intact. At Beddington the loose-knit village stands on higher ground to the south of the river itself (which has always been prone to flooding in this area); note the large house, Queenswood, and Queen Elizabeth's Walk, commemorating the royal associations at nearby Carew Manor, which at this time was in the middle of a 70-year period as a female orphanage. The rectory (which gave its name to Rectory Lane) can be seen in the south-west corner of the map, while the large chalk pit across the road is still a feature behind homes between Rectory Lane and Demesne Road.

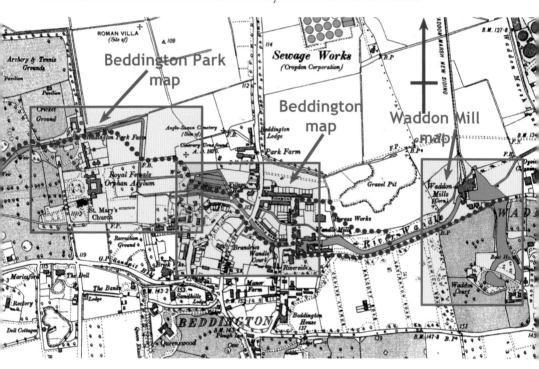

Carshalton

The 1867 map shows Carshalton dominated by the river and its springs and lakes, with evidence both of industry along the banks of the river and large houses surviving in some locations. At this time, the nearby hamlet of Wallington was centred far more closely on the river, from the then paper mill, past the manor house up to the new villa developments on Manor Road to the south, close to the *Duke's Head* Inn.

North Carshalton

The northern part of Carshalton on this 1919 map is still almost empty, but within ten years construction of the large St Helier Estate would be well under way here. The eastern (Wallington/Mitcham) bank of the river is more built up, notably in the vicinity of Beddington Corner with its mills. Apart from the three distinct mill sites on the map, there are allotments and watercress beds, and again, several large houses close to the river banks.

Ravensbury

The 1919 map shows an area also about to be overwhelmed by significant urban development. At this time, however, it remains largely rural, although villas line the London Road between the station (now Mitcham Tram stop) and the town centre to the north. The brewery is clearly visible close to the river, but the map area is dominated by the grounds of Ravensbury, with its ornamental watercourses downstream of the important mill site at Mitcham. The then newly built Ravensbury Manor can be seen on the south bank of the river. Ravensbury Print Works has gone by this time, but the water channels in its vicinity are still there.

Bennett's Hole area map

Beddington Corner Mills map

Culvers Island map

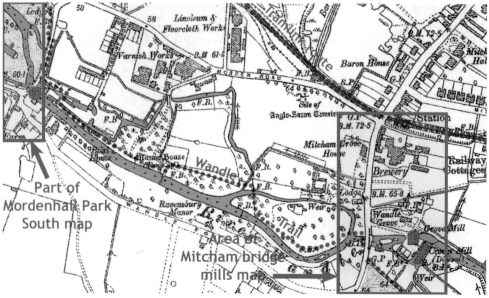

Part of Mordenhall Park South map

Area of Mitcham bridge mills map

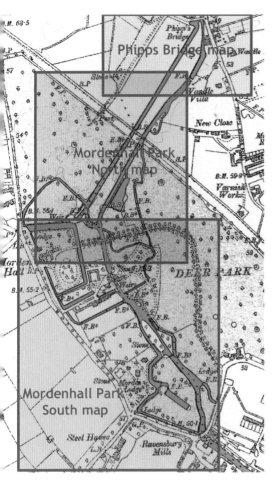

Morden

Morden is still a village just off the map to the west in 1919, while Hatfeild's Deer Park dominates this rural area.

Merton

In sharp contrast to the Morden area immediately south, London has spread over the northern part of this part of the Wandle Valley by the First World War. The extensive grounds of the sewage works can be seen, and much of the flood plain on either side of the river is still unoccupied, but terraced streets dominate elsewhere, except towards Phipps Bridge in the south.

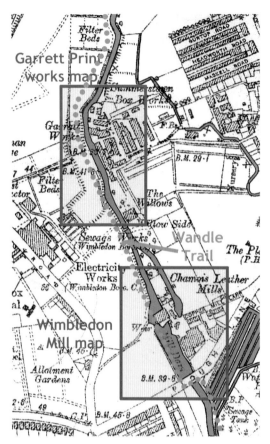

Summerstown

This stretch of the river in 1919 was occupied by a mixture of industrial and agricultural uses, with the river's flood plain offering a largely unattractive prospect for housing development. Sewage works and filter tanks are widespread, in stark contrast to the more attractive land uses upstream!

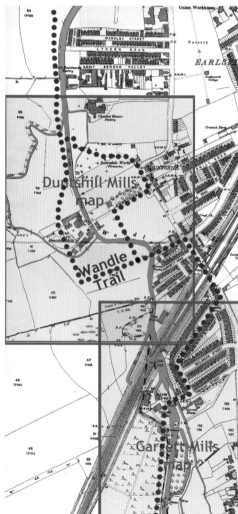

Earlsfield

An interesting mixture of land uses on this late Victorian map. On the east bank of the river, Victorian terraced streets and factories encroach the valley; whilst to the west, the scene is more rural-looking. Water mills survive on the river itself.

Wandsworth

This 1868 map of Wandsworth shows a sizeable town but one still surrounded by open space and parkland. The river, with its factories and mills, dominates the town. The marshy west bank of the river south of Wandsworth is empty of settlement, and today is occupied by King George's Park.

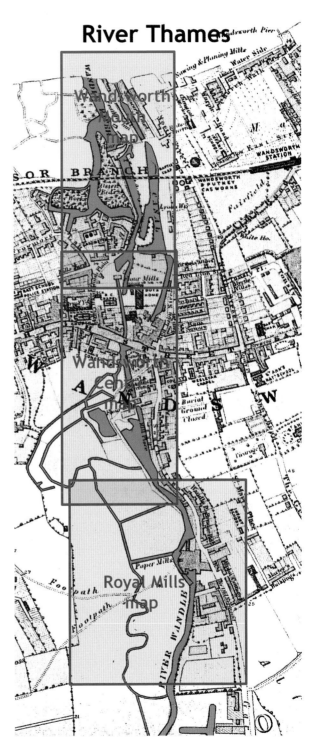

Detail from 'Croydon Parish Church' by R R Reinagle (1775–1862).
The river flows close to the church where today a busy road runs...

The Croydon Wandle:
west to Beddington

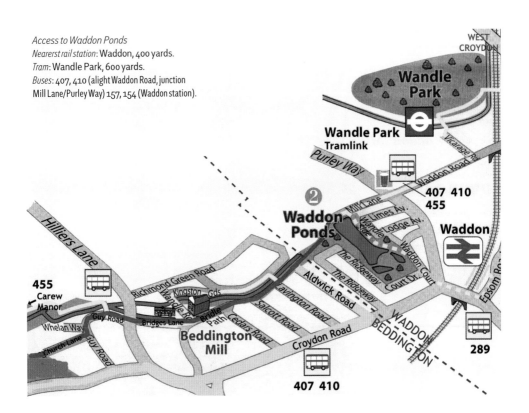

Access to Waddon Ponds
Nearerst rail station: Waddon, 400 yards.
Tram: Wandle Park, 600 yards.
Buses: 407, 410 (alight Waddon Road, junction
Mill Lane/Purley Way) 157, 154 (Waddon station).

We have noted in the introduction that, in geological terms, the
Croydon branch of the Wandle is by far the more significant; but
rarely has a town turned its back on its river to the extent that
Croydon has. The Bournes, or woe waters, referred to in that chapter
have always been intermittent streams within recorded history,
but within Croydon itself numerous springs and ponds were still
in existence in the nineteenth century, as the map (p. 127) shows.
The line of London Road between Purley and Croydon follows closely
that of the prehistoric Wandle, but for many centuries the Wandle
proper rose from a spring south of the present *Swan & Sugar Loaf*

public house, and flowed north past what is now Whitgift School before veering north west approximately along the line of modern Southbridge Road, the name of which suggested a stream or other obstacle. Writing in 1882, local historian J Corbet Anderson noted: *"The stream continued its course for a short distance along what is now the path on the west side of Southbridge Lane; when crossing the road, and entering the meadow, it separated into two branches, one of which ran through the field, while the other skirted the east side of Southbridge Lane. As it gurgled through the meadow, the Bourne appeared a lovely rivulet, about five feet wide, and from one to two feet deep, with a nice*

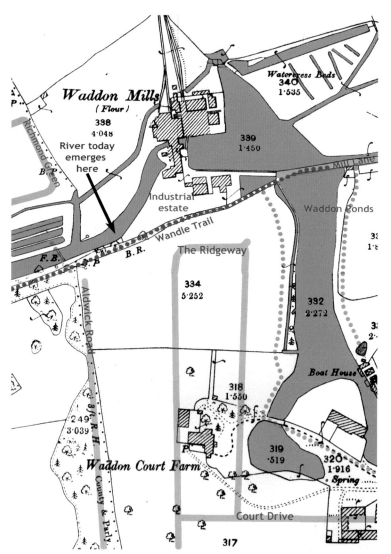

Waddon Mill

This map of the water courses of old Croydon is superimposed on a modern street plan. It shows the course of the Bourne joined by the Scar Brook and other feeder springs before being united in the Wandle below Harris's Mill Pond. Streams marked 'x' had disappeared by 1840, and all had gone by 1850 save for the Wandle north of the railway. By kind permission, Ken Maggs.

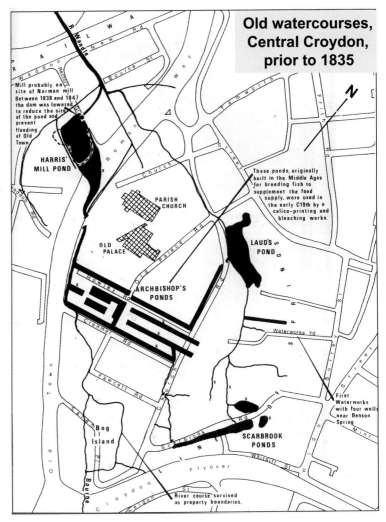

Old watercourses, Central Croydon, prior to 1835

Mill probably on site of Norman mill. Between 1838 and 1847 the dam was lowered to reduce the size of the pond and prevent flooding of Old Town

HARRIS' MILL POND

These ponds, originally built in the Middle Ages for breeding fish to supplement the food supply, were used in the early C19th by a calico-printing and bleaching works.

PARISH CHURCH

OLD PALACE

LAUD'S POND

ARCHBISHOP'S PONDS

Waterworks Yd

First Waterworks with four wells near Benson Spring

Bog Island

SCARBROOK PONDS

River course survived as property boundaries.

gravelly bottom for trout to spawn in; and here, sixty years ago, they used to catch trout a foot long". There is still a narrow lane, Meadow Stile, which drops west from the High Street today, even though, alas, the lovely rivulet has long gone. The modern Croydon flyover spans the river valley in which the Wandle once flowed, and the steep climb up to the High Street at Scarbrook Hill and Crown Hill to the east, or Southbridge Hill to the West, marked the edges of that valley. In-between, as the map above shows, lay a complex network of ponds and channels, fed by a series of springs issuing from a high water table along the line from South Croydon to Church Street. Corbet Anderson again: *"The Springs of those tributary heads of the Wandle, which arose from under the western side of the High Street and*

LAUD'S POND ON THE WANDLE. CROYDON.

fed the Scarbrook, were powerful. A noted spring of water also formerly gushed up opposite the west end of Sheldon Street, and a reminiscence of it still lingers in the name Pump-Pail." Some of the largest of the springs rose immediately west of Surrey Street, for example the Benson Spring which later, in 1851, became the site of Croydon's first waterworks supplying a million gallons of water a day. The castellated building of the old waterworks still survives. Nearby, you can still walk down Overton's Yard where in 1814 Henry Overton opened his brewery, making use of the water supply. In the early nineteenth century the ponds and watercourses in this low-lying part of Croydon made an attractive picture according to contemporary descriptions. Indeed, as a small child in the 1820s, John Ruskin (better known perhaps for his associations with Carshalton) wrote in his autobiography *Praeterita*:

"…under the low red roofs of Croydon, and by the cress-set rivulets in which the sand danced and minnows darted above the Springs of Wandel".

However, as the town grew, this sylvan scene changed rapidly and by 1849 the newly formed Croydon Board of Health reported that the Scarbrook Pond had become *"an enormous reservoir of filth… [like] Laud's Ponds in [its] occupation of spreading fever and death among the inhabitants".* The whole valley was often waterlogged, exacerbated by the fact that the water level in the pond at Harris's Mill (as it was then called) was causing the local water table to the south to rise. To combat this, the pond was reduced in height and size over

View of the Laud's Pond, in 1849, looking east towards the second Town Hall.

A romantic postcard of Waddon Mills.

the period 1838–47. Laud's Pond itself was in the grounds of the Archbishop's Palace, and one time fed fishponds to the south on land that is now occupied by nineteenth-century housing on Howley Road and Cranmer Road. These fish ponds eventually became an area of calico bleaching and there appears to have been a mill here engaged in the manufacture of silk and ribbons. The construction of a culvert in 1850–51 carrying the Bourne underneath the Old Town and north

Victorian photograph of Waddon Park House and Waddon Pond.

of the parish church enabled the waterlogged and unsanitary Old Town area to be drained, and Laud's Pond and other watercourses to be filled in, to the great benefit of Croydonians' health.

Croydon's mediaeval corn mill (Harris's Mill above) stood a short distance north-west of the church until 1849, across the site of the modern urban motorway, Roman Way. Beyond this, the river was culverted under Pitlake (meaning 'stream in a hollow') and emerged in what were a couple of marshy fields – Froggs Mead and Stubbs Mead. In 1890 these fields became Wandle Park. An artificial lake was constructed, the original intention being to divert the Wandle to run

A Victorian sketch of Beddington Mill, then known as Wandle Flour Mills.

through the lake and thus keep it full. However, it was found that, local springs would be sufficient to replenish it and therefore the Wandle was led through the park in a separate conduit so that stormwater and runoff would not end up fouling the water in the lake. It was, however, the falling water table in the twentieth century which led to the lake being filled in. The river eventually suffered the same fate, less excusably perhaps. A culvert was dug under the park in the 1960s and this still contains the river, which is now underground all the way until it emerges, a little indignantly perhaps, from its culvert at the Beddington border half a mile away. That it is still there is not in doubt: an article in the *Croydon Advertiser* in November 2008 told of a surreptitious expedition underground. Describing the river, the anonymous photographer said: "*The water was fairly clean. It didn't smell too bad, a bit like washing detergent… at the time there was less than a foot of water as we had just been through a dry spell. …during times of heavier rain I wouldn't be surprised if the level rose over a few metres.*"

Plans are afoot, however: Croydon seems about to cash in on the current climate of rehabilitating rivers. Wandle Park, which currently looks pretty forlorn and neglected, is about to get a significant injection of cash, partly from a £1m planning gain award. Then in

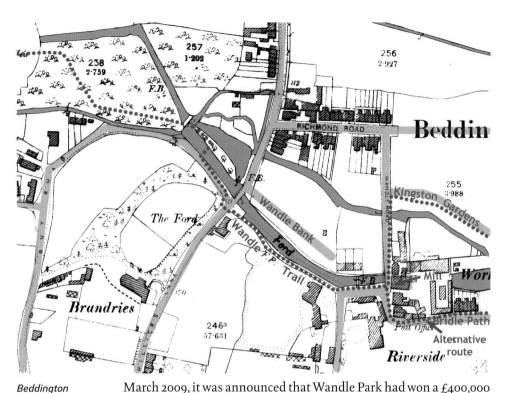

Beddington

Guard Room entrance, Archbishop's Palace, Croydon (see p. 54).

March 2009, it was announced that Wandle Park had won a £400,000 award in the Mayor of London's 'Help a London Park' scheme. You can read more about the plans for Wandle Park at www.wandlepark.com. These include a scheme to bring the river back to the surface, re-create the ponds, and restore the Victorian drinking water fountain. Nonetheless, at the time of writing, there is little or no evidence of the river in the town, save perhaps for some steep terraces, most notably maybe at Scarbrook Road at the southern end of Surrey Street. This despite the Croydon arm once being a pretty significant and powerful river, which flowed through the through the grounds of the Archbishop of Canterbury's Palace and into Wandle Park. The river then made its way towards Waddon, half a mile west, and into a large mill pond on the northern side of Mill Lane. This site is effectively the start of the Wandle Trail today, although technically the Trail is mapped as commencing at East Croydon station! Today, the two sides of Mill Lane by the ponds and garden present a stark contrast. Looking south, Waddon Ponds with its large weeping willows is fed by springs which make

up one of the sources of the Wandle itself. Waddon Ponds was part of an extensive estate of some 2000 acres for about 500 years. A large farm, Waddon Court Farm, stood on the western side of the ponds and served as a grand house where at least one owner, John Dewey Parker, entertained distinguished men of the day in the eighteenth century. Of the mill which named the road, no trace remains. Referred to in Domesday as a manorial corn mill, it stood inside the area of the current industrial estate, and must have been a significant enterprise, since it had a branch of the railway running to it from Waddon Marsh (now on the Tramlink) and a mill pond of over an acre which has now been filled in. From photographic and map evidence it was certainly a very large mill. The River Wandle had been dammed at the northern end to form a lake, but the river was diverted at the end of the nineteenth century to the north and east. The area of land created was used for watercress beds, then drained for allotments. Later it became the industrial estate it remains today. The mill itself ceased operation in 1928.

Guy Road, Beddington. The main river, left, re-united with the tail race from the former mill, right. Immediately downstream once lay a significant watercress bed. A new Wandle Valley Regional Park interpretation board can be seen on the far right.

The Wandle Trail follows an old path westwards from the northern end of Waddon Ponds, and 150 yards along here you pick up the flowing river for the first time. The linear strip of open space, Richmond Green, on the far bank once contained watercress beds, a significant Wandleside industry until fairly recently. Look out for Butterbur on the banks of the river along the Bridle Path. In early spring, the flowers can be seen before the leaves appear. By the autumn, the flowers have long since disappeared, but the leaves are enormous. Butterbur has male and female flowers on different plants and has lost the ability to reproduce from seed. This colony is female, which is very unusual, most colonies in the south are male; male colonies can be seen at Bennett's Hole and Watermeads, Mitcham.

We are now approaching Beddington; the trail crosses the river on the modern footbridge, although you can also continue on the southern bank and pick up the river again at Beddington Mill (see below).

Beddington is an ancient settlement of some importance which had four mills at the time of Domesday, but we have no real evidence of their location, and in recent history there was only one. This mill was situated on the east side of Wandle Road, where the last building on the site, a corn mill erected in about 1850, still stands. The history of this mill is hard to trace with certainty, but it's clear from records that in the late eighteenth century snuff was being made here, and we also know that at some date between 1813 and 1823 Charles Lambert, of the snuff milling family that later occupied Hackbridge Mill, Carshalton (see p. 161–163) took over.

His son Robert Lambert had taken over the management of the business by the time the 1851 census was compiled. Frederick Braithwaite in 1853 noticed that *"Mr. Lambert's mill employs two wheels, equal to 25 H.P., for grinding snuff."* He also mentioned the deplorable state of the river there:

"The mill head, like that at Waddon, is full of mud; at times, the water does not exceed 4" in depth, and the stench is only kept in check by a low temperature. The chief cause of this is the filth from Croydon, which finds its way through the wheel at Waddon mill."

Due to the sale of the great Carew estate in 1859, we have a detailed inventory of the mill from the contemporary sales catalogue:
"The Mills are brick-built and pantiled; and are worked by two breast water wheels, turned by the River Wandle. There are four separate mills, working sixty-one mullers, and a pair of edge stones; there are also two kilns and two drying places, with storing sheds adjoining, together with a millwright's shop. The whole is in good working order, in the occupation

of Mr. Robert Lambert, on lease (with the house, premises and lands)
for an unexpired term of fourteen years from Michaelmas 1848, at the
yearly Rent of £275." Around 1880 the mill passed to the family of
Wallis, who converted the mill to flour, and ran a business there
until some time between the World Wars when it ceased operating.

The Wandle Trail continues along the river westwards from the
mill past Mount Pleasant, a row of old weatherboarded cottages,
before following the river along a walled footpath leading to and
across the busy Beddington Lane into Guy Road. This was another
site where watercress was grown extensively until well into the
twentieth century. Cross the river again here to the northern side
and follow the path close to the river, both of which bear right into
a copse where a flood alleviation pond doubles as a wetland area
known as Carew Manor Wetland. Where the tarmac path veers away
from the river a little further on, take the unmade path (left) which
shortly crosses the river, and then heads diagonally across a field,
with the impressive buildings of Carew Manor as the backdrop,
to rejoin the river at the entrance to Beddington Park.

Beddington Park and Old Wallington

Access: Buses X26 stops at the Plough, Beddington (250 yards from the Trail). Buses 410, 407 at Beddington Church/Carew Manor. Nearest rail stations: Hackbridge, Wallington.

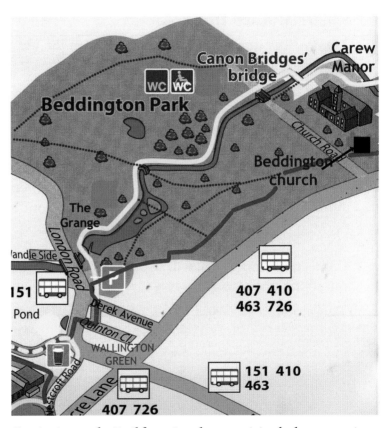

Continuing on the Trail from Croydon or arriving by bus or car via Church Road, you find yourself at the eastern end of Beddington Park, where Carew Manor and St Mary's Parish Church together represent a close approximation in layout to a mediaeval manor. The church appears in the Domesday Book and it's possible that a house existed at this time too. The association with the Carews dates back to the mid fourteenth century, when Nicholas Carew, who became a successful and wealthy courtier, took possession. Later Carews added to what became a deer park, and by the time of Sir Francis Carew (1530–1611)

An early engraving of Beddington Church and Carew Manor. Compare with the view below.

the park reached its greatest extent. Sir Francis laid out the gardens, which according to art historian and landscape designer Sir Roy Strong was an elaborate water garden with fountains and grottoes. Carew planted it with choice fruit trees, many procured at great expense from abroad. It's possible that his orangery, which was a wooden structure, was England's first, although oranges had been grown in the country before that. Part of the orangery wall (built later to shelter the orangery), in handsome brickwork and divided into several sections by pilasters, still survives in the garden.

In August 1599, Queen Elizabeth paid a visit to Sir Francis Carew at Beddington, for three days. Her visit is commemorated in Queen Elizabeth's Walk, a local street name.

As for the house, it has been altered and rebuilt several times (see box). The remainder of the buildings on show have a rather later origin. The early eighteenth century dovecote is the most noteworthy,

Carew Manor and the church today.

Beddington and the Carews

The Carews first came to Beddington in the fourteenth century, but the family was most important in the Tudor period. Nicholas, as the son of a royal official was a courtier and favourite of Henry VIII, a position he held for nearly all of Henry's life, unlike many well known to the king! He rose to become a Knight of the Garter in 1536 above the more logical candidate, the brother of the Protestant Queen, Anne Boleyn. Henry tired of Boleyn's political ambition and she was arrested and beheaded on a spurious charge of adultery. Nicholas who hated her, had been coaching Jane Seymour as her successor; however, Nicholas' success at this time of intense political jockeying was short-lived for Cromwell, jealous perhaps of his influence over HRH, plotted against him and managed to have him executed for treasonable conspiracy in 1538. Carew Manor then passed to the Crown, but when Mary came to the throne in 1553 and restored Catholicism, she remembered the Carews, and Nicholas who had been beheaded because of her, and she duly restored the estate to his son Francis. Francis wisely steered clear of politics and devoted himself to his garden. He brought back from France in 1562, myrtles, pomegranates, oranges and lemons, which he planted at Beddington; and at the time of his death in 1611, the garden was one of Elizabethan England's most striking.

It is likely that Richard Carew, who had the house from 1493 to 1520, was responsible for the crowning glory of the building, the hammer-beam roof over the great hall, probably built between 1510 and 1520.

By the beginning of the eighteenth century, the Carews' fortunes had started to decline, partly due to the accumulation of gambling debts, but the Carews had backed the wrong horse, the Royalists, during the Civil War. At this time the then owner, another Nicholas, decided to have the house remodelled. The Tudor courtyard house was opened out by demolishing the west wing, leaving the great hall flanked on either side by the long wings. Soon after the building work was complete, the north wing was gutted by fire and the whole interior destroyed. This part of the house remained as a shell for many years and was still largely empty in 1859, at the time the Carew Estate was sold after accumulated gambling and other debts.

A few years later it underwent heavy alteration to convert it into an orphanage, opening in 1866 as the Royal Female Orphanage Asylum, which function it served until 1939. Today, Carew Manor is in use as a school and the Great Hall with its wonderful arch-braced hammerbeam roof is the only Grade 1 listed building within a stone's throw of the river. It is embedded within a building that is largely nineteenth century in its current incarnation, and is occasionally open to the public. Ring 020 8770 4781 for details, or search for Carew Manor on the London Borough of Sutton website, www.sutton.gov.uk.

and difficult to miss; in a distinctive octagonal design and with some 1350 boxes it was unusually large for this kind of structure and may have provided an income in addition to supplying the house with eggs and meat. Nearby, the former outbuildings, now a smart terrace of houses, were converted in the 1980s: the author remembers one of them used, complete with old wooden frames, as an allotment hut in the early 1960s.

At one time the Carews' deer park stretched right up to Mitcham Common, but by the time the estate came to be broken up in 1859 the northern half had long been enclosed leaving the southern part as a deer park. Several years later, the great majority of the remaining park was sold to Canon Alexander Henry Bridges, who served as rector of Beddington from 1864 to 1891. Many of the surviving human and 'natural' features of today's park owe their existence to Canon Bridges: he filled in the long narrow lake (see map below) which stretched away west from in front of the house, although it's still easy to identify the depression it once occupied.

The dovecot at Carew Manor.

Beddington Park

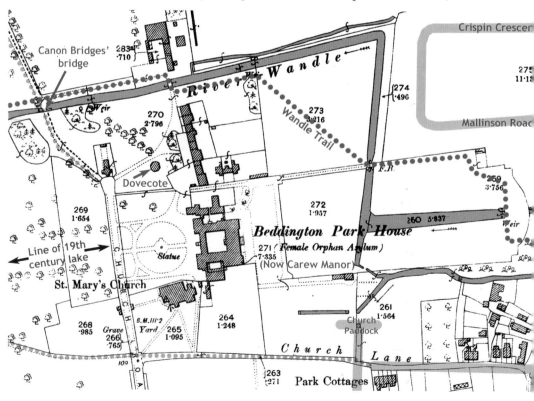

He also replaced many trees, and most of the older trees in the park today date back to his time, including the circular copses within it. In 1877 he had built the East Lodge at the end of Church Road near Carew Manor. This attractive Arts & Crafts-style gatehouse, which still stands, housed his gate-keeper. Also his doing is the terracotta bridge over the river near the dovecote, which bears his initials; and (very probably) the rather handsome flint and stone bridge further downstream. The former was very badly damaged by a fallen tree in the great storm of 1987, but has been faithfully restored.

We largely have Canon Bridges to thank for saving Beddington Park, one of the jewels of the Wandle, from the property speculators; although others played their part. It seems that George Payne, whose famous sweet factory stood in Croydon Road, was another, twentieth-century, benefactor; and Beddington & Wallington Borough Council acquired the park lands as and when they became available. The bulk of today's park, along with the adjacent Grange (see below) was bought from Major William Mallinson in about 1935.

As to the river itself, the first stretch of the river in the park, close to the old stables, has been extensively modified for flood control: if need be, water can be diverted into the retaining lakes on Beddington Farmlands, the channel which you can inspect by crossing the metal-sided bridge and following the path to the right for a short distance. This area north of the river is part of the Beddington sewage farm (see box on p. 89).

Downstream of Canon Bridges' Bridge the river flows freely through the park in one of its most attractive stretches, although in a

Canon Bridges' Bridge, Beddington Park.

A winter morning in Beddington Park: East Lodge is in the foreground.

more open parkland without the denser tree cover of some locations further downstream. Reach and pass the handsome flint bridge where the river veers south and flows into the former millpond of Wallington Mill. Look out for the little leat or artificial watercourse, which once served Kilburn's Mill (see below), running away at right angles to the long span metal bridge, which replaced a couple of rustic but rickety wooden affairs in about 1970. From this bridge, in some years, you can almost look into the nests of the breeding Grey Herons. Beyond this point lies The Grange, which has a distinctively different feel. This is because it was outside the Carews' deer park and laid out as a Victorian formal garden by Alfred Smee, who then described it in his book, *My Garden,* in 1872. Alfred's son later built the impressive house, also called *The Grange*, on the site; both house and garden were bought by the local council from William Mallinson in 1935, but sadly the house was consumed in a huge fire early in 1960.

The Grange garden, from across the mill pond, Wallington.

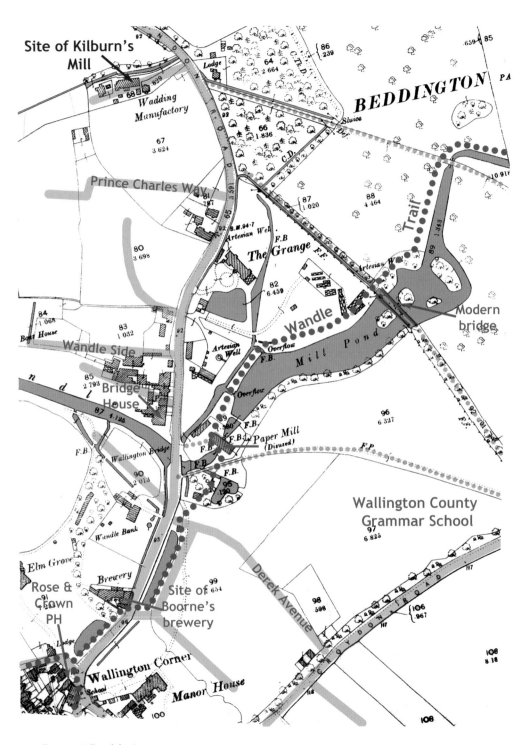

Wallington Mill and the Grange

The present building is a remodelling of the replacement and certainly an improvement on the harsh concrete lines of the typically 1960s effort. The gardens, which survive in altered form, contain a collection of trees, some of which are likely to have been planted by Smee. He also had an extensive fern collection and Royal Fern still grows widely in the water channels close to the formal pond. Smee's numerous glasshouses have unfortunately been lost.

The Grange lake as mentioned above was originally the mill pond of the village of Wallington. Wallington itself was originally a spring-line settlement which grew in linear form towards the green presided over by the *Duke's Head* Inn. The settlement has its origins in geology: like the parishes of Croydon, Beddington, Carshalton and Ewell, Wallington grew up around the clear springs that spurt out of the chalk. In time, the river was bridged at this spot. Only later, in the mid nineteenth century, did Wallington migrate south to cluster around the newly-opened railway station (which was then called Carshalton!). It's still possible to identify springs and wells here at Wallington: one, which may be an artificial bore, issues into a little pond by a leat very close to *The Grange*; another into the larger pond immediately south of Wallington Bridge. The mill stood at the west end of the lake, near London Road. It may well have been one of the mills in the ownership of Sir Francis Carew, mentioned by Giuseppi in his paper on the Wandle in 1610, and it had appeared on John Seller's map of Surrey in 1690. In a typically varied career its most celebrated owner was probably William Kilburn. Kilburn was born in Dublin in 1745, moved to London in 1766 and by the time he bought the Wallington factory in 1784 he was a well-known calico printer, who occupied printing works and grounds on a small

The slight depression running west from Carew Manor marks the site of a former lake.

*The river in
Beddington Park.*

tributary of the river a little to the north-west. He had the then
logwood mill rebuilt as a cotton spinning mill. It later became
Bourne's flour mill, but by the late 1850s had become a paper mill.
In the twentieth century the site had a brief life as the Helm chocolate
factory, not a unique instance for former Wandle mills. Sadly, nothing
remains, but the modern sluice gate and the large head of water
visible at the far end of the lake testify to the potential the wheel
would have had. As for Kilburn's calico printing works, the site is
commemorated in Kilburn's Mill Close, off the London Road, whilst
the water channel or leat survives in the park and can be followed
down as far as the lodge on the London Road, a worthwhile diversion.
Returning to Wallington Bridge, adjacent is the handsome *Bridge
House* completed in 1786 by James Newton, proprietor of Merton
Abbey Mills. It is now a care home. Excavations behind the building
suggested occupation during the later medieval/early post-medieval
period. Growing beside *Bridge House* is a fine example of a Swamp
Cypress (photo p. 73), probably the tallest on the river. Across the
river stands the early eighteenth-century *Wandle Bank*, one of the
finest domestic houses remaining close to the river. Note the
Victorian extension closest to the river, a studio (with a Venetian
window) by Arthur Hughes, the pre-Raphaelite painter.

Downstream of the bridge lies one of the few sections of the river which remains inaccessible to the public, as far as the unity of the Croydon and Carshalton branches of the river at Wilderness Island. So the Wandle Trail now follows the London Road south beyond *Wandle Bank*. Further springs fed the ponds which now lie on either side of the road just beyond *Wandle Bank*, and a small stream, which is visible on the old map, still runs in the front garden of the house. The more attractive pond is across the road, a survivor from the old Wallington Manor House grounds. Opposite this, just before you reach another pond, is *Old Brewery House*, a modern development commemorating the site of Boorne's brewery. No doubt taking advantage of the pure spring water, the brewery survived until it was taken over and shut by Ind Coope in 1934, although the buildings survived until 1968. The *Rose and Crown* pub, at what is still known as Wallington Corner a few yards further on, was once the brewery tap. The photograph on p. 43 shows the brewery after the 1904 rebuild. Note the wooden casks and the use of horses for delivery!

The Wandle Trail now follows Butter Hill to the right, past the little lodge to the former Elm Grove House (both shown on the map, p.141), but I would recommend taking the next road on the right, Westcroft Road, which leads into Carshalton, where one can pick up the Carshalton branch of the river.

Wandle Bank, London Road, Wallington

The Carshalton Wandle: from Carshalton Park to Wilderness Island

Access to Carshalton village:
Rail: Carshalton, ¼ mile.
Buses X26 from Kingston
and Croydon, local buses
157, 127, 407.

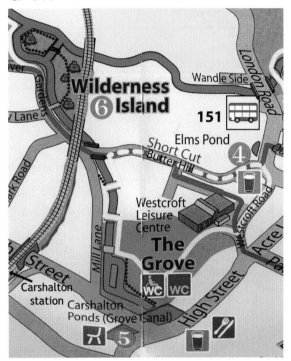

Carshalton Ponds are the natural starting point for any walk down the Carshalton river today, although the Carshalton arm once had its origins in the chalk to the south of the modern village centre. Accordingly, the first part of the walk description takes you on a tour of the remains of the early headwaters south of the ponds. You can skip this section if you simply want to get straight down to following the main river.

Carshalton's attractive ponds have long been crossed by a causeway, which was enlarged to carry vehicles in 1825. The lower East Pond was probably some sort of reservoir for the Upper Mill, on the site of Carshalton's ancient corn mill, although it also performed an ornamental function, as it does today. The ponds were fed by a series of springs and streams running in from all sides, but today would be no more if man had not intervened, first to waterproof the bottom of them in 1967 and to keep them topped up artificially by a water recirculation system.

The water table in the chalk, which feeds the whole Wandle system has, as we have already noted, been depleted by abstraction. The charming stone bridge under which the Wandle leaves the East or Lower Pond is attributed to the Italian architect Giacomo Leoni, and carries the Griffin crest of a well-known Carshalton family, the Scawens, who also occupied *Stone Court* (see below). Sadly, the magnificent Cedar of Lebanon tree, whose graceful branches fanned

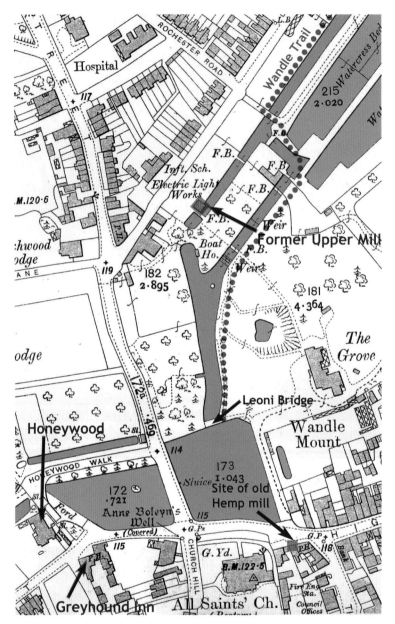

Upper Mill

out over the pond by the bridge for probably 200 years is no more, axed rather precipitately by Sutton Council in 2001 who claimed that it was actively tilting.

If you take the path over the bridge westwards towards the wall and road, you'll come in a few yards to a gate in the wall. Leaving via this gate and crossing the road carefully there is a road (Honeywood Walk) a few yards to your left, which runs along the north side of the

Carshalton Pond and Honeywood.

Upper or West Pond. By the War Memorial there is a good view across the pond to the attractively sited *Greyhound Hotel*, and further right the house called *Honeywood*, dating in parts to the seventeenth century, but much extended at the turn of the twentieth. It now functions as a heritage museum, with an adjacent tearoom. Carshalton's impressive parish church dominates the view. It is worth a visit: parts of the interior are many centuries older than the Victorian restoration that overlooks the pond, and tell of the former importance of this spring-line settlement.

At times when the water table is high, streams still run into the West Pond under *Honeywood* from a feeder channel which you'll find by continuing straight ahead at the end of Honeywood Walk into Festival Walk. Note also here the little gate house to another Carshalton mansion on the corner. *The Lodge,* a Victorian remodelling of a late eighteenth-century house, was bought by Carshalton Council in 1944 and has been used as offices and amenity land since. It is currently the subject of a vigorous campaign to retain it and its attractive grounds in community ownership and use in the face of planned disposal by Sutton Council. Dominating Festival Walk itself is a huge London Plane tree, although your eye will also be drawn to the handsome Queen Anne-style *Old Rectory,* which for many years has been a council building, although its future is also now uncertain. The stream channel, usually dry, leads us to West Street; and right across the road can be seen the unusual water tower, possibly designed by architect Henry Joynes, and which lies in the grounds of *Carshalton House* (see below). The tower contains a

Looking across to Carshalton House from the water tower.

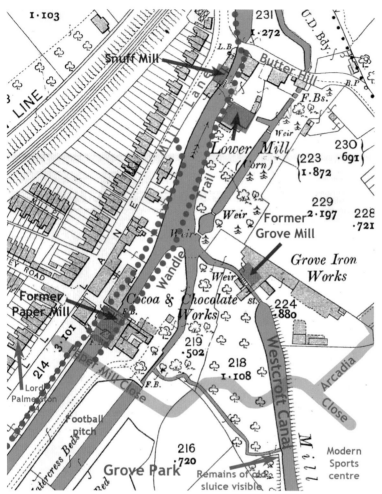

Lower Mill

suite of rooms, including a bagnio, or bathroom with its deep plunge bath and exquisite early eighteenth-century Delft tiles; a saloon looking out across to the house, and an orangery (without any oranges, however!). Also of significance are the restored remains of a water wheel here, within the wheel pit of the Pump Chamber. This powered the pumps which lifted fresh spring water, from below this chamber, into a cistern, housed in the tower. Unfortunately, access to the Tower and to the usually dry pond that acts as one of the Wandle's headwaters is restricted, usually to summer Sundays, although it's well worth a visit (see www.carshaltonwatertower.co.uk).

Carshalton House itself is in the premier division of surviving Wandle-side houses. Almost certainly a very early eighteenth-century house, its more prominent owners included, briefly, Dr John Radcliffe, physician and MP; Sir John Fellowes (of South Sea Bubble fame), Sir

Carshalton Water Tower, viewed from the lake. Sadly this lake is nearly always dry today.

Delft tiles line the walls of the plunge bath inside the remarkable bath room of Carshalton Water Tower.

Windows in the Water Tower offer lovely views towards Carshalton House.

Philip Yorke, Attorney General, and later Lord Chancellor Hardwicke and Admiral Lord Anson. The latter used it as a country retreat or second home, although history doesn't record whether the taxpayer footed his mortgage! The grounds include the remains of a formal landscape garden of 1716–20, laid out for Sir John Fellowes, possibly designed by the celebrated Charles Bridgeman (1690–1738), although little remains of this scheme today. A serpentine lake, now dry, with sham bridge was added in the later eighteenth century, replacing an earlier formal canal. *The Hermitage*, a listed and recently restored building in the grounds, probably dates from the early to mid eighteenth century. It is constructed of Reigate Stone (Lower Greensand) and chalk.

Having seen use as a military college and a private school, *Carshalton House* has been run by the Daughters of the Cross as a Catholic girls' school since 1893, and despite later additions the handsome main house is largely intact. There are occasional open days, for example on the annual *Open House* event.

Turning left at the end of Festival Walk and staying on the near side of West Street brings us in a few yards to Margaret's Pool at the road junction, on the left through the railings. This pool, again almost always dry these days, was beautified and endowed by John Ruskin, an early environmentalist who was very fond of Carshalton but less so of its inhabitants, whom he castigated as the *"human wretches of the place"* who cast their *"broken shreds of old metal"* and *"rags of putrid clothes"* into the stream. In 1876 he had it cleaned up and the surrounds beautified, and it seems that it was he who named the pool, and after

The Hermitage in the grounds of Carshalton House.

his mother. The adjacent inscribed tablet, installed against Ruskin's wishes by local historian George Brightling, reads:

"In obedience to the Giver of Life, of the brooks and fruits that feed it, of the peace that ends it, may this well be kept sacred for the service of men, flocks, and flowers, and be by kindness called MARGARET'S WELL. This pool was beautified and endowed by John Ruskin., M.A., LL.D."

Follow the road round to the left at Margaret's Pool, into Pound Street where the village jail once stood, although the site is now a garden. We're now heading back to the ponds and the *Greyhound*, Carshalton's enviably sited old inn; if we cross the road here with great care, we can follow the footpath past the pub and the parish church into the High Street by the *Woodman* pub, formerly a butcher's shop – note the old meat hooks outside! Immediately beyond it and just before the *Coach & Horses* pub stood a small mill fed by another one of the Wandle's headwaters. As we continue along Carshalton High Street, we are following the line of an underground culvert built to carry the young river from its source in Carshalton Park, which itself once extended to the High Street. It formerly flowed along the side of the street; it was, however, as one local historian put it, *"an attractive but hopelessly*

Westcroft Canal, Carshalton. Properly this is a mill race; it led to the Grove Mill, the only full-size overshot wheel on the river.

Old Grove Mill bypass sluice, Westcroft Canal.

uncommercial feature" of the High Street and so was buried in the interwar period. Pick up the old river valley once again at the junction of Carshalton Place in about 150 yards, turning right to follow the (again usually dry) valley until we reach a busy main road and cross with care to enter Carshalton Park through a gate. Ahead of us, the dry valley stretches for another 300 yards or so and if we walk up we can see the grotto from which the Carshalton branch of the river used to emerge. The grotto itself was at one time a fine feature, elaborately decorated with a mosaic including shells and flints, all presided over by a statue of Neptune himself, but it's in a very sorry state these days.

Carshalton Park had been acquired by Sir William Scawen, a wealthy city merchant, early in the eighteenth century. After his death in October 1722, his properties passed to his nephew Thomas Scawen, who had much work carried out to Carshalton Park, including the so-called Grotto Canal. The last part of our Carshalton trail is well worthwhile, but requires a bit of detective work. Return to the High Street and this time turn right and continue, keeping the *Fox and Hounds* pub on the opposite side, to a pedestrian crossing and cross over. Just to the left is another entrance to the Grove Park, but turning right walk down Westcroft Road, which forks left from the busy main road. At one time this was the main road to London from Carshalton; it now leads down to a sports centre, but it was also the route of another water channel drawn off the Grotto Canal and fed into a leat or mill race a little further down the road, just beyond Scawen Close. We can see this channel and walk alongside it as we approach the modern sports centre. Just before the building, a gate leads across the channel on a bridge and into the Grove Park.

The Westcroft Canal has a special place in the history of the River Wandle since it fed the only mill on the river with a full-size overshot wheel, that is, one where the water channel was conveyed over the top of the wheel, the most powerful arrangement, but obviously only possible if a head of water greater than the wheel diameter could be attained. The more intrepid reader can follow along the bank of the channel to a point where a couple of rusty sluice gate holders are set into some concrete on the park side. It is easy to see how large a head of water had been built up, for the drop down to the left is quite considerable. This sluice opened a bypass channel, which conveyed water (when the mill was not at work) down to the main stream close to Lower Mill. Grove Mill itself was a short distance ahead in the area now covered by the modern housing estate. It had a monster 20' wheel and was a snuff mill for most of its life, with possibly a pair of adjacent mills; it was converted to iron making in 1867 and remained as the Grove Iron Works until its demise following a disastrous fire in 1944. Brayley, in his *History of Surrey* (1850) called it '*very powerful*' although he was probably taken in by the size of the water head. In his section on the Wandle, R.T. Hopkins in *Old Watermills and Windmills* (1938), describes the mill, although he misplaces it to Mill Lane, as follows:

Tail race from Upper Mill, Carshalton.

"*The Great Water Wheel in Mill Lane is the 'lion' of Carshalton, and you will hear him roaring long before you see him. The curious creaking of a water-wheel added to the boom of the water racing over the pond-head is a unique sound, and a sound that awakes in mankind dim, unconscious memories of primeval life, when the people crushed their corn with cumbrous wooden grinders and lived perilously with sweat and suffering. Now as you walk up Mill Lane you will hear that primitive sound – the creak, creak, creak of the wheel and the row of the water as it wrenches and worries over the paddles. Later, through a space between some cottages, you will perceive the mill-wheel ponderously revolving on the opposite bank of the Wandle. A veritable giant of a fellow, twenty feet in height and eight feet across the paddles. The great wheel has been turning quite a long time; hundreds of years, and it will turn for hundreds of years to come.*"

Well he was wrong about its future longevity too as it had closed within six years; and he also got it wrong about the leat, assuming that was its original function, stating it had been built hundreds of years before. In fact, it first appears on Rocque's map of Surrey in 1760, close to 1777 when the first record of the mill appears; but at least his prose is good! The photograph on p. 31 shows the towering but rather rickety-looking timber-clad mill, but there were also several

Butter Hill to Strawberry Lane

outbuildings and houses associated with it, on a surprisingly steep slope which has since been levelled off and lies somewhere along the line of the footpath running up from the new pedestrian bridge over the river 50 yards downstream of Paper Mill Close (see below).

By walking at right angles away from the channel across the park – which may be muddy, in which case a tarmac alternative leads to our left in a horseshoe – we will arrive back in a few moments at the site of Upper Mill, just downstream from the Leoni bridge (see map p. 146). This, along with central Croydon, is one of the few sites to appreciate a visible river valley with terrace above a sloping drop to the flood plain.

The heavily altered and restored mill was in its last incarnation actually a small power station, replacing a flour mill which was demolished in the 1880s. This explains the rather diminutive structure on the site today; but this is very probably the location of Carshalton's original corn mill, mentioned in Domesday. The site of Upper Mill also shows a clear layout of the mill race, the deep pond immediate upstream of the mill site, and the bypass channel, now the waterfall. The tail race of the mill was converted by the last owner of the Grove estate, Samuel Barrow, into a swimming pool. It's a pleasant 5-minute circuit up to the Leoni Bridge and down the far side back to the mill to inspect the site. On the site of the lawn on the west side of the river here, there once stood *Stone Court*, a large mansion, one of many in the Carshalton area. It was demolished 200 years ago and in 2006 the site was excavated by archaeologists.

Returning to follow the river downstream, pass a smaller cascade on the river as it curves round to re-unite itself at the end of the mill tailrace. As the river's gradient here in Carshalton was particularly

Ansell's snuff mill, Carshalton – probably an early twentieth-century view.

steep it's no surprise that this stretch of the river had one of the largest clusters of mills. Turn sharp right onto a modern path, which follows the river closely with new houses to your left. Until the early 1990s this site was part of a large industrial area which, in turn, occupied old mill land. Trees and shrubs have quickly re-colonised the banksides and the river flows briskly through a narrow riffled channel; so much so that the Wild Trout Trust have identified this stretch as one of the best on the river for the fish. It should be possible to identify habitat enhancement works they carried out along with the Wandle Trust and volunteers early in 2011.

Where the path crosses the next road stood a large paper mill. This was a sizeable mill site, and for at least some of its life had a pair of breast-shot wheels. The mill turned out high-quality paper and was leased by William Curteis in partnership with his sons John and Thomas, before a long period under the stewardship first of Charles and James Ansell (1782 until around 1820), then the Muggeridge family, until 1894. In 1853 Frederick Braithwaite noted that the mill had a water wheel of 15 horsepower and also a back-up steam engine of 12 horsepower. Fifty years later Giuseppi wrote (*Victoria County History of Surrey*, 1902) that:

> "The business now consists of the manufacture of the finest hand-made paper, well known in the trade with the watermark 'C. Ansell', and ledger paper, writing, drawing, and loan papers are made. There are five vats in use on the premises, and the Carshalton mills are now the only ones in the county for hand-made paper."

The Grove Park, Carshalton

The attractive Grove Park which sees the Wandle on its way is the remains of the Stone Court Estate, which was acquired by John Cater in 1697. It was he who built *Stone Court* (see main text) on the site of an earlier house. In 1729 *Stone Court* passed to Thomas Scawen. Thomas's uncle Sir William Scawen had been a successful city merchant and financier, and the family were to become very important in Carshalton. Among other things it was he who built the graceful Portland Stone bridge which crosses the river by the pond. It was most probably the design of Italian architect Giacomo Leoni and carries the griffin from the Scawen coat of arms. Scawen probably created a grove of trees and classical temple on the land to the east of the river where *The Grove* now stands.

In 1856 The Grove, with the eponymous house built in the early Victorian period, was leased to the Reverend Cator, Rector of Carshalton. Cator may have created The Grove's Victorian garden, the structure of which is still largely intact, and contains an old group of yews. His wife Aurelia, after his death in 1884, bought *Upper Mill,* which she demolished and replaced with a water-powered generating plant to supply electricity to light both *The Grove* and her home at *Stonecourt* (not the big house which was demolished but the outbuildings which still carry the name today on the corner of North Street and Mill Lane).

Mrs Cator died in 1894 and both houses were leased to Sir Samuel Barrow, a wealthy tanner, from Christmas Day 1895. He later acquired the freehold. He made many improvements to the estate and developed several outbuildings as well as embellishing the grounds; but like many wealthy industrialists Sir Samuel lost a lot of his money in the postwar slump, and in 1923 the Grove Estate was put up for sale. The auction particulars suggested the potential returns from the development of the grounds as blocks of flats, but fortunately for us all the estate failed to reach its reserve price, and the following year was bought by the Carshalton Urban District Council for the princely sum of £14,600. The Council used the buildings as much-needed staff accommodation, whilst they vowed *"to preserve [the grounds] as an open space for ever ... and also to obtain control of the beautiful ornamental waters which form such an attractive centre to the area".* The old Urban District Council had a very good record of acquiring and maintaining buildings and open spaces for public benefit, something their successors at the London Borough of Sutton might do well to remember as they currently seek to dispose of several important sites close to the Wandle in Carshalton.

Left: *Old and new at Butter Hill Bridge: the historic sluices and weir pictured with the first fish pass on the river, installed in spring 2011 to enable trout to reach the upper reaches of the Carshalton arm.*

The mill closed down in 1905 and, after short spells as a cocoa and chocolate works and later a pencil factory, it was absorbed into the chemical works of the Distillers Company Ltd, in turn bought out by BP Chemicals until the site was developed for housing in 1991. The road you've just crossed is called Paper Mill Close *in memoriam*.

Follow the path along the river for a further short distance, crossing the next footbridge so that the river is now on your left. The swiftly flowing stony-bottomed stream has already slowed right up and the bed is covered in increasingly deep mud deposits in anticipation of arrival at a weir and the remains of sluices, with a much altered old mill building on the opposite bank. There were mills on each bank, and even today you can see the remains of both wheel pits, one now occupied by a lariner fish pass installed in 2011 to enable trout to pass into the upper reach of the river. On the east (right-hand) bank stood a small mill which was possibly built by George Ansell in the late eighteenth century and which for most of its working life, was a calico printing works, although it seems that initially it was concerned with cloth weaving. Records suggest the building was still in use as a store in the late nineteenth century, although neither Braithwaite in 1853 nor Brayley in his 1850 inventory of Carshalton mills mentions it as a functioning mill. The building on the opposite side of the river is the much altered remains of Ansell's Mill, as it is often called even though the Ansell family had interests in several mills. In 1790 shortly after the first reference to it, the mill was then described as a *"Madder & Snuff mill under one roof"*. It was indeed a snuff mill for most of its life, although latterly it became a parchment and vellum mill, the latter being in demand for drum heads by the twentieth century!

Just upstream of the snuff mill and sharing the same dam stood Lower Mill (map p. 148), which turned out a range of goods including copper, calico and paper in its long life. It seems that this was the mill occupied by Christopher Patch and his son, the celebrated paper makers, (see p. 41) in the late eighteenth and early nineteenth centuries. In a photo from around 1900 (p. 30) it is Denyer's flour mill, a tall building dwarfing Ansell's mills below it. As with the whole of this area, the twentieth century mill buildings were absorbed into what became Vinyl Products Ltd, who alongside BP Chemicals occupied a substantial riverside area prior to their closure in the late 1980s and the subsequent development of the modern housing estate.

Downstream again, cross over the very old, but much-altered, Butter Hill Bridge. No trace now remains of the tail race from Lower Mill which passed under Butter Hill to the right (east) nor of the

Wilderness Island, Carshalton: from fish and osiers to Local Nature Reserve

The 'watersmeet' where the Carshalton and Croydon branches of the river come together is one of the most interesting localities on the river today. Wilderness Island, as it is now called, is one of the success stories of public access on the river and has been a Local Nature Reserve for about 20 years, but has had a chequered history. The history of the site has been extensively documented elsewhere* but in brief it was part of a large estate at one time in the ownership of George Shepley, who had commercial interests in the adjacent Hackbridge Mills. The earliest useful maps of the site show that the two branches of the river separated again almost immediately below the site of the mill(s) here and finally made one stream by the Hack Bridge (according to Sutton's heritage manager John Phillips the bridge took its name from the old English for the narrow sliver of land made an island by these two channels). This simply reinforces a point made several times in this book that very few stretches of today's river are unaltered in their channel. Indeed, the construction of the railway embankment here in 1868 necessitated a considerable diversion of the Croydon arm of the river, which formerly meandered in a far more pronounced loop. The ponds on the island, which still exist today although heavily silted up and rather overgrown, appear to have been fish ponds, with osier beds between. Osiers are willow saplings which were coppiced to make baskets, etc. The 'Cut' as we know it is in existence by the late eighteenth century, although it may have been made up to a century earlier. The theories of previous historians that it was to improve/switch water supply between the mills here seems hopelessly improbable and unscientific; I much prefer the theory of John Phillips, who suggests it was excavated simply to keep poachers out! When the estate was sold off for housing in 1932, the parcel of land between the two river branches and the Carshalton to Hackbridge railway line was spared development by a combination of poor access and its wet and low-lying nature. It seems that later in 1932 a restrictive covenant was placed on what is now called Wilderness Island preventing development, and it is this covenant that we can thank for having the nature reserve we enjoy today. As a result the Carshalton Urban District Council acquired the lands in question, and a few odd corners on the western bank of the river, from the developers of the estate for the princely sum of £300! We know that the 'mainland' section of the land was used as a wartime dump, which is why this part of the site is now several feet higher than the river, and indeed it was even referred to as 'the dump' in minutes of the Carshalton Urban District Council!

There was certainly no public access however, and references to the site in the post-war years were nearly always concerned with keeping people out.

The Island was nearly used in the early 1960s for sheltered housing for the elderly; but the council was thwarted in the ensuing Public Inquiry because of the covenant referred to above. Similarly, a decade later, by which time Carshalton was now part of the London Borough of Sutton, there were plans to turn the area into a formal public park. These met with a surprisingly hostile reaction from local people and again the whole proposal went to a Public Inquiry. In 1978 it seems that residents including children (and a petition containing the signatures of 72 children who used the area as an informal play area was presented) had a higher regard for what we might call wildscape than the authorities! Once again the council suffered an embarrassing defeat at the hands of the Inspector and, although progress during the 1980s was painfully slow, monies released as part of the Manpower Services Commission Community Programme helped to unlock the dormant plans for what was now called Wilderness Island. Volunteers put in long hours of work at this time, nobody more so than Mrs Pat Selby, who played a key part in the successful 1978 campaign. The Sutton Conservation Group[1] emerged as a body for conservation volunteers and, coupled with the transfer of the site to the management of the London Wildlife Trust in 1987, we were well on the way to the open access reserve that we have today.

In 1990 the site was declared a Local Nature Reserve and enjoys greater protection as a result. Today, conservation volunteers work monthly at Wilderness Island under a management plan presided over by the London Wildlife Trust. Details are on the noticeboard at the entrance to the site, which is now accessible to the disabled via the radar key scheme. The highlight of the reserve is the island itself, accessible by a bridge over the Cut, which having been dredged recently is in a healthy condition. A leaflet giving information about the island is available from the London Wildlife Trust.

* In *Wilderness Island – An Historical Review* by Andrew Skelton & Bob Steel, for London Wildlife Trust, 2004.
1. Now Sutton Nature Conservation Volunteers

The Carshalton arm of the river at Wilderness Island.

bleaching grounds that once lay between the channels and are now occupied by modern flats. Pass under the impressive three-arch bridge of 1867 carrying the railway across the river, and look out for the much-altered *Strawberry Lodge*, one of Carshalton's oldest houses. It was built by Josias Dewye, a noted gunpowder manufacturer, although sadly it has long since lost its riverside garden and now operates as a church and conference centre. Opposite is the entrance to Wilderness Island Nature Reserve. A detour here is highly recommended (see box). On leaving the island, the Trail continues along River Gardens; at the sharp left turn in the road, you can look across the river to Wilderness Island. Here the river becomes wide and deep, the former mill head for what was one of the key industrial sites on the river some 150 yards downstream. To reach it, the Trail leaves River Gardens on a signed riverside path a few yards further on.

Wilderness Island to Goat Bridge

Access to Wilderness Island:
By rail to Carshalton then
½ mile walk via Denmark
Road. Alternatively, bus to
Carshalton then follow
Wandle Trail from Grove Park.

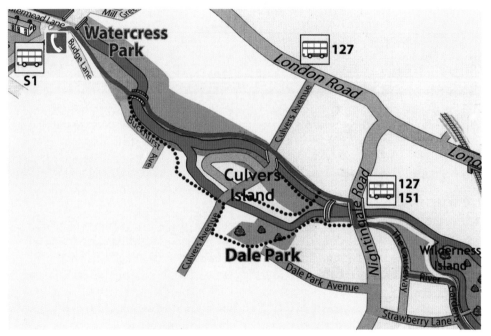

Arriving at the large fenced culvert, which carries the river briefly underground opposite Wilderness Island, one stands at a significant site on the river for two reasons. Here is the union of the Croydon and Carshalton branches, the former joining after swinging around the eastern side of Wilderness Island (a second culvert is visible from the island a hundred yards east). This is also the location of the former Hackbridge Mills, an important site in the economic history of the river (see Hackbridge Mills box pp. 162–3). Even though it is barely a quarter of a mile below the Butter Hill mills, a good head of water was available here as the drop into the culvert testifies.

The two culverts locate the approximate position of the wheels of the two mills which latterly stood here, but at the time of writing the site is derelict after the latest of several fires, which have all but destroyed the historical interest here.

It's a couple of minutes' walk down to the road crossing at the Hack Bridge. On this stretch, look out for the yellow flowers of Marsh-marigold in early spring, and trout spawning in early winter. It was on this stretch that trout fry were caught in March 2010.

The area around the Hack Bridge was a very different one even in recent history. Shepley's branch of the Surrey Iron Railway ran down here to his mills, while nearby stood the old hamlet of Hackbridge, just along the road where the old cottages and *Old Red Lion*

The Hackbridge Mills, Carshalton

A look at the chequered timeline of this significant site shows how, typically, Wandle mills have been adapted over time for a diversity of production in line with economic and social changes.

There is an early reference in the Carshalton Court Rolls to this site operating as a fulling mill in 1361, in which usage it continued until 1569, when it was sold and converted to a Brazil wood grinding mill. This function produced dyes for the textile industry, which was of course an important Wandle industry in its own right. In the early 1650s, possibly at the commencement of the First Dutch War in 1652, the Brazil mill was converted to gunpowder making, and then, or later, two other mills were built nearby for the same purpose. They were later (in 1661) acquired by the well-known powder manufacturer, Josias Dewye, who had been manufacturing at the important Chilworth Mills in Surrey; and he continued making gunpowder at the three mills on the site until around the end of the century. We know that some time around 1710 two of the three mills on the site were then converted to copper making, the third reverting to dyewood grinding. This in turn was converted to a leather dressing mill in 1738:

leather mills on the river were often associated with linseed oil – the skins being placed in a trough of oil and pounded by hammers to soften them. This was the start of a long association with this industry since, moving forward into the nineteenth century in 1825 an oil mill was built here adjacent to the leather mill; but not before the site had come into the possession of the man most closely associated with it, George Shepley. Shepley, a Yorkshireman, entered into a joint lease of all the mills on the site in 1765; and on or before this time the two former copper mills had also been converted to leather dressing. A detailed description of the site at the time of the renewal of the lease in 1773 makes it possible to identify the buildings on the site accurately for the first time: *"Immediately to the north of the confluence of the Carshalton and Croydon streams of the Wandle, on the west bank, was the former Great Copper Mill, now used for drying skins."* On the east bank opposite this mill was the former Lesser Copper Mill, now used for skin dressing. A little to the south of this, on the east bank of the Croydon stream was the mill that had formerly been used for *"rasping wood for Coulourmen and Dyers"*,

Left: *Hackbridge Mills*

pub face each other across Hackbridge Road. The author remembers as a child sitting in a dingy but atmospheric room in the latter, still wholly unspoilt. The old cast iron bridge has been gone for a century; this was a very old bridging point but in addition, a ford is still identifiable immediately north of the bridge. This is also the area where several large riverside houses stood until well into the twentieth century (see map, p. 164, which shows all six of them; and Chapter 4, pp. 60–62). On the west bank of the river a footpath follows the riverside along the line of the old driveway to *Hackbridge Lodge*, but no trace of the house, or adjacent *Hackbridge Cottage*, survives. Adjacent to the Trail on the east bank, *Hackbridge House* was a Territorial Army barracks in its later life and was finally pulled

now used for dressing skins. There had originally been a gunpowder mill, of which only a conduit remained, a little way upstream from the former wood-grinding mill. There were various ancillary buildings including one "*part of which was formerly used as a Melting House for Copper*", a charcoal house, a lumber house, a brew house, a barn, and several workmen's cottages. By the terms of the lease, the landlord undertook to erect a dwelling house for the tenants, to be included with the premises on lease. This house, which later became known as Shepley House, was located in the vicinity of the present Shepley Close, off River Gardens, and survived until these streets were laid out in the early 1930s.

At some time before 1778, George Shepley converted one of the mills to oil milling, so that he could become self-sufficient as regards the supply of oil. The work was completed by 1779 since he insured an oil mill in that year. Shepley's period of tenure also saw fires razing the mills, a common occurrence to wooden mills on the Wandle and elsewhere, but they were soon rebuilt. It seems however that there were now two mills, an oil mill and a leather mill, and although Shepley died in

1807, a few years after the Surrey Iron Railway, which was largely down to his vision, had been completed, the mills continued in oil and leather operation. The mills changed hands several times before the mid-nineteenth century when, following a period of inactivity, they were acquired by one Robert Lambert, who was already producing snuff at Beddington, and who converted one of the mills to that function. His son Alexander built the business up to such an extent that in 1900 the *Royal Magazine* stated: "*[it was] one of the largest if not the largest in the United Kingdom. It is quite a usual occurrence for as much as five tons of snuff to be sent out by Mr Lambert in a week.*" The 1898 Ordnance Survey map (opposite) shows the large mill at the confluence as a leather mill whilst that on the east side of the Croydon arm is shown as the snuff mill. Leather working in some form continued at the leather mill (although the Shepley lineage petered out in the 1880s) until just before the Second World War. The snuff mill continued under Lambert's occupancy until 1912 when it was acquired by Messrs. Arthur Coles & Co., a firm of calico printers, who occupied the site until the Second World War.

down in 1970 to make way for the modern flats of Corbet Close. The public benefit was the new footpath on the east side of the river from the white bridge to Culvers Avenue, now part of the Wandle Trail. It's worth leaving the Trail here, however, and detouring over the bridge to

Culvers Island

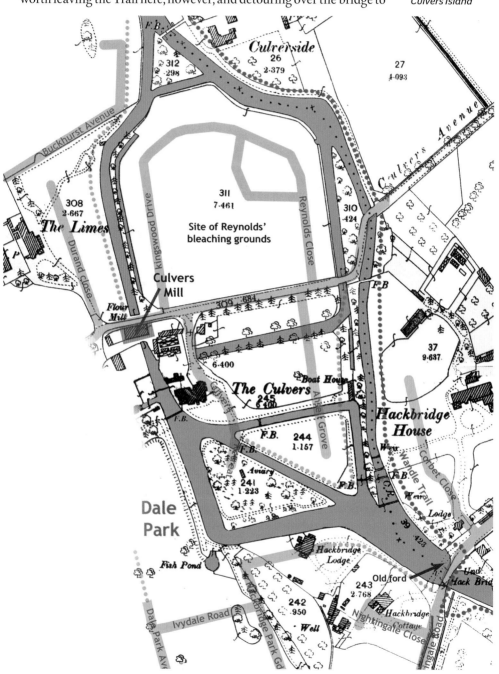

follow the western arm of the river, which is an artificial cut created to power a mill (see below). The path follows what was (see map opposite) until the twentieth century the edge of a channel cut to create a couple of small islands laid out as pleasure gardens with an aviary, in the grounds of *The Culvers*. In fact, the layout of the water courses at that time was very complex: the line of another, now vanished, channel followed the line of the service track running from Culvers Retreat across Ansell Grove.

The Culvers was an impressive house almost certainly built for banker Samuel Gurney in 1850 (Box, p. 166, *The Reynolds of Carshalton*), but it may occupy the site of an earlier house. In 1886 the house and estate were bought by Peter Gassiot, another wealthy Carshalton man and a friend of John Ruskin, who himself was a regular visitor to the village. The house lasted a good deal longer than the estate which went under bricks and mortar throughout the early twentieth century; older residents remember it being referred to as the 'Spanish House' in its later years, since for several years before and during the Second World War the house was used to house Basque children, refugees from Franco's fascists in Spain. This came about because of the generosity of Carshalton Urban District Council, who

The Cut, Wilderness Island Carshalton.

The Reynolds of Carshalton

The records of the Quaker family of the Reynolds go back to Chichester in Sussex, but by the mid eighteenth century Thomas Reynolds was established in Southwark as a cloth maker. The calico industry on the Wandle really took off in about 1760 and it was shortly after this time that Thomas's son Foster appeared on the scene at Carshalton. Foster took over his father's prosperous business upon the latter's death in 1771 and moved first to Mitcham and soon afterwards to Carshalton, where he bought the Culvers Estate. At this time the estate was very large – 280 acres; and he set about developing his calico firm into what allegedly became the largest in the world. The estate had three significant houses: *The Culvers* itself (the word means 'pigeons' or 'doves'; a culverhouse is a dovecot), dating back at least to the early seventeenth century; *The Limes* built by Foster in 1786, (it stood on the site of modern Cherry Close and Limes Close); and *Culverside*, formerly *Wallington Cottage*, which was on the site of modern Mullards Close.

Foster Reynolds had eight children including three sons. Two of these, William and Jacob, carried on the calico business whilst the oldest, Thomas Foster, became an eminent figure, a co-founder of the Royal Horticultural and the Zoological Society. William along with two of his children all married into two significant Quaker families: the Gurneys, well-known bankers of the time, and the Frys. Elizabeth Fry (née Gurney) the great prison reformer was linked to the Reynolds family through three marriages. It was one of these, that of William's daughter Ellen to Samuel Gurney, nephew of Elizabeth, in 1837, that had significance for Carshalton, since they came to live at *The Culvers* and had the house rebuilt on a much larger scale (in 1850).

It was William's son Charles who had the last connection with Carshalton, but it was not a happy one: under his stewardship the great calico business was about to collapse due to events elsewhere, and in any event Charles, along with Sam Gurney, were not great businessmen. The latter did not have the financial acumen of his more famous father, also Samuel. They preferred to lead the lives of gentry, in *Culverside* and *The Culvers*, respectively. The collapse of the Overend Gurney bank in 1866, with liabilities of some £11 million, rocked the financial world and precipitated the sale of the Culvers Estate, including the great bleaching grounds. The Carshalton calico industry nose-dived to its death a few years later, but like many other eminent former Carshalton citizens Reynolds' name lives on in a street name, Reynolds Close, on Culvers Island.

The western arm of the river at Culvers Island, Carshalton, from the site of Culvers Mill.

also made space available in the Oaks, the large house in the park of the same name. There is more information about the Basque 'Colonies' on the Internet at www.spanishrefugees-basquechildren.org (Follow the links to 'Basque Children' and then to 'Colonies in Britain'.)

The Culvers was pulled down in 1960 and the modern town houses of Culvers Retreat were put up on the site. You can gain access to the river bank at the point just before Culvers Retreat joins Culvers Avenue. Here stood Culvers Mill, marked on older maps as 'Carshalton Mill'. It appeared for the first time in the mid-eighteenth century in connection with the recently established bleaching grounds. In October 1781, Foster Reynolds purchased the freehold of the mills and grounds. James Edwards in his *Companion from London to Brighthelmston* (Brighton) of about 1789 reported that at 'Carshalton Mill', "*Mr. Reynolds carries on a very extensive trade of whitstering, or bleaching, of linen. Sometimes 40 or 50 acres of land together may be seen almost covered with linen; which to a stranger at a distance, is oftentimes mistaken for snow*". William Foster Reynolds (see box) died in 1838, and via this we have a good surviving description of the then corn mill:

"*An entire brick erection, with walls of great substance, slated roof and three-storey high. The mill building measures at the base about 50-feet in front and 33-feet in depth, worked by a powerful 15-feet undershot wheel, 8 feet 10 inches wide, with a large head of water – without the liability of floods – which drives three pair of French Stones, with all proper dressing*

View downstream from the Hack Bridge towards Culvers Island, Carshalton.

A view downstream from the Spencer Road footbridge towards the wetlands.

and other machinery ... capable of grinding twenty-five loads of wheat weekly. The interior of the mill is finely timbered, and altogether finished and fitted in the best manner, so as to promote the objects of the trade, and afford ample accommodation for the storage of corn, &c."

It ceased production in about 1900; some buildings survived until 1960, when some of the mill stones were re-sited at the entrance to Millside, a few yards west along Culvers Avenue. There are the remains of the wheel pit where the river flows under Culvers Avenue. Opposite Culvers Mill, north of the road, was the carriageway to another large house, *The Limes* (photo, p. 61, and box, p. 166) . It was demolished in 1913 and the land built over, the area nearest the river becoming, after the Second World War, an area of 'prefabs' (the prefabricated homes which sprung up across the country to provide a supposedly temporary solution to the postwar housing crisis). These asbestos homes were in turn removed in the mid 1960s to be replaced by the prefabricated towers of Durand Close, themselves now undergoing demolition!

Remains of old plateway at Spencer Road Wetland, an old watercress bed. This moved watercress around the site.

Culvers Avenue ('The Avenue' on old maps) itself originated as a private carriageway to *The Culvers*. The Lodge at the Hackbridge

entrance to the road survives. At the Carshalton end (by the junction with Greenwrythe Lane) a large house, *Avenue Lodge*, stood but this was pulled down at the same time as *The Culvers*, in about 1960.

Continuing from the site of Culvers Mill, you can either carry straight ahead on the signed path opposite to rejoin the official Trail where the two branches re-join in 300 yards; or walk down the road to your right until you meet the main branch and pick up the Trail opposite the allotment gates. Note the new (2011) Regional Park information board and 'gateway' stiles here. Taking this option and continuing downstream, one passes another site which has undergone great changes recently. Here stood another very sizeable riverside house, *Wallington Cottage*, which later became known as *Culverside*.

Sluice at southern end of Beddington Corner mills site.

This site was transformed in 1927 by the construction of Mullards factory. The Mullard Radio Valve Company was set up in 1920 by Robert Stanley Mullard. In 1925 the Dutch firm of Phillips took over the company but it was always known by its old name. This tall, modern electronics factory employed over 5000 at its peak, making Mullards the largest single employer on the river. For a detailed history of the factory refer to 'Memories of Mullards' (see Bibliography). The factory was closed in 1993 and demolished soon afterwards; and the modern housing estate built on the site. This allowed new public access and it's now a pleasant riverside walk down to the new wooden footbridge. Just before this bridge, the two branches of the river re-join; the area hereabouts was once known as Rushy Meadow,

Hackbridge: Culvers Island left, former Mullard's site on the right

and from about 1780 until around 1825, there were bleaching grounds and a calico printing works here. Later on, around 1895, Louis Doerr had built a patent leather factory nearby; although it was known as Doerr's mill, it may not have been a mill in the strict sense, and was all in probability there simply to tap a supply of water from the river. Interestingly, the orchard which occupied the site on which latterly allotments, and now Culvers House School stands, was known locally until the mid twentieth century as the 'Miller's Orchard'; but this may have referred to the mills at Beddington Corner instead. Louis himself lived at nearby *Culverside* for a time, and died in 1927, so it can be assumed that the factory was wound up then or some time before.

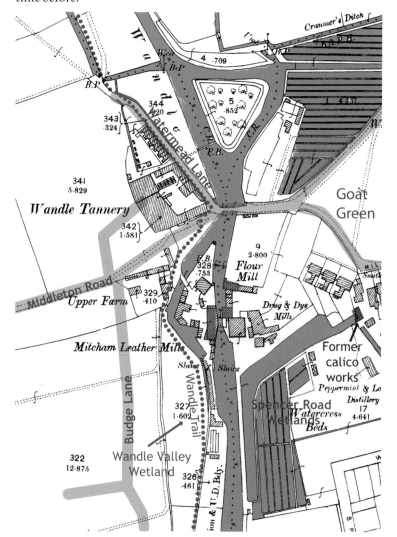

Beddington Corner Mills

The site of Beddington Corner mills today.

Just downstream of the bridge lies the small Spencer Road Wetland, a Local Nature Reserve administered by the London Wildlife Trust (restricted public access, on advertised Workdays and Open Days only, via the right fork in the paths before the wooden bridge, across Watercress Park and then left on Spencer Road). This lies on the site of a former watercress bed. One interesting survivor in here are some old railway tracks, which were used to push carts laden with cress to the site exit. Across the new bridge, the Trail swings to the right alongside another Local Nature Reserve, the Wandle Valley Wetland. The heavily fenced-off site has an interesting mix of open water, scrub, marginal vegetation and seasonal pools. Again, access is restricted (information at www.sutton.gov.uk). Now the interest switches to the right-hand side of the path as it runs alongside a rather grim old industrial building which, although heavily altered, was part of the former leather skinning works here at Beddington Corner. As the map shows, this was another very significant industrial site, with three main mills here along with another large calico bleaching wash mill; although by the time of the map this site was being used as a lavender and peppermint distillery, and continued producing essential oils until around 1960. With the leather tannery across the lane, this was a veritable industrial village, complete with some handsome villas, and workers' housing further away. Some of the big villas known as Crief Villas survive in Mill Green Road, along with a nearby manager's house which we pass on the Trail by the entrance to the site, which is still in industrial use today. As for the mills, the original buildings have gone or been altered beyond recognition, but the sluices, by-pass channel and other buildings of interest survive on the site. Unfortunately, there is no public access. The leather mill was interesting in that it was in the long time ownership (in the eighteenth and into the nineteenth century) of the Savignac family, whose name suggests possible Huguenot origins. It is also one of the works which Braithwaite in his 1853 paper savages for its severe pollution: "*A great deal of filth is constantly being discharged from these works…the taint [is] perceptible for a considerable distance down the stream, and pieces of skin were also observed floating on the surface.*"

Goat Bridge to Mitcham

Access to Goat Bridge:
Rail and Tram: Mitcham
Junction, then 10 mins.
walk via Carshalton
Road/Goat Road, or local
buses 127, S1.

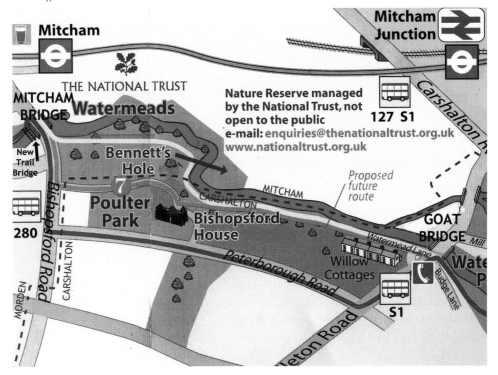

Cross the busy Middleton Road by the crossing and pick up the trail almost opposite, passing some cottages on Watermeads Lane. These cottages were probably associated with the Wandle Tannery (map p. 170), which was first referred to around 1853, but which was later run as a parchment and leather manufactory by the firm of George Gibbs & Sons, and known as Gibbs' Mill or Mitcham Parchment Works. They were last recorded in 1935. It's not clear that there was ever a water wheel associated with this factory, however, and in fact one contemporary account around 1900 states: "At Beddington Corner [stands] a picturesque building in which parchment and vellum are made. Here the water of the Wandle is used *but not for power*" (my italics).

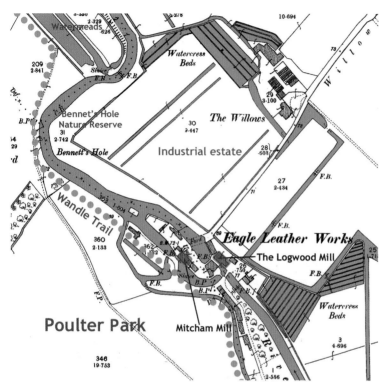

The river here occupies an artificial channel cut in the mid 1960s as part of a flood alleviation scheme. Prior to this the course of the river was farther to the east, in an earlier artificial channel constructed in about 1702 by Richard Bond, then the occupier of a logwood mill (see below). In turn, Bond's 'new cut' superseded the original course which ran some distance to the *west* of the current channel, and west of the tannery. Until recently it was possible to discern what could have been traces of this channel to the left just after passing the kissing gate at the end of Watermeads Lane, although this land has recently been cleared and levelled. The outfall of the modern treatment works joins the river here today from the east after traversing land that was yet another watercress bed until well into the twentieth century.

On your left now is Poulter Park, which accompanies the Carshalton bank for about half a mile. It was laid out as a public open space at the time of the building of the St Helier housing estate in the inter war years. Some 300 yards along the riverside path, at a point where Willow Lane comes down to the river on the opposite bank, was another significant mill site. Reference to the map will show that once again the river channels were artificially altered to feed water to two mills. One of these was the logwood mill, first recorded in 1685,

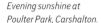
Deed's Leather mill, Carshalton.

and rebuilt around 1700 by Richard Bond. It was he who created the new channel for the river referred to above. On an island in the river partially created by this new channel a second mill was built some time later, known as Mitcham Mill – despite being in Carshalton parish! This latter started life as a copper mill, although it later turned to corn. For much of the nineteenth century the corn mill was owned and operated by John Searle of Carshalton, and (briefly) by his son William. The dyewood mill appears to have retained that use for most of its life, at one time being owned by James Sprules, of the well-known Carshalton family of herb growers and distillers. In 1884 both mills were acquired by J. S. Deed & Sons, leather workers. They expanded the site and operated the whole complex as the Eagle Leather Works.

The old corn mill building survived until as late as 1965, and in fact, Deed's continued with leather working in other buildings on the Mitcham bank until 1989. Hillier, in *Old Surrey Water Mills* [1951], described it thus: *"It has a brick base up to the first storey, tarred weatherboards above… a large external breastshot wheel of mid-nineteenth century date drove the mill, and still remains, having the normal Wandle diameter viz. 18 feet, with four sets of compass-arms spanning its 10 feet width, the whole wheel of cast-iron, with L-shaped floats…"*, although he went on to note *"the cross-beams are now studded with tenterhooks whereon the leather-dresser stretches his skins"*.

Evening sunshine at Poulter Park, Carshalton.

The river at Bennett's Hole Nature Reserve, Mitcham.

On the Mitcham bank is a large industrial estate named after the little rural lane that used to run down to a ford by the mills. Willow Lane was also the site of a calico bleaching industry, which had its origins in about 1600. It was fed by a meandering channel taken from the river at Goat Bridge; it was probably cut by John Cranmer, a member of an important Mitcham family. By the early eighteenth century the works were owned by a Thomas Selby, whose son built the big house known as *The Willows* in 1746. It was also known as the *Red House*. Thomas Reynolds, whose family was later to acquire the Culvers bleaching grounds, bought the business on the death of Selby junior in 1751. By the nineteenth century when records show that it was a substantial business, Samuel Makepeace was in occupation from about 1720 to 1745. The last record of the Willow Mills was in 1861, but the wheel and part of the chimney of the print works survived until after the Second World War. The house (prominent on the 1894 map) had been demolished well before the War.

From Watermeads, c.1900, looking towards cottages near London Road.

Entrance to The Cut on Watermeads from Bennetts Hole.

1. More information on the St Helier railway can be found in a paper by John Williams in the 1980 Bulletin of the Wandle Group, held in Sutton Local Studies Centre.

Heavily restored weatherboarded cottages at Mitcham Bridge.

As the river approaches the curve at Bennett's Hole, now a nature reserve (see box p. 180), it widens and assumes a delightfully rural aspect despite the proximity of the industrial land on the opposite bank. Interestingly, the 1933 map shows a railway line crossing the river at this point! This in fact was a temporary railway to serve the construction of the St Helier estate.[1]

Up on higher ground to the left, the modern flats in the park occupy a much altered *Bishopsford House*, a Victorian pile which was later absorbed into Poulter Park and, prior to falling into dereliction and becoming victim of a fire in 2001 served as a pavilion for the adjacent sports fields. The park itself represents the remains of the grounds of the house, and after passing through several hands following the sale of the estate, the land was bought in 1928 by the Greater London Playing Fields Association, with a £5000 gift from Reginald Poulter, hence the name. Back on the river, the Wandle Trail now departs from the river bank and shortly runs alongside the boundary fence to Watermeads, a National Trust reserve with very restricted access. The incessant cries of young Grey Herons begging for food can be heard in early summer. If you look carefully through the fence, you may even be able to see the nests at the top of the trees. Watermeads is a complex site and those who are interested in it should look at E N Montague's detailed work on the Mitcham Mill and Watermeads area (see bibliography). It was one of the earliest acquisitions by the National Trust, in 1913, after a campaign by among others Octavia Hill, one of the Trust's founders, who sadly died the year before the formal presentation. The Trust also in 1915 received two acres donated in her memory on the far side of the road bridge which, like Watermeads itself, was once part of the extensive Mitcham Grove estate (see p. 183) at one time owned by banker Henry Hoare. This small slice of land on the Morden side of the river is known rather grandly as Happy Valley!

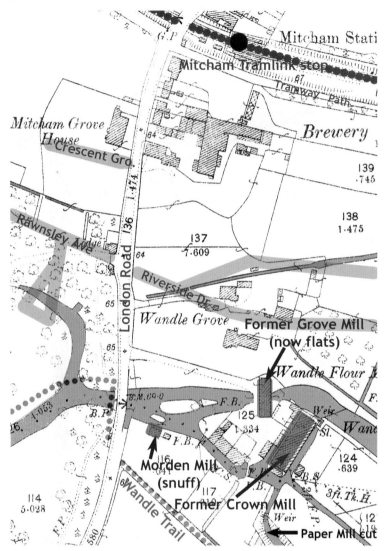

At the time of acquisition Watermeads was an area of meadows and clumps of trees, as evidenced by contemporary photographs. Several decades later it had become quite a dense mass of wet woodland. Although Watermeads remains to this day in the ownership of the National Trust, there has been no public access for many years. In the past, one could apply to become a key-holder and, in the near future, once work being undertaken to improve habitats as part of the London Wildlife Trust Water Vole Project is complete, it is thought the National Trust intend to reintroduce a similar scheme.

Inside Watermeads lie the sites of two mills that were operating in the early nineteenth century: the snuff mill on the Morden bank was situated about 25 yards above Mitcham Bridge, and its remains

Old Grove Mill building, Micham.

can be seen on the south bank of the river shortly after entering into Watermeads from the main road gate. As in the case of the paper mill, it was established by Richard Glover, and probably built in around 1800. It was referred to as 'long disused' a century later, however, and finally pulled down in 1922. A millstone survives. The other mill, of which no trace remains save for the long straight cut leading to it, visible on the 1894 map, and the tailrace at the end, was a paper mill. Like the snuff mill it was almost certainly built by Richard Glover, the same person who took over the lease of the corn mill on the Mitcham bank opposite in 1774. There is documentary evidence of Glover as a miller, paper maker and snuff manufacturer here in the early years of the nineteenth century. On his death in about 1825 his son, also Richard, took over, but no evidence has come to light as to the demise of the mill. The rectangular 'Jack Pond' (presumably so named as it contained Pike) at the top of The Cut was almost certainly originally constructed to provide additional water for the mill; in the late twentieth century it served as a well-stocked lake for Mitcham Angling Club. The mills on the Mitcham side of the river here, technically not in Watermeads itself, have a well-documented, if typically complicated, history with the usual wide range of goods having been produced here over time. Like many other sites on the Wandle, copper-working took place here at Mitcham in the first half of the eighteenth century. Interestingly, it seems that the first ball and cross on St.Paul's Cathedral were made at Mitcham – presumably here – in 1708. By the time of the 1895 Ordnance Survey map, the corn mill had probably recently been amalgamated with a third mill and rebuilt. It was advertised a few years later as a 'three-storey water

Looking upstream from Mitcham Bridge, c.1900. Fisheries cottage on left, Glover's Snuff Mill on right.

Bennett's Hole

Bennett's Hole is the name given to the riverside area on the Mitcham bank of the river opposite Watermeads. It's a Local Nature Reserve and well worth a visit. The most convenient access is via a public path and gate at the far end of Riverside Drive (take first right having turned right onto the Bishopsford Road at Mitcham Bridge).

The name may well derive from the slight hollow in which the river flows at this point. The land here has been used for typical Wandle-side activities of cloth bleaching and watercress, but parts of the site, like Wilderness Island Nature Reserve, have also apparently been raised by dumping of wartime debris. The site became a Local Nature Reserve in 1993, following involvement of the London Wildlife Trust. Management of the site has improved the diversity of the plant and animal life so that this, with Watermeads opposite, is perhaps the most secluded stretch of the whole river, and a good spot to watch for Kingfishers if you are patient.

corn mill' with a breast-shot water wheel and six pairs of grinding stones. This mill became known as Grove Mill, and is the one that survives today as flats inside the gated development, its formerly handsome brickwork now painted white. The river used to flow under the mill, but a 1960s channel diversion left the mill some yards from the modern course. The adjacent large 'felt factory' became known as Crown Mill. From about 1910 until 1930 both mills were in the ownership of the same company, producing artificial fibres, although Crown Mill had a couple of other occupiers before it was destroyed in a savage fire in 1964. No traces remain.

The handsome, if heavily altered, weatherboarded cottages seen upstream of the bridge are the Mill Cottages. Two of them date back to the mid eighteenth century, the double-fronted house facing the bridge is about a century younger. They were probably built for mill workers, but for a while around the turn of the twentieth century one of them, Wandle Cottage, No 475 London Road, was briefly tenanted by one Henry Bourne, who was bailiff to the short-lived Wandle Fisheries Association, a vain attempt to promote and conserve fish stocks, which were in steady decline. It was this connection that probably gave the group of cottages their now common alternative name of the Fisheries Cottages.[2]

Finally, the house shown on the Mitcham Mills map as 'Wandle Grove' survives today, with a modern extension, in Riverside Drive. It was built around 1800 but has been used for offices for several decades now.

2. Eric Montague in his book 'Mitcham Bridge, The Watermeads and the Wandle Mills' attributes this name to an estate agents' advert in 1993 for No 479 London Road as 'Fisheries Cottage'.

Ravensbury

Access
Tram: Mitcham, then 5 mins.
walk via London Road.
Bus 118 (Morden—Brixton)
stops in Wandle Road
and London Road.

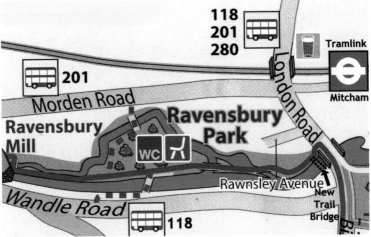

From the Watermeads, cross the road and take in a new footbridge (2009) which leads behind the estate wall of *Mitcham Grove* (see box p. 183). The modern houses which now occupy the site date from the 1970s and before that the area was part of the Hovis sports ground. The demolition of the great house in 1846 led to the estate's acquisition by George Parker Bidder, a prominent civil engineer who added to this the Ravensbury estate in 1855, the year the Wimbledon to Croydon railway line was opened. He demolished the old manor house (see below) and had built his new house, *Ravensbury Park*, a rambling and rather ungainly Victorian pile which stood near the junction of modern-day Seddon Road and Bishopsford Road. It survived until the late 1940s having been a convalescent home during its twentieth-century existence, but in the meantime his grandson Harold Bidder had built the third house, the short-lived *Ravensbury Manor*, in 1912. This was a handsome house in a neo-Queen Anne style, in a lovely riverside setting approximately at the junction of Wandle Road and Morton Road. It lasted only some 20 years before the area was overwhelmed by inter-war housing.

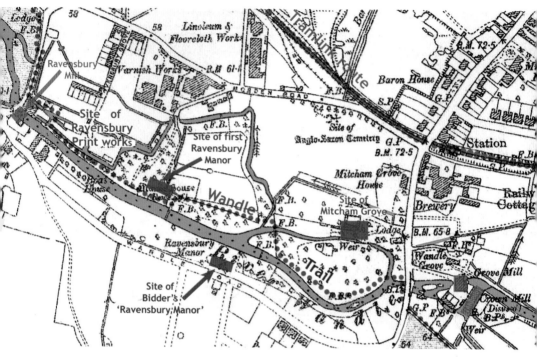

Ravensbury (1919 map at smaller scale)

The water channel you cross on a footbridge leads to an artificial lake in front of the modern houses and is part of flood protection works, although the handsome cedar tree opposite dates back to the days of *Mitcham Grove*. The lake is one of the most regular nesting sites for Mute Swans along the river and their cygnets may adorn the river in summer. Look out too for Fritillaries flowering in April. The flower resembles a snake's head and is a rare plant of water meadows, but was introduced here.

The Ravensbury estate was once very extensive, but as noted already it was overwhelmed by the inter-war suburban housing boom. The park bearing the name is merely the rump of that estate, purchased by the local councils in 1930. Beyond the first metal bridge, the Wandle Trail bears left here to follow the main river, not the smaller branch which bears off to the right and follows a circuitous course around the modern park. Braithwaite's report has the answer to the question as to the origin of this winding watercourse: *"Below Mitcham Bridge the river divides itself into two streams, the western branch proceeding to Mr. Rutter's snuff mill, at Ravensbury, the eastern branch to Messrs. Dempsey and Hind's print works, serving in its course, through Mr. Gifford's grounds, for an ornamental water, in which trout is very abundant."* The map above shows the site of the print works

Mitcham Grove

This fine house, which occupied the site of an earlier one was probably built in the mid sixteenth century for Thomas Smythe, an official in Queen Elizabeth I's court. It must have been a sizable house, for under the Surrey Hearth Tax, a contemporary form of council tax, his great-grandson George was assessed for 14 hearths, and of course, if they all related to this one house, it would have been considerable. The house was inherited by William Meyers in 1725 from George's widow and at this time the late Elizabethan building was enlarged, but it was in 1774, when occupied by Alexander Wedderburn, the Solicitor General, that none less than Robert Adams upgraded the House again. Wedderburn appears to have been gifted the house by Clive of India in recognition of his successful defence of Clive in a Commons censure motion following his conduct in India. Wedderburn was elevated to Lord Loughborough in 1780 and sold the house

and estate to banker Henry Hoare for £18,000. Hoare was a very different man with a large family who, unlike Wedderburn, became a prominent and philanthropic member of the local community, as well as being a skilful and capable professional. He pitched fully into local life, particularly to the benefit of the poor and of children. When Henry died in 1828, the house and the attached estate amounting to some 620 acres was sold to what turned out to be its last significant resident, Sir John Lubbock, another prominent banker. The artist John Hassall, in his *Picturesque walks and rides* (1817) refers to the *"immense groups of large trees"* in the grounds and to the smaller channel leaving the river just downstream of the bridge which conveyed water to the house. He also noted the *"numerous and large"* trout in the river. Alas, after Sir John's death in 1840, the house failed to find a buyer and was demolished in 1846.

This cedar tree stands in the former grounds of Mitcham Grove.

(see below) in relation to this branch. Close to the footbridge over the river further along is the site of the old *Ravensbury House*, also known as the *Manor House*. A branch of the Garth family (see Morden Hall Park) seems to have occupied it briefly in the early seventeenth century; it was later occupied by the Arbuthnott family, who operated the textile printing works nearby. The house was demolished in about 1860 when George Parker Bidder, who had acquired the estate, built *Ravensbury Park* (see above). Interestingly, the old road from Mitcham to Morden formerly crossed the river close to this point. It was diverted in around 1750 at the request of John Arbuthnott, who bore the cost of the new crossing by Ravensbury Mill further west. Just behind the brick wall was the site of *Ravensbury Print Works*, in its time a very significant centre of the textile bleaching and printing industry that flourished on the banks of the Wandle hereabouts. Peter Mauvillain, a calico printer of French extraction, claimed in a submission in 1719 to have employed over 200 people here at

The Lake,
Ravensbury Park.

The river flows through the formal gardens at Ravensbury Park, Morden.

Ravensbury and at Wandsworth. These works were still going strong in 1853 when Braithwaite visited; however, shortly afterwards, in the face of competition from mills in Lancashire and elsewhere, the works closed down. Like other works of that kind on the river, the Ravensbury Print Works was frequently involved in disputes about pollution since the washing of the cloth impregnated in dyes turned the river various shades of pink and purple – hardly conducive to good trout fishing!

Almost nothing of interest now remains of the site of the factory save a short stretch of wall and one of the old water channels that runs behind it on your right as you walk down towards the exit of the park. Here until the 1960s stood *Ravensbury Cottage*, occupied by William Williams, the bailiff of the Hatfeild estate (see Morden Hall Park). He had a lovely garden, which stretched along the land between two water channels, but sadly this was destroyed during the council's flood protection works already referred to.

Immediately below the large weir, partially obscured by modern housing, Ravensbury Snuff Mill survives. Unlike many Wandle mills, this one seemed to be used for the same purpose for most of its life. In 1805 the mills here were taken over by John Rutter and his family, who were well known for tobacco and snuff in London. They occupied the site until Rutter & Co. left Mitcham in about 1925. It was at Ravensbury that the popular tobacco *Mitcham Shag* was manufactured. Note, alongside the Trail at this point, the reconstruction of the arrangement of 'edge runners' in a snuff mill. (For more about snuff see the section on the industrial river, pp. 38–41). The mills were occupied for over 50 years by Whitely Products who manufactured a wide range of goods and who until at least 1960 used the river as a power source. Plans to use the old mill buildings as a new home for the Wandle Industrial Museum have been stalled for several years.

Old Ravensbury Snuff Mill, Morden.

Morden Hall Park

Access: To Morden Road entrance by Surrey
Arms: 12 mins walk from Morden Underground
station. Buses 201 to Surrey Arms, 118 to
The Drive then 5 mins walk via Wandle Road.
To main pedestrian entrance opposite Aberconway
Road: 5 mins walk from Morden station.
Buses from all parts to Morden. Also direct access
into the park from Phipps Bridge Tramstop.

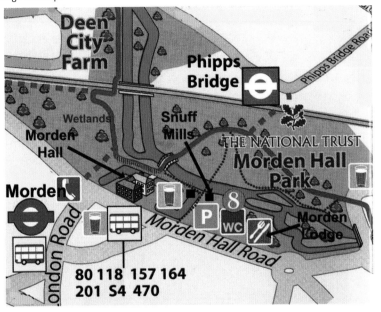

There's a good case to be made that Morden Hall Park is the
highlight of the Wandle; so it would make an ideal first visit for the
newcomer to the river. Entering the park through the gate by the
lodge opposite Aberconway Road is to be immediately transported
into a different world. The traffic-free roadway leads alongside a
backwater of the river towards the workshops, the renovated stable
block and, beyond, the former snuff mills.

However, this is jumping ahead a little for those who are following the river from the previous section, as reference to the maps will
show. The exit from Ravensbury Park onto Morden Road is several
hundred yards upstream. From this point, the Wandle Trail now
follows the road for about a hundred yards to the right (but note the
frontage of Ravensbury Mill to the left). On the bend stands the late
eighteenth-century *White Cottage*. This handsome weatherboarded

Morden Hall Park

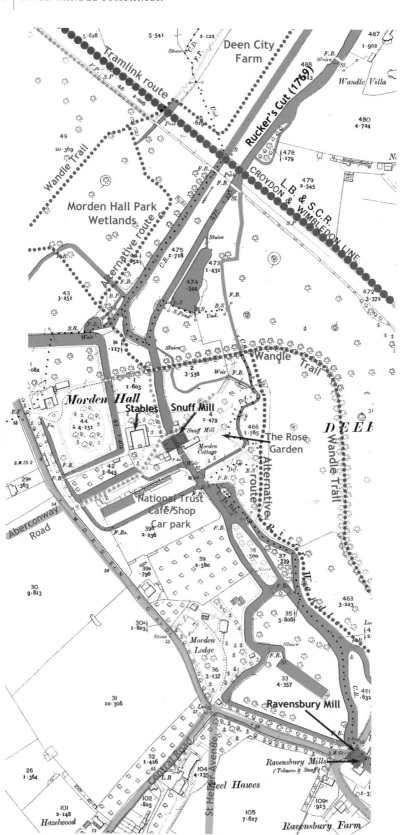

A Portland Stone statue of Venus the Goddess of Love, with her child Cupid, recently returned to a site in Morden Hall Park after a 20-year absence. Vandals decapitated the original and new heads and arms have been re-carved.

Autumn in the deer park at Morden Hall.

house is a rare survivor of a vernacular style once widespread in northeast Surrey. Adjacent is the *Surrey Arms*, a 1930s rebuild of an earlier inn which stood alongside a row of weatherboarded cottages. The gate to Morden Hall Park is immediately before the pub, by the still-inhabited *Keepers Lodge*.

The park owes its existence to Gilliat Hatfeild senior, a wealthy tobacco and snuff manufacturer who bought the mills and *Morden Hall* in around 1870 and acquired the land for his park thereafter. Thirty years later, the 'Deer Park' is shown on the Ordnance Survey maps, and the tree-lined carriage drive survives as a central feature. It was his son, also Gilliat, who when he died in 1941 bequeathed the park to the National Trust.

It is a more rewarding route to bear left upon entry into the park, leaving the wide drive almost immediately, following a narrower path; bear left again after a few yards to reach the river at one of its most attractive stretches: upstream through the trees you can catch glimpses of Ravensbury Mill, although the drone of traffic intrudes on the otherwise sylvan scene. Immediately downstream, recent conservation work has created a backwater to improve habitat diversity. On the opposite bank are the wooded grounds of *Morden Lodge*. This shy but handsome stuccoed villa with its low slate-hipped roof also features an attractive porch with slender fluted Doric columns and a decorative fanlight above. It was built in 1820 close to the site of *Growtes* (see p. 55). Hatfeild bought the house in 1929 to preserve the privacy of his estate, and his married sister took up residence. The Lodge is still leased today by the National Trust. You can see the Lodge through the trees and across another stretch of water for there are islands in the river here, as the map indicates. There is also a heronry on the opposite bank, so look out for their large nests and the trees, white-washed from the youngsters' droppings.

Easier to see now that they have recently been restored are the two eighteenth-century listed statues, *Venus* and *Neptune*, the former re-sited early in 2011 after an absence for repairs of some 20 years.

Two main channels from Ravensbury join together here, but throughout the park the river again

A quiet reach of the river in Morden Hall Park, looking into the grounds of Morden Lodge.

divides into separate branches and channels due to a combination of milling, cloth whitening and ornamentation. You can follow the river as far as the weir before turning right under a great plane tree, where you may spot an old Mitcham parish boundary marker. Then it's through the gate into Hatfeild's rose garden where the white building on the left is *Morden Cottage*. Continue ahead on the path with a small channel on the left, leaving the rose garden to join the main carriage drive. If you continue along the stream, you'll find a good example of modern conservation work on the riverbank where wooden revetments have been removed and new planting has taken place. Either way, work your way round to the core of the estate where *Morden Cottage* and the old snuff mills stand side by side.

The first reference to a mill here is in 1750 and it seems likely that west mill occupies the site of an earlier medieval mill. Taddy's assumed the lease in 1845 and Alexander Hatfeild, whose father had married into the Taddy family, took control in 1854. (For more on the Hatfeilds, see box opposite, and also the section on snuff, p. 38–40.)

Old parish boundary marker, Morden Hall Park.

Morden Cottage, home to the last of the Morden Hatfeilds.

The Hatfeilds

Gilliat Hatfeild was a wealthy tobacco merchant and a one-time owner of Taddy's, a well-known contemporary purveyor of tea, tobacco and snuff. He bought Morden Hall in 1867 and the double snuff mills shortly afterwards. As the Squire of Morden, he acquired over 1000 acres of land, some of which he embellished as a deer park, but which also included the Ravensbury Print Works and a part interest in Ravensbury Mill.

The estate was inherited by Hatfeild's son Gilliat Edward, who lived the life of a country bachelor in *Morden Cottage* rather than in the Hall. Alongside his home he laid out the rose garden. In London he was regarded as a fair and benevolent employer who, as the owner of Taddy's, ensured that wages and conditions were superior to those of his rivals. However, in the early 1920s his workers joined a national cigarette industry strike in sympathy; and after they ignored Hatfeild's request to return to work, he shut the factory. Thereafter he lived as something of a recluse, but upon his death in 1941 he left the bulk of his estate to the National Trust, and this survives as one of the most intact estates in the London region. The southern part of his estate at Ravensbury, however, was broken up, sold and is now built over. As an aside, cigarette cards from Taddy's are among the world's most sought-after for their rarity!

The wheel of the west mill has now gone, but the paddles on the wheel of the east mill have recently been replaced. It's very easy to gain an impression of the potential power of the water running through the narrow confines between the two buildings. As part of the Heritage Lottery Fund's £2.5m *Heart of the Park* project, a new hydroelectric screw turbine has been installed in the river near the mill to generate power for the new Living Green Visitor Centre (see below). This turbine, an Archimedes screw, is probably the first of its type in

One of the pair of former snuff mills, with its new paddles installed in summer 2011.

London. Sadly, the waterwheel is not suitable, for technical reasons, to be adapted for the generation of electricity.

There are two streams leading off over weirs from the mill-pool above the wheels, one on each side of the river. The one from the right bank runs through the rose garden, then into the public part of the park to rejoin the river at the tramway. The one from the left bank runs by a circuitous route to *Morden Hall*.

Many of Hatfeild's estate buildings survive, including lodges for his estate managers, and the mill manager's cottage adjacent to the west mill, which itself has, since 1990, housed the *Snuff Mill Environmental Centre*. Adjacent to Mill Cottage stands the picturesque bothy, once used as a dormitory to house estate workers. In front stands a newly reconstructed set of edge runners, as the stones to grind stuff were called, after their vertical configuration. Tobacco kilns survive in the buildings adjacent to the east mill although these are not open to the public.

Opposite the snuff mill complex stands the stable block, built around a courtyard and entered via an arched gateway surmounted by a clock tower. In November 2011 it was open to the public for the first time, as a 'sustainable living centre', part of the Trust's *Heart of the Park* project. Note the trout-shaped wind vane: fishing was one of Gilliat Hatfeild's passions. Further along to the left, the rather handsome workshops are now occupied by a variety of craft enterprises just before you go through an archway to the National Trust's cafe and shop. Sadly, the kitchen gardens which once employed over a dozen workers, have not survived and these are now

The attractive Snuff Mill cottage and Bothy in Morden Hall Park.

Morden Hall Park in winter.

Ornamental bridge
and Morden Cottage,
Morden Hall Park.

covered by the car park and garden centre ahead of you through the archway. Back outside on the entrance lane, the lodge on the left just before reaching busy Morden Hall Road, clearly bears the initials 'GH' between the first floor windows.

Morden Hall itself lies in the trees just to the north, but is best seen by walking back along the entrance lane as far as the ornamental white bridge, for the carriage drive led straight into the hall itself. The present building is an eighteenth-century mansion, which was in the hands of the Garth family, lords of the manor, until 1872 when Gilliat Hatfield bought it. It has been a school, a hospital and more recently council offices. Now, however, it is privately leased, which helps generate funds for the maintenance of the park itself. The interior still has some features of interest, notably a large fireplace and a substantial staircase. Continue on the path signed to Deen City Farm, noticing the complexity of the water channels at this point, as well as a couple of pretty little folly bridges to the left. To the right are the two straight cuts, which take the river down towards Bunce's Meadow.

Morden Hall bathed in
winter sunshine.

The right hand one is Rucker's Cut, named after the calico printer who had it excavated in 1769 for his bleaching grounds downstream. Although most of the Park today is managed as meadow or woodland, there is an attractive and extensive wetland area which can be seen to best advantage by bearing right at the next junction of paths and crossing another small bridge. The wetland area, a remnant of the river floodplain immediately on the left, enjoys active conservation management encouraging regular inundation of this habitat, which includes several species of sedge. The wetland supports a rich biodiversity including breeding Reed Warbler,

Reed Bunting and occasionally Water Rail. The path then bears left and right in turn before crossing the former Wimbledon to Croydon railway line, now the Tramlink route – take care at this open level crossing.

The Wetlands at Morden Hall Park, in summer...

...and in winter.

For events at Morden Hall Park, go to www.nationaltrust.org.uk/main/w-mordenhallpark-2 and click on events.

Wandle Trail to Merton Abbey Mill (3/4 mile)

Morden Road tram stop

Caution: trams crossing

Phipps Bridge tram stop

North Park

Hay Meadow

Wetlands

South Park

Hay Meadow

A24 Morden Road

Wandle Trail to Ravensbury Park

A24 to Morden town centre, tube and bus stations

River Wandle

A297 Morden Hall Road

Morden Road

Key

1. Stable Yard Visitor Centre
2. Snuff Mill Education Centre
3. Second-hand bookshop
4. Morden Cottage
5. Morden Hall
6. Shop & cafe
7. Garden centre
8. Arboretum
9. Rose garden
10. Picnic area
11. Natural play area
12. Deen City Farm

© NATIONAL TRUST

The Merton river – from Bunce's Meadow to Merton High Street

Access: Tramlink to Phipps Bridge (then via Morden Hall Park) or Morden Road; by bus to Morden (see Morden Hall Park) or Merton (by bus garage/Sainsbury's) then walk upstream. Underground: Colliers Wood or Morden.

Everetts cottages and the folly, Phipps Bridge Road, Mitcham.

Once across the tramway and out of Morden Hall Park, the Wandle Trail path runs through Bunce's Meadow with the five-acre Deen City Farm on the left. The popular urban farm moved here in 1994 and showcases rural and agricultural activities to an urban community. There are plenty of animals, so it's a great hit with kids – and there's a café. Online, go to www.deencityfarm.co.uk for more information, and there's a picture gallery at www.urban75.org/london/deen-city-farm.html

The ground on the right where the two parallel cuts of Wandle run was once a bleaching ground, and, until the 1950s when the level of the meadow was raised by Mitcham Borough Council, traces of the old ditches and channels were still visible. Until relatively recently this area retained a rural feel and Phipps Bridge Road even today has several old buildings of interest. It's worth crossing the river by the farm entrance to see them, but all trace of a mill at this site, once owned by Merton Priory, the 'Pippesmoln', has long since disappeared.

Upstream from the bridge on the right is a terrace of early nineteenth-century cottages, *Everett's Place*, buttressed on the near end by a flint folly which was erected later. Just beyond is *Wandle Villa*, a substantial house built in 1788 by John Rucker, who made his fortune from developing new textile printing techniques in his works behind the house. As stated elsewhere it was Rucker who had the parallel river cut

made and who developed the associated
bleaching grounds. Later, it was briefly
the home of Gilliat Hatfeild senior before
he bought the Morden Hall Estate; it was
Hatfeild who eventually demolished
Rucker's works, by then a silk printing mill,
to improve the vista over the river from the
house. No trace remains either of the remarkable 'Patent Steam Washing Factory', a very
large three-storey affair '214 feet by 61 feet'
according to contemporary tax records, which
was erected alongside the cut just north of *Wandle Villa* in around 1825.
Recent research[1] shows it was built to cash in on the enthusiasm at
that time for a new technique in domestic laundry of washing using
steam; and that 150 women were briefly employed there. It was plagued
by technical and administrative problems and was probably far too
big and geographically mis-sited, and three years later the business
was bankrupt. It seems the building was later used for textile printing,
but was destroyed in a big fire in 1848. Drawings of it survive and can
be inspected in the Merton Heritage Library photo collection at Morden.

Reference to the Phipps Bridge map shows that there was a
'Japan & Varnish' factory north of Phipps Bridge. Japanning is a
protective and decorative technique using natural, or, more commonly
in Europe, imitation lacquers. This was the works established by
William Harland, one of several varnish and paint firms in the
Mitcham and Merton area. Harlands survived until the 1950s and
it was William's grandson Samuel who built a substantial house,
Homefield, overlooking the river nearby (see map). This house
met the usual fate of 1930s demolition for housing development.

The Wandle's course has been much
altered over the years to provide, in particular,
good mill heads, and as we continue on the
Trail, we follow a significant one, which leads
the river to the once important mill complex
at Merton. On the right and hardly visible,
a sluice takes the original course of the river
away to the east of Merton Abbey. This is now
called the Pickle Ditch and it is probably
better seen on the map. It marks the ancient
boundary between Merton and Mitcham;
the curious name is likely to derive either

*The River near Phipps Bridge
in late Victorian times.*

1. By Peter McGow who
uncovered an interesting
sequence of articles and letters
in *The Times* of the period.

*The Pickle Ditch near
Phipps Bridge, Merton.*

from 'pike and eel' or from the Old English *pightle* meaning a piece of land, according to local historian Eric Montague.

The main river now follows a straight course to and beyond Windsor Avenue, where on the left (west) the former bleaching grounds (visible on the late nineteenth-century map) are today covered by the large Lombard Industrial Estate. A few minutes beyond we reach the Merton Abbey Mills market, which occupies an historic site of great significance on the river. Stane Street, the Roman road from London to Chichester, crossed the river here. No visible trace of this remains, but what does survive is the wheelhouse on the site of the Merton Abbey print works associated with Littler and Liberty's (see p. 37) and built in the old Priory grounds.

Phipps Bridge

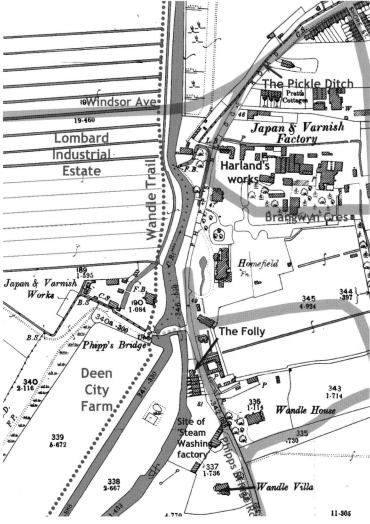

Its undershot wheel is currently the only wheel on the river that can still turn. Beyond this towards the centre of Colliers Wood lay an area of bleaching grounds and, during the nineteenth century, Thomas Bennett's calico printing works, which were taken over by Edmund Littler in 1833. Bennett had married into another local printing family, the Leaches, eventually taking over the works and focusing upon the printing of colourful handkerchiefs using madder. Madder is a plant of the coffee family, and the roots have a long history of use as a natural plant dye, yielding a vivid red colour. The handkerchiefs were much in fashion among users of snuff at the time! The works are shown on the late Victorian map. After they were demolished, in around 1910, the ground then became a watercress bed, in time-honoured Wandle tradition.

The Wheelhouse at the Merton Abbey Mills site has the last working wheel on the river. Behind is the gable of the Colour House, one of the oldest remaining Wandle-side buildings.

Merton Abbey – World Heritage Site?

It's very hard to visualise today as you cross the busy road by Merton Abbey Mills that this site was once occupied by a priory church the size of Westminster Abbey, and that this site has been put forward as a candidate to be London's fifth World Heritage Site.

The manor of Merton was given to the Augustinian canons by Henry I and the Priory was founded by Gilbert le Norman, sheriff of Surrey in 1115. Thomas a Becket was educated here in the late 1120s, and wore the black cowl of the canons of Merton on becoming Archbishop of Canterbury in 1162. Here too, in the Chapter House, was concluded the peace between Henry III and Louis, the Dauphin of France. The Priory also has wider significance since here on 23rd January 1236 Henry III met with the Archbishop of Canterbury, and various earls, bishops, and canons to discuss 'the common good of the realm'. Thus it can claim to be the first instance of a recognisable 'Parliament', although of course the common people were excluded and it was very much the House of Lords only! The *Statute of Merton*, which resulted by agreement from this meeting, is the first English Statute Law, and in effect, like the Magna Carta, was another restriction upon the rights of the monarch. There is also a connection here with Oxford's earliest collegiate institution: Walter de Merton attended the priory as a student and later worked for the prior as a clerk; hence his name. He set up in 1264 a house of the scholars of Merton on his manor at Malden. It started as a way of educating his numerous nephews, but about a decade later moved to Oxford and became Merton College.

The priory was suppressed in the reign of Henry VIII and the church demolished soon afterwards, although some buildings and sections of the old wall survived. And so to the present time, when excavations

Pickle Ditch and old Priory wall, Colliers Wood.

The only relic of these older times is another small ditch which runs at the back of houses in Runnymede (for more on Bennett & Leach, see p. 36).

The now popular craft market grew up during the 1990s, but more recently a new development of apartments and the almost mandatory array of national retailers intrude very closely on the old workshops. A couple of buildings, now listed, predated Liberty, the oldest of which is the quaint colour house whose unusual construction might derive from ruins of the old priory. But Liberty demolished many of the old buildings, and replaced them with purpose-built workshops, many in the Arts & Crafts style. They were restored after a period of decay and now house the Abbey Mills market.

revealed the ground plan and remains of the Chapter House, the administrative centre of the priory. Also, more than 700 bodies were found on the site.

Some archaeologists contend that Merton Priory's remains are comparable in significance with the medieval remains at Westminster Abbey, and moreover they are at ground level. They have, however, been violated on several occasions: first by the railway which cut across the site in 1868, and subsequently by a sewer and by factory buildings. The new Merton High Street bypass road, Merantun Way, was at least raised a little to preserve the Chapter House remains beneath it when it was built in 1989. Nonetheless, the ruins are only accessible a few times a year via a dingy underpass adjacent to a car park. No wonder that the archaeological consultants engaged by Merton Council in 2009 to produce a vision for the future development of

the site commented: *"The site is presently a disgrace... grotesquely deformed by culturally illiterate modern buildings, pointless roads and intrusive electricity pylons."* Indeed. To be fair, Merton Council now appear to be trying to do something about the site, and the document talks of reclaiming the site to create a Merton Priory Park with the potential to form one of the proposed Wandle Valley Regional Park's most significant features. As this book is being written, the site is awaiting the outcome of the long assessment process, which may result in it going forward to UNESCO as a candidate for inscription as a World Heritage Site. Given the scale of work needed, it must, however, be open to doubt whether this will be even partially realised in the near future, given the current political and economic climate.

A railway line, derelict sidings of which provided the land for this development ran along the alignment of the fast new road, Merantun Way, which now severs the former Liberty site from the Abbey Wall fragments and the former mills to the north, as well as burying the remains of the Priory's Chapter House. To make matters worse, the road is flanked by a frankly hideous cocktail of fast food kiosks, petrol stations, pylons and retail boxes, dominated by the Sainsburys/M&S warehouse whose former name, the *SavaCentre*, captures the spirit and values of the age succinctly. Given the enormous historic significance of the area with the Priory site, a World Heritage Site candidate (see box p. 198) and the connections

Detail of the wall to the Colour House, Merton Abbey Mills, showing the old flint and brick work

Merton Abbey

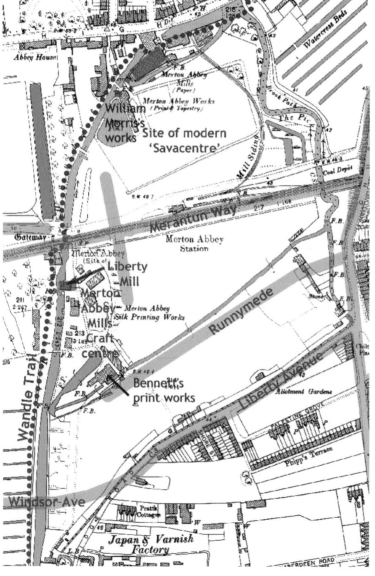

with Nelson, William Morris and Liberty, and to cap it all the line of Stane Street, it's fair to say that Merton Council's handling of this historic and sensitive site has been pretty disastrous. Moreover, a good deal of the 'planning gain' that was promised via the development, including the move of the Wandle Industrial Museum to a new home on the Liberty site, failed to materialise.

Nelson at Merton

Between 1801 and 1803, Nelson shared *Merton Place* with his lover Emma Hamilton, and her husband, Sir William, (a former diplomat and patron of the arts), who was some 35 years her senior. This bizarre domestic arrangement scandalised British society, but it doesn't seem to have affected his acclaim among the local population. It was the only house he ever owned and lived in, and he called it his 'dear, dear Merton'.

It was in 1801, before they came to Merton, that Emma gave birth to Nelson's child, Horatia, and while still at sea Nelson asked Emma to find 'a little farm', close enough to London for him to keep in touch with the Admiralty and public affairs. He gave Emma full responsibility for choosing the right house, knowing, he said, that he would be happy with any choice of hers. It was she who discovered *Merton Place*, an 'elegant and very commodious brick edifice' and, despite the advice of his surveyor, Nelson went ahead with the purchase *in absentia*. *Merton Place* was built in about 1750 and was originally known as Moat House Farm; it was enlarged and had two further owners before Emma acquired it and moved in. The great man himself didn't arrive home until the 23rd October 1801. Nelson acquired another 100 acres of land to protect his privacy, ending up with a sizeable estate; and Emma had the house extended once again. Sir William

meanwhile having become old and frail, moved out to his own home in Piccadilly where he died soon afterwards. Nelson himself was soon back at sea and that is where he remained for most of 1804 and 1805. Although he had a brief period of leave in the summer of 1805, he was soon off again, on the 13th September, for what would be his final voyage, to the seas off Cape Trafalgar, Spain. It was at Merton on 6th November that Emma received the news of her lover's death, but she soon recovered and continued to run up huge debts on her extravagant lifestyle. She tried and failed to sell the house and land although eventually friends stepped in and bought the house to help her out. She died in poverty in Calais in 1815 and sadly the house was pulled down in 1823, whilst the land was parcelled up and sold. Nelson's name lives on in 'Nelson's Fields' the district of small terraced houses that cover the land once occupied by the great house. The actual site of the house is now occupied by flats of the High Path estate, whilst two local pubs, The *Nelson Arms* and the *Trafalgar Freehouse*, also commemorate his name. The former has some very fine tilework and murals depicting Nelson and his ship, the Victory. A trail devised by Merton Council visits these and other sites connected with Nelson's brief local presence.
(See www.merton.gov.uk/visiting/attractions/nelsontrail.htm.)

William Morris

Cross the nasty new road, opened in 1989, via the controlled crossing passing through a replica gateway on the site of a twelfth-century predecessor that led to the Abbey house. A section of the old priory wall survives here. The Trail hugs the river as it runs fast on a curve around the *shopperama* on the opposite bank. This was the site of the works that William Morris, the great designer, writer and social reformer, ran from 1881 until his death in 1896. Apart from his famous chintzes, the factory turned out a range of goods including carpets, hangings, tapestries and stained glass. His move to Merton was in part prompted by the fact that he found the waters of the river ideal for dyeing; and with other craftsmen at Merton Abbey he developed the technique known as indigo discharging.

Priory wall and gateway, Merton.

Morris's concern for protecting old buildings was manifested here: when he moved to Merton, he refused to pull down any of the existing buildings. Instead, he adapted the (mainly timber) buildings on the picturesque seven-acre site to suit his needs.

Morris didn't live here, but he commuted from his home in Hammersmith to nearby Merton Abbey station, which had opened in 1868. His biographer J W Mackail referred to the works:

> the riverside garden … rambles away towards the millpond with its fringe of tall poplars; cottons lie bleaching on grass thickly set with buttercups… the long low buildings with the clear rushing little stream between them… trout leap outside the windows of the long cheerful room where the carpet looms are built…

This fascinating picture shows the scene, looking west, at Merton Abbey in 1929. In the foreground is the Pickle Ditch, with Merton Abbey Station and goods yard behind. In the background, buildings on the Liberty site.

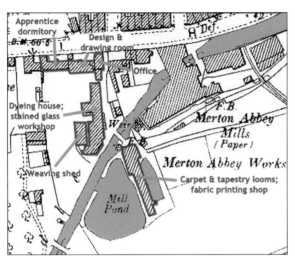

Late Victorian map showing layout of Morris's works.

The riverside pub back across the road at Merton Abbey Mills, in the old block-house of the former Liberty Print Works, is named after the great man, but otherwise it is beyond the imagination of most to link the scene described above with the oversized temple of consumerism that occupies the site today.

Close by for six years from 1882 to 1888 were the works of the celebrated artist William De Morgan, a life-long friend of Morris, who designed tiles, stained glass and furniture. Research by Judith Goodman has established that De Morgan's premises stood in Colliers Wood close to the junction with Byegrove Road.

At the time of Domesday, there were two mills on the royal estate, linked to the Priory. By the sixteenth century two riverside mills here were known as the Amery mills. They were probably corn mills, but by the late seventeenth century there is a reference to a Brazil or dyewood mill and in the early eighteenth century copper smelting had also become established here. The artificially straightened channel upstream ensured a good head of water here and made this site a powerful one. The site between the High Street and the Priory wall had a complex array of buildings with forges, hammers, furnaces, stables and a nailmaker's shop, covering an area of an acre.

Liberty's Mill and Abbey House, Merton, from an old print.

Braithwaite, visiting in 1853, remarked that the copper mills, by then owned by the Shears family, were working around the clock, sometimes backed up by a 40-horsepower steam engine due to the usual Wandle problem of water shortages. In late Victorian times the site was taken over by the Metropolitan Paper Co., which in 1897 was producing about 30 tons of paper a week. After occupancy by Albert Reed, the founder of Reed International, the site became the Merton Board Mills, which dominated the area until as late as the mid 1980s, latterly being involved in recycling of cardboard and waste paper. The site was then controversially redeveloped to spawn the *SavaCentre*.

At the front of the shopping centre, the river runs along the High Street for a short distance, past Merton Bus garage. As it's easily accessible, it's a popular stretch for anglers. The Pickle Ditch (see above) is re-united with the main river just before the Wandle heads north under the road into Wandle Park.

SITE OF ENTRANCE TO MERTON PRIORY PRECINCTS

THIS ARCHWAY WAS BUILT IN 1988 CLOSE TO THE SITE OF A NORMAN ARCH DEMOLISHED WHEN MERANTUN WAY WAS CONSTRUCTED. THE ORIGINAL ARCH BECAME THE GARDEN ENTRANCE TO ABBEY HOUSE, WHICH STOOD TO THE SOUTH OF MERANTUN WAY AND INCORPORATED PART OF THE ANCIENT GUESTHOUSE OF THE PRIORY. ABBEY HOUSE WAS DEMOLISHED IN 1914. SECTIONS OF THE MEDIEVAL PRECINCT WALLS CAN STILL BE SEEN EITHER SIDE OF THE PRESENT ARCH.

merton
moving ahead

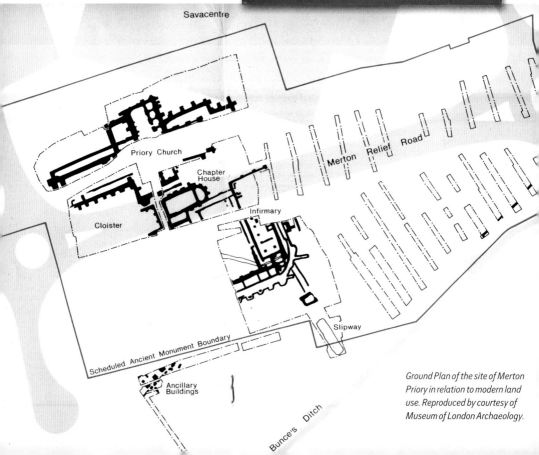

Ground Plan of the site of Merton Priory in relation to modern land use. Reproduced by courtesy of Museum of London Archaeology.

Colliers Wood to Earlsfield

Access: Underground to
Colliers Wood; bus 57 from
Kingston, Wimbledon and
Streatham; 470 from
Sutton and Epsom.

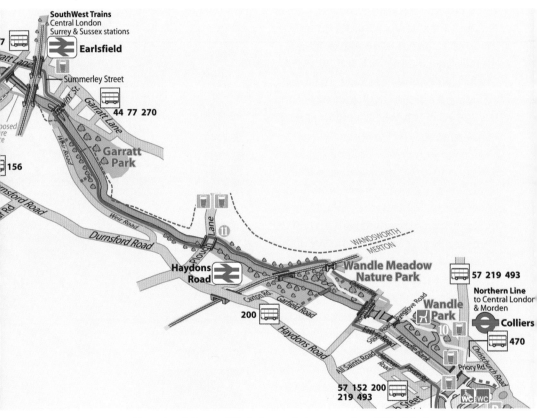

Crossing Merton High Street brings one into Wimbledon,
albeit a remote corner of the old parish, and in fact, as you cross the
river to enter Wandle Park, the district is Colliers Wood, or Merton
Singlegate as it once was, the name recalling an old toll gate on
the road. The straight cut of the river north of the bridge leads
to the former Merton Mill, whilst the original course of the river,
replicating the situation south of the road, winds through the park.
Merton Mill, actually in Wimbledon parish, may, according to
Peter McGow's research, be one referred to in Domesday as part
of the Wimbledon holdings of the Archbishop of Canterbury.

In the sixteenth century there appear to have been three mills on this site, one a corn mill and the others fulling mills.

The fact that there is a park here today is due in no small measure to early campaigners for open spaces including Richardson Evans, a local man who wrote in the *Pall Mall Gazette* but also played a part, along with Octavia Hill, in the founding of the River Wandle Open Spaces Committee. In 1907 Wimbledon Corporation bought the ten-acre estate of *Wandle Bank House* when it came onto the market. The price, including the house (see below) was £6000. It was officially opened as a public park on 13 July 1907, by H R H Princess Louise, Duchess of Argyll. *Wandle Bank House* itself (photo p. 56) survived until 1962. It was home to more than one prominent figure: one of them was the philanthropist Robert Fenwick who lived with his family in the house from 1867 until 1895. One of the fountains in the park, in Italian marble, with granite steps and a Portland Stone base, commemorates him. Perhaps the most important resident, however, was James Perry, proprietor of the *Morning Chronicle*, once an influential newspaper, founded in 1770. Perry, a friend of Admiral Lord Nelson, lived here from 1791 until his death in 1821. He leased the mill in 1796 and converted it to the manufacture of cloth. This was short-lived, however, and the mill was rebuilt in 1798 as a corn mill. And, after buying the freehold of the mill in 1803, Perry had a private siding built from the newly opened Surrey Iron Railway, which crossed the present Bygrove Road just west of its junction with Mead Path, to his mill.

Writing in 1805, James Malcolm (*Compendium of Modern Husbandry* [Vol 1])

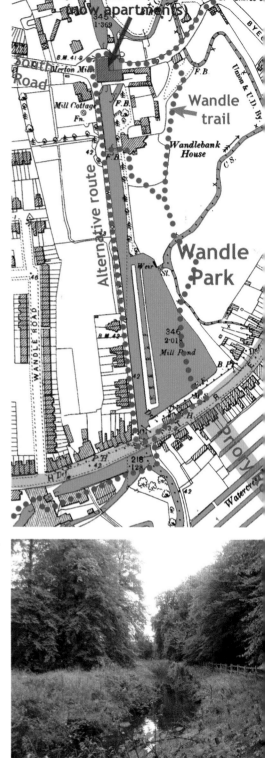

In Wandle Park, Merton.

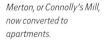

Left: **Merton Mill**

wrote of "*the very spacious flour mills belonging to Mr. Perry of Merton… These mills work seven pairs of stones, and the whole interior of the works … are said to be the most complete of their kind in England; and in order that a constant supply of water may be had at all seasons to assist the river in carrying on such an extensive concern, the proprietor has dug out the soil from an adjoining field and formed it into a large basin of some acres in extent, which, being full of springs, contributes greatly to the supply.*"
In other words, Perry dug the mill pond to ensure against water shortages – and reference to the 1894 map shows the mill pond and the straight cut leading directly, as it does today, to Merton Mill. The meandering stream visible on the map was replaced by a dismal concrete-lined conduit that led water through the park. Recently, the conduit was removed and natural channels restored. The opportunity was also taken to create a reed bed with the hope that it might attract Reed Warblers to nest.

You can exit the park either over a footbridge to Wandle Bank, crossing the river just upstream of the mill, or into Bygrove Road at the northern end of the park by the lodge. In the latter case turn left to reach the old mill. The mill ended its working life as Connolly's Leather Mill, but was converted into flats in 1994. The map shows a 'patent leather works' north of the mill on the west bank of the river: this site was yet another calico printing factory for some 150 years until the mid nineteenth century, when it was converted to leather dressing.

There have been plans to take the Wandle Trail along the river north of the mill alongside this new housing estate and across via a new footbridge into the Wandle Meadow Nature Park, but at the time of writing these have led instead to a new folly, a half-bridge that projects across the river but stops in mid air! So, the current Trail

Merton, or Connolly's Mill, now converted to apartments.

route follows Bygrove Road east from the mill, and left on a signed path where it meets Denison Road. In about 200 yards, beyond the houses, bear left through the kissing gate into the open space which is now part of Wandle Meadow Nature Park. You can now walk over to inspect the bizarre folly bridge from below! Crossing under North Road, you enter the main part of the reserve. Until 1970 this area had been a sewage treatment plant with no public access, and it represents one of the success stories in the efforts to open up the riverside. The site was derelict until 1993 when work started on the nature reserve, aided by a Derelict Land Grant. Many of the subsurface structures are still in place as you can see walking around the reserve, but the transformation is striking and, if you pick up the path along the river itself, this stretch has been improved immensely. The revetments are still in place, but have been softened by vegetation, and some fine trees, notably several mature Crack Willows, overhang the river. A useful interpretive map near the Chaucer Gardens entrance to the site gives an idea of the opportunities and constraints offered by the site, which although not as pretty as some riverside areas further south has nonetheless made great strides in 15 years. In this context one can forgive the gigantic electricity pylon that sits right in the middle of it!

If you've followed the river bank, you will have to bear right either by the footbridge or shortly afterwards, since the northern end of the reserve is hemmed in by the railway embankment. Follow the Trail under the railway line where a path picks up an outflow of the tiny River Graveney, which flows in a rather grim concrete culvert to join the Wandle in some 200 yards. This section of the Graveney is entirely artificial: old Ordnance maps show the river meandering close to the Wandle and not joining the latter for another mile or so, north of Garrett Print Works in Summerstown. A new metal viewing platform offers a good place to inspect the 'watersmeet'. The name Graveney derives from the De Gravenel family whose lands eventually became Tooting Graveney. The parish gave its name to the small stream, which was not large enough to support any mills. The Trail continues for 400 yards on a path following the east bank of the river, again with some attractive riverside poplars and willows and, on the far bank, allotments, softening the urban landscape until you reach Plough Lane. The pine trees between here and Plough Lane are Monterey Pine: they are commonly planted in the south-west because they favour a mild climate; however, they seem to be doing

Confluence with the Graveney.

very well here too. Look for the remarkable fist-sized cones, some even attached to the main stem; they remain tightly shut for years: a condition known as serotiny. Only after a fire will the cones open to release their seeds that grow to replace trees burnt down in the fire.

This section had no settlement or industry prior to the twentieth century, but immediately north of Plough Lane, behind the modern car dealership, stood an important mill site. There appears to have been a mill here as early as the fifteenth century, used for fulling,

Wimbledon Mill

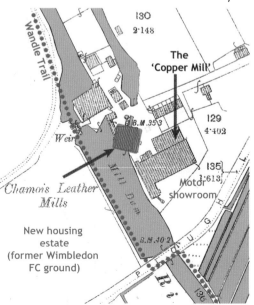

and later in 1634 according to Peter McGow, converted to iron. However, it was as a copper mill that this mill site is best known, despite the 1895 map showing it as a chamois leather mill. A lithograph in Wandsworth Heritage Library shows the *Pontifex Mills* at Wimbledon; Edward and William Pontifex produced copper vessels and utensils, including large brewing coppers, here for some 45 years in the Victorian period. They were later known as Garrett Copper Mills, just to confuse us with the Garrett Mills further downstream! The water wheel here was a monster, allegedly Europe's second largest at one time.

The map was published shortly after the mill became Chuter's Chamois Leather Mills, and production continued until the works closed in 1968; the mill and mill house were demolished some years later. It's apparent that the works was in good shape well into the twentieth century since an article in the *Leather Trades Review* of March 1936 refers to the large working mill wheel, and describes the Toll House on Copper Mill Lane *"still standing in a remarkably good state of preservation"* and carries pictures suggesting at that time a site full of interest with several venerable buildings – a sad contrast to the dismal state of the site today.

The surviving building, behind the car dealers in Copper Mill Lane, is an early to mid nineteenth-century leather dressing factory, not an old copper mill as the plaque on the wall suggests. It's worth a look for its attractive first floor windows, although the top floor has clearly been rebuilt at some stage. The surrounding urban landscape is frankly a mess despite its Conservation Area status.

Summerstown, the district to the east, is first mentioned in 1801 and had grown to a fair-sized hamlet by the time the 1851 census recorded economic activity. The occupations recorded in the census suggest that it was closely linked to the mills here at Plough Lane.

The river near Garrett Park.

There is no riverside path on the east of the Wandle here: from Plough Lane Bridge, pick up the good track on the west bank of the river, which now runs for the best part of a mile to the Wandsworth Borough boundary at Trewint Street Bridge in Earlsfield. It's fair to say that this path and the associated wild margin alongside the river is a very happy treatment, far more nature-friendly than the fencing and lighting which seem to prevail in Wandsworth. New housing occupies the site of the old Wimbledon FC ground on your left, later giving way to an industrial area. On the opposite bank no trace now remains of the mill site, except for a stretch of old brickwork at water level. The same applies to the Garrett Print Works (see map), which turned out printed cloth from around 1770 until 1895, when it then became a cardboard box factory. In 1850 Brayley in his *Topographical History of Surrey* wrote that the factory *"...employs about a hundred...who print annually 25,000 pieces or dresses. This establishment has existed between eighty and ninety years,*

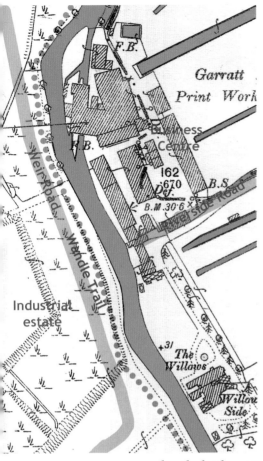

and is fitted up with the usual improvements in coppers, copperplate presses, cylinder, and padding machines, &c." Braithwaite in 1853 was less enthusiastic, remarking on the pollution caused by dyes entering the river.

The print works site is now an industrial estate, shielded to an extent from the riverside path by a sufficiently wide green ribbon on the west bank to soften the harsh urban landscape. Further north on the opposite bank, allotments front the river. These occupy a site which at one time was marshy common land by the outflow of the Graveney River. Beyond the allotments lies Garrett Park. The name Garrett is now associated with Garrett Lane, but at one time it was a separate hamlet, around the area occupied by the *Leather Bottle* pub. For many years it was the scene of a comic election for the 'Mayor of Garrett', which Samuel Foote turned into a two-act farce in 1763.

Garrett Print Works

Old Garrett Mill site, Trewint Street Earlsfield.

Shortly after the allotments the Trail reaches the bridge at Trewint Street where the Garrett Mills once stood. All that is visible today is an islet in the channel either side of the bridge. The late Victorian map (p. 212) shows the complexity of water channels at this site – and interestingly the line of the parish boundary (a dashed black line), which is often a clue as to the past river course – suggests considerable alteration, perhaps precipitated in part by the construction of the railway. Note the former tight meander at the northern part of the map extract. Peter McGow's research informs us that the straight cut around the present bridge was made by one James Lloyd to serve two gunpowder mills of his in the mid seventeenth century. In turn, these were built a little south of the main mill, first recorded in 1756, also making gunpowder at this time. The buildings apparently later fell into disuse and either collapsed and/or were demolished, but in

around 1730 two new mills were erected to produce oil, primarily from linseed.

Writing at about this time, David Hughson gave an account of the oil production here:

> The first operation is that of grinding the linseed under large stones, during which the seed is wetted, in order to prevent its discharging the oil; it is then dried over a furnace in an iron pan, after which it is poured into long bags, closed up in leathern cases; these are inserted perpendicularly between wedges, which are driven down by upright shafts, thrown up by a horizontal one, then suffered to fall by their own weight, after which the seed is taken out, again ground, and passes through the whole operation as before, the oil running off through small pipes into a receptacle under the floor, and the refuse of the seed is sold to the graziers for the purpose of fattening sheep and oxen. The concern is of so profitable a nature, that the last mentioned article is said to defray the whole expense of the operation ... The seed is said to be imported chiefly from France. A quarter of seed produces from twenty to twenty three gallons of oil.

These mills were important enough for a branch spur to be taken off the Surrey Iron Railway, running close to the line of Garrett Lane, to be run to the mills in the early nineteenth century. Braithwaite's 1853 paper contains the last reference to a seed (crushing) mill, since the 1865 map shows *Garrett Paper Mill* standing in open country. This activity was quickly succeeded at the mill by bone crushing and tallow melting, but the main mill was destroyed by a great fire in 1890, hence its absence from the 1894 map. By 1920 no water wheels were in operation anywhere on this site. At present there is no public access north of the bridge at Trewint Street, and the Trail leaves the river to the east on the road, and first left into Summerley Street, which leads to busy Garrett Lane at Earlsfield.

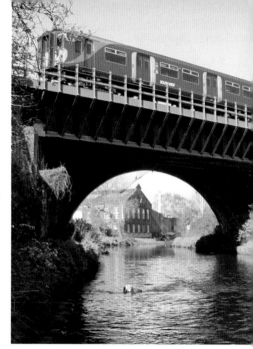

An inaccessible stretch of the river, downstream of Trewint Street, Earlsfield.

Garrett Mills

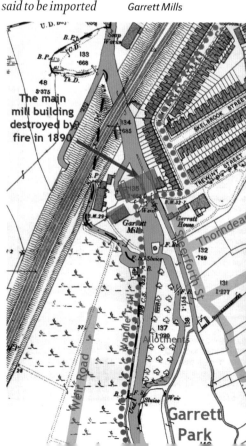

Earlsfield to King George's Park

Access: By rail to Earlsfield (Waterloo line).
Bus 44 from Mitcham, Wandsworth and Battersea.
Bus 270 Putney Bridge to Mitcham.

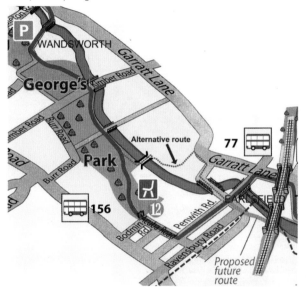

To regain the river from the busy Garrett Lane at Earlsfield, we need to walk under the railway bridge and bear second left into Penwith Road. There's not a great deal to be gained from walking down the first turning, Thornsett Road, to view the river over a concrete flood embankment. The river at Penwith Road Bridge couldn't be called pretty, although compared with 50 years ago it has improved considerably. The dual concrete-lined channels here date back to a flood control scheme for the old London County Council in around 1960. Enthusiasts can access the river south of here during working hours by detouring first left into Ravensbury Terrace and, at the first corner, left again into a small industrial estate. Walk past some attractive old warehouses near the entrance to reach the river, which can be accessed on a narrow grassy ledge via some steps. A long-discussed connection to this point from the Trewint Street Bridge not far away would be a great improvement to the Trail.

Back on Penwith Road, the Trail 'officially' continues down to the junction with Acuba Street (second right) and thence straight into the sports grounds and back to the river via the cycle track. However, I would recommend an alternative route (see map p. 214): bear first right into Strathville Road/Duntshill Road, which gives you another view of the river by the sharp bend; then, before the road turns sharply right, take a brief detour into the close of modern buildings, Flock Mill Place. This leads to another former mill site and commemorates

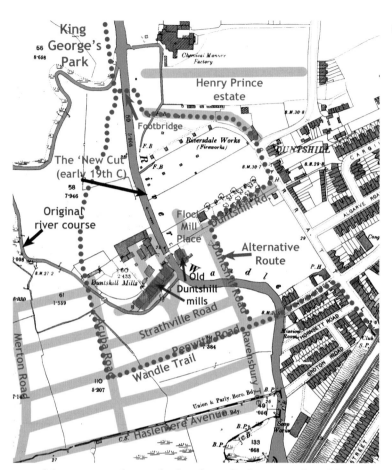

one of the activities that took place here: flock was produced from
rags and scrap textiles and could be used as cheap stuffing as well as
an ingredient in paper making. The 1894 map clearly shows the
meandering former course of the river (although even in the 1850s
Braithwaite found this to be a shallow muddy channel) and the
New Cut, as the Wandsworth tithe map identified it, striking north at
the Duntshill Mills site. As was often the case, there was more than
one mill here – on both the original channel and on the New Cut.

Although the site is first mentioned specifically (as a calico
printing works) in 1802, a typically wide variety of activities
seems to have been carried on here, including parchment making
and colour dye manufacture. The modern building straddling
the river is the rehabilitated remains of an industrial building
used by *Kenco*, the coffee firm, in the 1970s. The only surviving
building from the original Duntshill Mills complex, a warehouse,
is currently undergoing a sensitive restoration for commercial

Riverside warehouse at Earlsfield.

uses, using some very eco-friendly heating and insulation technology. It's named after one of its more recent uses, a sawmill. Exasperatingly, the Wandle Trail could quite happily follow the river here but for a metal railing: the difficulties appear to be political rather than practical. Across the river, the possible future removal of government buildings could unlock a path into King George's Park on that side of the river. For now, however, one needs to return to Duntshill Road and walk down to Garrett Lane, bearing left. Now take the left turn into St John's Drive where Garrett Lane bends away to the right. This leads under three blocks of flats of the Henry Prince Estate and into a riverside garden where a footbridge, built in 1973, carries us across to the west bank of the Wandle again to rejoin the official Trail.

Much of the land alongside the river north from here was wet and inhospitable in former times, so early maps indicate a lack of buildings and little economic activity, although the map shows factories by the late Victorian period, and there were bleaching grounds further north in the vicinity of modern-day Kimber Road. Certainly, in comparison to the southern reaches of the river, this was not the sort of site to attract rich merchants to erect their country seats! Today, the Wandle Trail here is pleasant enough, thanks to a hard-fought decision to replace the gang-mown grassland with a wild margin being encouraged in the interests of biodiversity; although the riverside margin is fenced off and views of the river are limited as the vegetation thickens. Cross Lydden Road and continue through more playing fields towards Kimber Road.

The dual concrete
channels carrying the
river though Earlsfield.

North of Kimber Road, the Trail curves away from the river
around an area of commercial land. Reference to the map shows
that this was historically an area of old settling tanks and filter beds.
The Trail now continues directly ahead into the main part of
King George's Park, which today is an extensive urban open space.
The name was a hasty replacement for 'Southfields Park' when
HRH deigned to come down and do the honours of opening the park
in 1923! The enclosure and laying out provided much-needed work
in post-war Wandsworth. An open-air swimming pool survived until
1994. Note the old water channels running across open land west of
the current river course (see Wandsworth overview map, p. 123).
These may well relate to the original, or at least an earlier, course of
the main river; but by the time of the late Victorian map these were
little more than a straight series of ponds.

To hold to the river, a more interesting path, signed *Riverside
Path* branches right alongside a modern nursery and leads to a
footbridge across the river directly downstream of the old site of
the former Adkins Mill, later the Royal Paper Mills (see map).
It is probably one of Wandsworth's Domesday Mills, but the first
specific reference is in the fourteenth century. It has a typically
chequered history, more so in fact than the town's other mills.
The list of uses includes fulling, copper, iron, paper and corn.
When in use as Henckell's Iron Mill (he took over the premises
in 1777), it later gave its name to nearby Iron Mill Place. It is said
that cannons used at Waterloo were forged here.

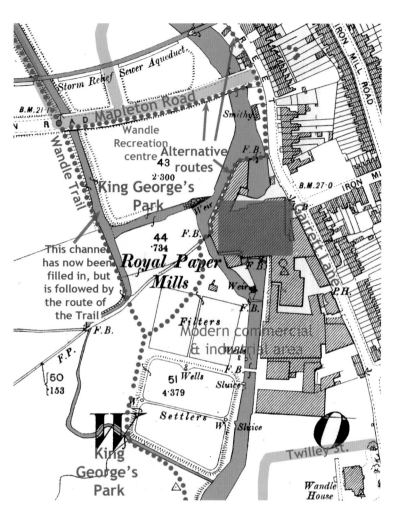

Royal Mills

David Hughson in 1808 gave a dramatic description of the activities carried out at the mill:

> *At these mills are cast shot, shells, cannon, and other implements of war; in another part of it the wrought iron is manufactured, and the great effect of mechanical power is exemplified in all their operations, in the splitting of iron bars of prodigious length; in a pair of shears which will rend asunder pieces of iron more than two inches in thickness; and in the working of a hammer, which weighs from five hundred and a half to six hundred pounds.*

Another contemporary at this time remarked that the mill proprietor *"told me, that, to supply the excessive evaporation* [from working in the heat] *some of them found it necessary to drink eight or ten pots of porter per day."* Good business no doubt for the nearby *Old Sargeant* pub, which still occupies the same site today!

View upstream from Kimber Road Bridge, Wandsworth.

The mill was converted to paper making in around 1838, and eventually became the Royal Paper Mills shown on the late Victorian map. A surviving photograph shows the tall chimneys of the mill presiding over the fields which later became King George's Park, around the turn of the century. Much of the mill was destroyed by a savage fire in 1903, and although it was rebuilt and re-opened briefly thereafter, it had closed for good by 1909 and was demolished soon afterwards. The footpath leads across the river affording a good view of the old mill tail, and then joins busy Garrett Lane just south of the Mapleton Road junction as we arrive in Wandsworth Town.

The tail race from the former Royal Paper Mills rejoins the river at Wandsworth.

Wandsworth

Access: To Mapleton Road, buses 44 and 270 (see Earlsfield). Bus 156 from Wimbledon to Buckhold Rd. To Central Wandsworth: Use National Rail to Wandsworth Town (connects with bus 44).

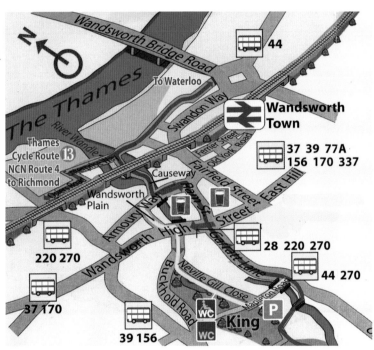

Mapleton Road was at the southern edge of Victorian Wandsworth, although today the boxy mass of the *Southside* shopping centre, not to mention the towering nearby flats, dominate the scene. Just north of the junction, you can walk about 50 yards further before riverside access is lost and the river disappears under the shopping centre shortly afterwards. Buried under it lies the site of Wandsworth's Upper Mill (see below), and, just south of the point where Mapleton Crescent joins Garrett Lane, Williamson's dyehouses. Dyes were made here for some 200 years, the latter hundred in the Williamson family, until about 1830. Manufacturing continued on the premises (shown on the 1894 map as the Wandle Colour Works) until the 1970s.

Reference to the Royal Mills map shows that, approximately at this point, a storm relief aqueduct ran east–west across the Wandle Valley.

This curious structure, having been built in the 1880s to carry a sewer across the river, was not demolished until 1968. Wandsworth had the same urgent need of proper sewerage that the river's other large town, Croydon, had as we have noted earlier. In fact, Croydon was probably quicker off the mark than Wandsworth, where in 1854 up to 80 people died in a cholera outbreak.

It's perfectly possible to follow the road down to the centre of town past the *Southside*, but the Wandle Trail follows Mapleton Road back into King George's Park taking the right turn along Neville Gill Close, with the attractive park and water gardens on your left. Worth seeking out is an apple hybrid, Purple Crab, the only tree on the Wandle that appears as a Britain and Ireland Champion on the Tree Register. It had a girth of 3' in 2001 and is the largest of three Purple Crabs on the north side of the bridge across the water garden. It is at its best in April when the tree is a mass of red–purple flowers.

The site on your right here was, until the 1960s, occupied by the 20,000-seater Wandsworth Greyhound Stadium, which along with the buildings of the old

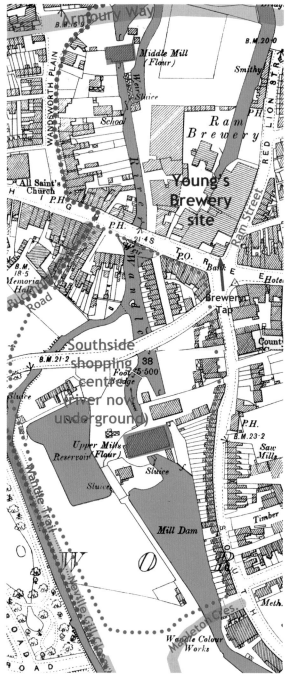

Wandsworth centre

Upper Mill were swept away to be replaced by the *Brave New World* of the *Arndale Centre*. *Southside* had opened in 1971 as the *Arndale Centre*, then the largest indoor shopping centre in Europe. The US mall-style Arndale 'experience' was one that swept Britain in the 1960s and 1970s, and was down to two Yorkshire entrepreneurs, **Arn**old Hagenbach and Sam Chippin**dale**. The high-rise tower blocks

The northern section of linear King George's Park, alongside Neville Gill Close, is the most attractive.

built above the mall were good for business, but the whole thing was dubbed by the Wandsworth Historical Society as 'one of London's great architectural disasters', a view with which the author would not disagree.

Wandsworth Upper Mill, first mentioned in the sixteenth century, was, unusually, two mills under one roof. The mills were associated for much of the eighteenth century with the families of the brothers Jacob and Michael Papineau, and George Shepley who we met earlier at Carshalton (and reciprocally the brothers, and their son, had the lease of one of the Hackbridge Mills in that village at the same time). In fact, the two families were related since George Shepley married Michael's daughter Mary in 1763. Shepley had the mills rebuilt in about 1770 when the eastern part was an oil mill and the west part a corn mill. They were acquired by Daniel Watney (related to the brewing family who later produced the keg beers so detested by late twentieth-century real ale drinkers!) in the early nineteenth century and rebuilt in brick as a corn mill in 1818. Watney also acquired the Middle Mills (see below) around the same time. Interestingly (probably due to the water supply problems discussed elsewhere), by 1898 the Upper Mill was using electricity and gas rather than water power and apparently even the traditional millstones had been superseded by steel rollers! Yet another fire, in 1928, marked the end of nearly a millennium of flour milling in Wandsworth.

Neville Gill Close runs into ugly Buckhold Way and, in turn, very quickly to the High Street. Although the Trail crosses almost directly north into Wandsworth Plain at the corner, it's worth a short detour to the right to the cross roads (where once the Surrey Iron Railway crossed on its journey to the Thames) to view the site of Young's Brewery.

Young's 'Ram' brewery (named in fact after a local field) had a long history dating back to least 1670, although a discussion in Dorian Gerhold's book *Wandsworth Past* traces brewing on the site back to 1576. Either way, Young's claimed with some justification that the site was the longest continuous brewing enterprise anywhere in the country. It came into the Young family's possession in 1831 and the business grew steadily into the largest and most successful of the Wandle breweries. In the twentieth century Young's survived the takeover mania and after the birth of CAMRA, the Campaign for Real Ale, in 1971, they flourished as one of the few breweries that had never transferred to the gassy 'keg' product.

Rapid change followed the death of long-serving chairman John Young in 2006. Plans had already been announced to close the brewery and move production to Bedfordshire. Some of the buildings on the site are listed, but the site of the old Ram Brewery has been approved for redevelopment into a new shopping and business centre.

The river flows past the old Youngs Brewery site, Wandsworth.

The now disused Young's Brewery still sits by the river at Wandsworth.

The brewery was certainly an important feature of Wandsworth and made good use in earlier days of the river and its associated basins and wharves. Across the street, the *Spread Eagle* is probably the most impressive of Wandsworth's remaining inns – built as a coaching inn in 1780 and rebuilt in 1898. The interior is still a remarkable place with some fine screens between the separate drinking areas.

It's possible of course that the new development may open up the riverside, but for now there is no public access, so return down the traffic-choked High Street (there's a tiny 'garden' by the river bridge where currently you can view the river encased in concrete by the remains of the brewery) and right into Wandsworth Plain. Church Row on the right has eighteenth- century houses built for prosperous merchants, which have somehow been overlooked by the planners, but it's a brief respite before you pass the studios (which are earmarked for development as part of the Young's site) and come to the wide and very busy Armoury Way town-centre bypass. It crosses the river just to the right. It's not a location that many would wish to dither at, except that a short distance upstream from the bridge stood Middle Mill.

The Middle Mill was first listed in 1504 as a corn mill, but later in the century it was converted into a Brazil Mill, that is, rasping Brazil wood to produce a powder used to dye cloth. Wandsworth became well known for the scarlet dyes made here, so much so that the mill continued to be known as the Brazil Mill long after the mill reverted to corn some time around 1600, which function it retained (save for a short period manufacturing oil) until its demise, despite a chequered pattern of changing ownership. Middle Mill was equipped with a windmill in the 1650s, but a painting of 1825 shows it without its sails. Although it was in a poor state of repair at the beginning of the nineteenth century, when new owners Shepley and Papineau commissioned a survey, Middle Mill had something of a nineteenth-century renaissance. In 1850 Brayley, in his *Topographical History of Surrey* wrote:

> *Messrs. Watney and Wells, at the Upper and Middle mills, now work thirty-one pair of stones, which, at the average of 1000 quarters per pair, will produce 60,000 sacks a year, to the value of £150,000. Although the operations of grinding, boulting, &c. are performed partly by steam and partly by waterpower, the business employs 26 work-horses, and 10 or 12 nags, but with so much economy of labour not more than 50 men are required to prepare and distribute flour for 50,000 persons.*

LONDON AND RICHMOND RAILWAY.—THE WANDLE VIADUCT.

Later in the century, Middle Mill and Upper Mill were acquired by the Aerated Bread Company, who leased it to the progressive firm of George Pimm, and although milling ceased at Middle Mill some time in the 1890s, Pimms continued milling at Upper Mill as late as 1930.

In a nice example of industrial linkage, nearby stood the Blackmore Bolting Cloth Factory (from 1814 until 1919). A boulting or bolting cloth was a sieve used to remove the coarser particles from the milled flour and lighten the texture (see also p. 46).

Cross the Armoury Way race-track with great care, by the controlled crossing. There's no trace now of the canal, or the Cut, as the large dock basin and wharf built for the Surrey Iron Railway was originally called. As the map shows, it crossed roughly at the junction with Ram Street a hundred yards or so further east, and was a prominent feature. It was filled in during the 1930s by the Wandsworth Gas Company, who owned a very large site to the east of it. Just beyond the pub, *The Armoury* (formerly *The Crane*), take The Causeway which still retains some of the character of the past. It has benefited from 'Section 106' monies received by the council from riverside developments. A short distance down, Bell Lane Creek swings under the road to the left. Unlike The Cut, this channel survived plans to fill it in – the land on either side is a part of a council depot; but plans to create an urban marina and moorings have surfaced here from time to time. If you arrive at low tide, however, you'll see one of the problems – wide areas of filthy mud along the banks, not exactly an

A Victorian engraving of the railway viaduct at Wandsworth. View from the north – The Cut on the left, the river on the right.

Low tide at Bell Lane Creek, Wandsworth.

THE CAUSEWAY

WAS THE ROAD FROM THE VILLAGE SQUARE AT THE END OF WANDSWORTH PLAIN TO THAMESIDE WAREHOUSES AND STRIP FIELDS. A TIDAL MILL STOOD HERE ON THE CAUSEWAY FROM MEDIEVAL TIMES UNTIL DEMOLISHED IN 1892. TO THE WEST OF THIS PLAQUE THE MOUTH OF THE WANDLE WAS A MARSHY DELTA, TO THE EAST RAN MCMURRAY'S CANAL FILLED IN c.1937 WHICH CONNECTED THE RIVER THAMES TO THE SURREY IRON RAILWAY. NEARBY STOOD THE FEATHERS BOAT HOUSE & PUB.

WANDSWORTH SOCIETY MAY 1997
MARKING IMPROVEMENTS BY
LONDON ELECTRICITY

Plaque near mouth of Wandle, Wandsworth.

attractive spot! The Wandsworth Local Development Strategy envisages improved public access along the river banks at this stretch, which is known as Causeway Island, but today the more pressing issue is that land nearby may be requisitioned by the proposed Thames Tideway Project, a super-sewer project to improve water quality in the Thames.

The weir by the bridge is interesting: in 1993 a micro-hydro turbine was installed, connected to a local primary school, together with a bell rung by the tides. This was part of the Delta Project, and according to advisors, the Intermediate Technology Development Group, this was the first time micro-hydro technology had been used in a rich-world, inner city river context. Above the weir, which at one time acted as a bypass for the Lower Mill, an inscription reads: *"Salmon, Swan, Otter, Heron, Eel"*. The Wandle Delta at one time would have been a feeding ground and breeding place for a wide range of molluscs, insects, fish, birds and mammals. *"Today the range of inhabitants in the river and on its banks are greatly reduced, but in honour of those that remain here and in memory of those that might return, their names have been carved in stone affixed to the sluice gate structure"* according to PLATFORM, the co-ordinators of the project.

Beyond the weir, the road leads down to and under the railway bridge; just beyond, the Trail meets the Thames Path at a footbridge over the Wandle. This is the spot where Lower Mill once stood. It was different from the other mills on the river in that it was affected

Wandsworth: the river negotiates an intensely urban landscape close to its mouth.

by the tides. Braithwaite's 1853 paper refers to it thus: "... *the lower or tidal mill.. is prevented, by the flow of the tide, from working during six to eight out of twenty-four hours. The power is derived from three wheels, collectively equal to 45 H.P. and a steam engine equal to 18 H.P. ... At the mill head, there are two overfalls, over which the tide frequently flows from the River Thames.*" For the greater part of its life (and the first reference known to a mill here was in 1371) it was a corn mill.

The mouth of the river at high tide.

Just beyond is Wandle Mouth, the appearance of which will depend heavily upon the state of the tide. The half-tide weir was built in 1991 to impound water at low tide to aid recreational boating, but has recently been partially removed (*see box below*).

The Wandsworth Half-Tide Weir

The weir is formed of a central metal gate housed within a concrete frame on either side. It was designed to operate automatically; the metal gate drops on the rising tide and rises on the ebbing tide. The raising of the weir led to the installation of traffic lights. Is the Wandle the only river to have traffic lights at its mouth? The weir has had an effect on the ecology of the river, particularly the build-up of silt, such that, ever since it was built, there has been pressure for its removal. In December 2009, the volume of water from the combination of a high tide and heavy rainfall forced the metal gate out of its frame wedging it at an interesting angle. This event proved a catalyst for Wandsworth Council to begin the process of removal – starting with the metal gate, which was removed in September 2010. The Environment Agency, Port of London Authority and Wandsworth Council are concerned that the silt build-up is deep and potentially contaminated, so do not want it flushed into the Thames all at once.

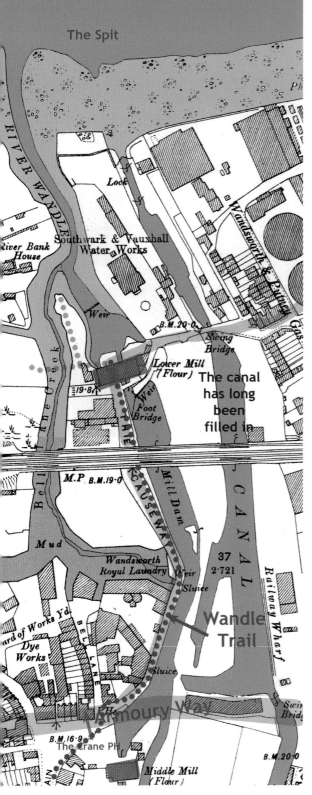

The mouth at Wandsworth always has something to interest the birdwatcher, particularly in winter. The built-up silt from the half-tide weir attracts Teal, Gadwall and occasionally Pintail. Pintail were first seen in 1995 and as many as 20 were seen in November 1999. They are a scarce winter visitor to London and such numbers are very unusual. Some of the birds are ringed and they are considered to come from the feral breeding population in St James's Park. Little Grebe are joined by Great Crested Grebe that sometimes try to build a nest, but are always thwarted by the daily tidal movements. Common Sandpiper, a wader that usually spends the winter in Africa, can sometimes be seen. Finally, look out for Cormorants that often perch on the traffic lights!

The little garden here occupies a tiny peninsula known as the Spit, between the mouth of the main river and that of Bell Lane Creek. Like the footbridge and other work in this area, the garden and small wetland planted areas on the spit were enhanced by monies from the Wandsworth Challenge Partnership, a regeneration body, in the 1990s. In good weather it's a pleasant enough spot to sit and try to imagine what a hive of activity the area would have been at one time. At Feathers Wharf, the eastern bank of the mouth, 1980s plans for a new park have been

Wandsworth mouth

reneged upon and the current proposal is for a mere three-yard walkway alongside a big new development. You can reach the Thames along a new path that has been recently opened along the west bank, which marks the end of the Wandle Trail. If you want to celebrate completing the Trail continue walking west along the Thames past the moored boats until the first road on your left, Point Pleasant where a well-earned drink can be had at the *Cat's Back* pub!

The 'Bason at Wandsworth' by an unknown artist. The tracks of the Surrey Iron Railway are visible in the foreground and a string of wagons is visible behind the man. Two dockside cranes are visible in the background. This is the only known painting of the Surrey Iron Railway, and probably dates to *c.*1820.

Select bibliography

Alfrey, P. R., Milne, B. S. & Coleman, D. A. (2010) *The Birds of Beddington Farmlands*, Beddington Farm Bird Group.

Baca Architects with BRE. (2000) *The Life Project. Long-term Initiatives for Flood-risk Environments*, IHS BRE Press.

Baker, H. (1984) 'The Status of Canada Goose in the London Area', *London Bird Report*, **49**, 111–126.

Barton, N. (1992) *The Lost Rivers of London*, Historical Publications Ltd., London.

Braithwaite, F. (1861) 'On the Rise and Fall of the River Wandle: its Springs, Tributaries and Pollution', *Institution of Civil Engineers Proceedings*, **20**, 191–258.

Brayley, E. W. (1850) *A Topographical History of Surrey*, Tilt and Bogue, London.

Burton, R. M. (1983) *Flora of the London Area*, London Natural History Society.

Carter, M. G. & England, J. A. (2004) 'Freshwater fish in London's rivers'. *London Naturalist*, **83**, 77–85.

Chambers, S. A. (1930) *The Birds of Beddington Park*, MS held in Sutton Local Studies Collection.

Clenet, D., Britton, B. & Game, M. (1988) *Nature Conservation in Croydon*, London Ecology Unit.

Cluett, D. (n.d.) *Some notes on Hackbridge House and its neighbours on the River Wandle.* Undated MS held in Sutton Local Studies Collection.

Coleman, D. A. (1985) 'The Coot population at Waddon Ponds, 1980–1986', *Surrey Bird Report*, **33**, 53–59.

Coleman, D. A. & Boyle, M. K. (2000) 'The status and ecology of the Hornet Moth, Sesia apiformis (Clerck) (Lepidoptera:Sessiidae), in suburban south London', *British Journal of Entomology and Natural History*, **13**, 99–106.

Coleman, D. A. (1994) 'Waterways Bird Survey of the River Wandle between 1983 and 1994', *London Bird Report*, **59**, 184–195.

Collins, G. A. (1997) *Larger Moths of Surre,* Surrey Wildlife Trust.

Corbet Anderson, J. (1882) *A short chronicle concerning the parish of Croydon*, Ballantyne, Hanson & Co, London.

Follett, P. (1996) *Dragonflies of Surrey*, Surrey Wildlife Trust.

Gent, J. B. (2002) *Croydon Past*, Phillimore & Co. Ltd, Andover.

Gerhold, D. (1998) *Wandsworth Past*, Historical Publications Ltd., London.

Giuseppi, M. S. (1908) 'The River Wandle in 1610', *Surrey Archaeological Collections*, **21**.

Greater London Council (1985) *A Green Chain: the Wandle Valley Area of Opportunity.*

Hewlett, J. (2002) *The Breeding Birds of the London Area*, London Natural History Society.

Hillier, J. (1951) *Old Surrey Water Mills*, Skeffington and Son Ltd, London.

Hobson, J. M. (1924) *The Book of the Wandle. The Story of a Surrey River*, G. Routledge and Sons Ltd, London.

Ingle, R. W. (1986) 'The Chinese mitten crab *Eriocheir senensis* Milne Edwards – a contentious immigrant', *London Naturalist*, **65**, 101–105.

Jones, A. E. (1973) *An illustrated Directory of old Carshalton.*

Jones, A. E. (1965) *From Medieval Manor to London Suburb – an obituary of Carshalton.*

Lancaster, B. (2001) 'The "Croydon Case": Dirty Old Town to Model Town. The making of the Croydon Board of Health and the Typhoid Epidemic of 1852–3', *Proceedings of the Croydon Natural History and Scientific Society*, **18**, 145–206.

London Natural History Society (1957) *The Birds of the London Area since 1900*, Collins, London.

Lousley, J. E. (1976) *Flora of Surrey*, David & Charles, Newton Abbot.

Manning, O. & Bray, W. (1814) *The History and Antiquities of Surrey.*

McCrow, B. J. (1974) 'The biological effects of pollution on a stretch of the River Wandle 1970–71', *London Naturalist*, **53**, 17–33.

McLauchlin, J. & Fookes, G. (1996) 'The River Wandle: Distribution of its Flora', *Proceedings of the Croydon Natural History and Scientific Society*, **18**, 117–128.

Meadows, B. S. (1971) 'The recovery of the Kingfisher in London after the 1962/63 hard winter', *London Bird Report*, **36**, 60–66.

Merton Historical Society, Edited by Goodman J. (2008) *Coal and Calico: Letters and Papers of the Bennett and Leach Families of Merton and Wandsworth.*

Mills Whipp Archaeological Consultancy (2009) *The Merton Vision: reclaiming the Priory.*

Montague, E. N. (2007) *Colliers Wood or 'Merton Singlegate'.* Merton Historical Society in association with Merton Library & Heritage Service.

Montague, E. N. (2005) *Mitcham Bridge, The Watermeads and the Wandle Mills*, Merton Historical Society.

Montague, E. N. (2006) *Phipps Bridge*, Merton Historical Society.

Montague, E. N. (2008) *Ravensbury*, Merton Historical Society.

Montier, D. J. (1977) *Atlas of Breeding Birds of the London Area*, London Natural History Society.

Palmer, K. H. (1982) 'The Breeding Season Status of The Grey Wagtail in the London Area 1979–1981', *London Bird Report*, **47**, 106–122.

Phillips, J. (n.d.) *Beddington Park History*, Unpublished MS.

Phillips, J. & Burnett, N. (2005) 'The Chronology and Layout of Nicholas Carew's Garden at Beddington, Surrey', *Garden History Society*, **33**, 155–188.

Plant, C. W. (1993) *Larger Moths of the London Area*, London Natural History Society.

Prentis, W. H. (1970) *The Snuff Mill Story.*

Price, S. M. & Price, J. H. (1983) 'The River Wandle: Studies on the distribution of aquatic plants', *London Naturalist*, **62**, 26–58.

Richmond, L. & Turton, A. (1990) *The Brewing Industry: A Guide to Historical Records*, Manchester University Press.

Rivers Restoration Project. (2009) *The London Rivers Action Plan*, http://www.thercc.co.uk/lrap.php.

Saxby, D. (2008) *The Mills of the River Wandle*, Wandle Valley Festival.

Saxby, D. (1995) *William Morris at Merton*, Museum of London Archaeology Service.

Shahbazian, C., Kowalik, R. & Woodcock, S. (2009) *A Water Vole Reintroduction Feasibility Study for the River Wandle*, London Wildlife Trust.

Skelton, A. & Steel, R. (2004) *Wilderness Island. Local Nature Reserve, Carshalton*, Historical Review, London Wildlife Trust.

Smee, A. (1872) *My Garden: its Plan and Culture: together with a general description of its geology, botany and natural history*, Bell and Daldy, London.

Thurston Hopkins, R. (1930) *Old Water Mills and Windmills*, Philip Allan & Co Ltd, London.

Towns, M. (1972) 'The albino form of the grey squirrel in the London Area', *London Naturalist*, **51**, 22–25.

Wandle Group. Edited by Twilley R. & Wilks. M. (1974) *The River Wandle: a guide and handbook*, London Borough of Sutton Public Libraries.

Wandle Group. Edited by Cluett D. & Phillips J. (1997) *The Wandle Guide*, Sutton Leisure Services.

Wandle Group. *Wandle Bulletins* vol 1 (1974)–vol 20 (1992)

Wandle Industrial Museum. (1996) *The Wandle Trail.*

Wandle Trail Partnership. (2003) *The Wandle Trail.*

Wandsworth Society. (1998) *The River Wandle: past, present and future?*

Wheeler, A. C. (1957) 'The Fishes of the London Area', *London Naturalist*, **37**, 80–101.

Yarham, I., Barnes, R. & Britton, B. (1993) *Nature Conservation in Sutton*, London Ecology Unit.

Yarham, I., Dawson, D., Boyle, M. K. & Holliday, R. (1998) *Nature Conservation in Merton*, London Ecology Unit.

Index of names

Bold numerals refer to principal references

Main index

Wildlife index

(restricted to more significant species)

Credits